Navigating
Change for
International
NGOs

Navigating Change for International NGOs

A Practical Handbook

James Crowley
Morgana Ryan

Kumarian Press

A Division of Lynne Rienner Publishers, Inc. • Boulder & London

Published in the United States of America in 2017 by
Kumarian Press
A division of Lynne Rienner Publishers, Inc.
1800 30th Street, Boulder, Colorado 80301
www.rienner.com

and in the United Kingdom by
Kumarian Press
A division of Lynne Rienner Publishers, Inc.
3 Henrietta Street, Covent Garden, London WC2E 8LU

Library of Congress Cataloging-in-Publication Data
A Cataloging-in-Publication record for this book
is available from the Library of Congress.
ISBN: 978-1-62637-559-8

British Cataloguing in Publication Data
A Cataloguing in Publication record for this book
is available from the British Library.

Printed and bound in the United States of America

 The paper used in this publication meets the requirements
of the American National Standard for Permanence of
Paper for Printed Library Materials Z39.48-1992.

5   4   3   2   1

Contents

List of Tables and Figures   vii
Preface   ix

Introduction   1

1   The Basics of Navigating
    Organizational Change   7

    The Aims of Chapters 1 and 2, *9*
    Level 1 Thinking: The Basics, *11*
    Practical Hints and Tips for Navigating Change, *25*
    Pointers for NGO Leaders Contemplating a
    Change Process, *29*

2   The Art and Science of Complex
    Organizational Change   33

    Level 2 Thinking: Managing Complexity, *33*
    Level 3 Thinking: A Deeper Investigation and
    Appreciation of Context, *44*
    Level 4 Thinking: The Art of Exploiting
    Organizational Rhythm, *53*

3   The Essential Components of a
    High-Performance Organization   63

    A High-Performance Organization, *64*
    Architecture of a High-Performance
    Matrix Organization, *67*
    Key Differences and Implementation Choices, *72*

4   Getting Serious About an Agency-Level
    Theory of Change   83
    The Situation, *85*
    The Architecture of an Agency-Level Theory of Change, *91*
    Organizational Resistance:
      Overcoming Barriers and Blockages, *101*
    An Approach to Developing a Theory of Change, *106*
    Stretch Ideas and Disruptive Thinking, *109*
    Summary, *116*
    Case Study, *118*

5   Working With and Alongside the Private Sector   125
    Why Does Collaboration Matter? *130*
    What Has Been Happening in Terms of
      Private Sector Collaboration? *135*
    Where Are the Real Collaboration Opportunities? *143*
    What Should NGOs and Private Sector Firms
      Do Differently? *147*
    Conclusions, *154*

6   Why NGOs Have So Much Trouble with IT   159
    Why Do NGOs Have So Much Trouble with IT? *162*
    Basic Elements of an IT Project, *170*
    Key Considerations for IT Success, *175*
    Frequently Asked Questions, *178*

7   Making Sense of Mergers in the Development
    and Humanitarian Sectors   187
    Consolidation Rationale and Barriers, *189*
    Stages of an Integration Process, *196*
    Risks, Success Factors, and Some Hints and Tips, *202*
    Conclusions, *205*

Bibliography   207
Index   209
About the Authors   223

Tables and Figures

Tables

1.1	Why Change? Common Drivers for NGOs	13
1.2	Articulating "Strategic Shifts" as a Practical Way of Aiding Communication	18
1.3	Overcoming Resistance to Change	21
2.1	Selecting the Right Mix of Approaches	39
2.2	High-Impact Leadership	41
3.1	Comparing a Simple Structure with a High-Performance Matrix Model	68
3.2	Potential Lines of Expertise	69
3.3	Organization Strengthening Self-Evaluation Template	80
4.1	Hierarchy of Theories of Change	91
4.2	Summary of Components of an Agency-Level Theory of Change	93
4.3	Change Canvas: Illustrative Outcome Areas for Navigating and Tracking Change	98
4.4	Possible Barriers and Blockages to an Agency-Level Theory of Change	102
5.1	Ten Key Trends in Private Sector Engagement in Development	137
5.2	Four Levels of Private Sector Investment in Developing Countries	139
5.3	Seven Opportunity Areas for Deeper Collaboration Between NGOs and Private Sector Firms	148
5.4	Potential Collaboration Conflicts Between NGOs and Private Sector Firms	151
7.1	Typical Arguments Mapped to Four Key Benefit Areas	190
7.2	Questionable Arguments in Favor of Mergers	194
7.3	Selected Barriers to Consolidation and Possible Responses	195
7.4	Mapping of Key Strands of Work Against Stages of an Integration Process	200

Figures

1.1   The Four Levels of Thinking About Organizational Change   10
1.2   How Will Front-Line Staff Respond to Proposed Change?   19
1.3   Valley of Despair During a Typical Change Process   27
2.1   Project, Program, and Journey   34
2.2   Interrelated Dimensions of Progress   36
2.3   Balancing Push and Pull, Macro and Micro   38
2.4   Disconnected Agendas and Priorities   40
2.5   Aligning Approach, Context, and Content   43
2.6   Concept of Organizational Glue   45
2.7   Organizational Life Cycle Model—PAEI   46
2.8   Reinventing Your Agency Before It's Too Late   47
2.9   Segmentation Framework: Motivation and Ability   49
2.10 Social Style Model   51
3.1   Do You Have a High-Performance Agency?   64
3.2   Interlinked Factors that Contribute to a
      High-Performance Agency   65
3.3   Lines of Expertise Mapped to Geography   70
3.4   Remit and Levels of Decisionmaking for Lines of Expertise   73
4.1   The Problem We Are Trying to Solve   86
4.2   Components of an Agency-Level Theory of Change   92
4.3   Example of Strategic Change Canvas   99
4.4   How a Theory of Change Permeates the Key Pieces of
      Any Agency   101
4.5   Flywheel Approach to Economic Development and
      Pro-Poor Growth   119
4.6   Overview of Context-Analysis Framework   121
4.7   Example Program A: Market-Linked Program   123
4.8   Example Program B: Institutional Capacity Building   123
5.1   A Simplified Illustration of a Positive Development Cycle   131
5.2   Impediments to a Positive Development Cycle   134
5.3   Stimulating a Positive Development Cycle   135
5.4   A Pyramid of Firms: The "Missing Middle"   141
5.5   A Pyramid of Firms: Intended Directions   141
5.6   Four Groups of Stakeholders with Overlapping
      Interests and Priorities   143
6.1   Example Phases and Activities for IT Implementation
      for NGOs   171

Preface

The development of this book has been a delight and a challenge. Building on the warm reaction to our earlier volume, *Building a Better International NGO*, we are delighted to tackle some topics that we did not manage to address in that book, particularly the topic of change. In our discussions with senior executives and leadership teams, the topic of navigating change emerged as the single biggest area they wanted to unpack. There seems to be a voracious appetite to explore this subject.

As to the challenge, navigating change is a very broad and complex subject. We have tried to cover a fair amount of ground, seeking to pull out the most useful ideas and tools for insight and help for large NGOs.

In a couple of chapters we tackle topics where our views may be somewhat controversial. In particular, we know that our views on agency-level theories of change may not be everyone's cup of tea—and the same may be true of the chapter on private sector collaboration.

There are some consistent themes throughout both of our books. In our previous publication, we emphasized three core messages. We called on each international NGO to re-evaluate its role and contribution to the development process—this is to respond to evolving thinking on good development practice, the need for local ownership of solutions, greater private sector interest and participation, and a myriad of exciting possibilities through new technology. We called on international NGOs to strengthen and modernize their organizations and management approaches. We also pleaded for NGOs to reach out for the bigger prize—to play their part in the pursuit and discovery of mega-scale breakthroughs in the fight against poverty and injustice.

However, the demands and realities of the world we live in are continuing to evolve. The number and severity of humanitarian crises has dramatically increased. Instances and levels of injustice are exploding across the globe. Inequality seems to be getting more pronounced. At the same time, the funding available to the sector has stalled, and trust in civil society and particularly NGOs is being severely tested in the eyes of the public, our governments, and particularly the governments in the developing world. Furthermore, the rapid pace of technological change is constantly shifting the context in which NGOs operate. We wonder if our organizations are changing fast enough; the accusation of "catching up with yesterday's demands"—is a phrase we hear far too often.

On a stylistic note, throughout this book we use the terms *NGO, international NGO*, and *agency* as seems to fit best in each situation. Readers should not be overly concerned with the differences. Though our experience over the past ten years has predominantly been with international NGOs in the development and humanitarian arenas, we feel that much of the content here applies to national and local NGOs as well. We also hope that a number of the chapters might be useful to private sector firms of all sizes.

* * *

There have been some positive constants in the course of our work. The wonderful British Library has continued to be the creative zone where much of this material was drafted and shaped. This was the place where the two of us started out on our writing journey in 2010. We are delighted that Kumarian Press, now part of Lynne Rienner Publishers, has continued the collaboration, and we particularly thank Lynne for her friendly support and advice. We are pleased to continue our association with Alzheimer's Research UK, which will again be the recipient of the net proceeds of this new project. This is a cause to which we remain committed, as it is one of the underplayed issues of our time.

We especially thank those organizations we have had the privilege of working with over the past decade or more. In particular we acknowledge World Vision (International, UK, and Australia), Plan (International, UK, and Australia), AMREF Health Africa, Voluntary Services Overseas, Catholic Relief Services (CRS), Amnesty International, the Asia Foundation, Oxfam (International, Great Britain, Novib, and Australia), Save the Children (International, UK, and Australia), Habitat for Humanity International, the International Rescue Committee, CARE International, the International Federation of the Red Cross, the Australian Red Cross, Action Against Hunger, Australian Volunteers International (AVI), the Fred Hollows Foundation, ChildFund Australia, Trocaire, Traidlinks, and ActionAid.

We also thank a host of individuals, many from those organizations, who provided invaluable encouragement, reflections, input (sometimes without knowing), and guidance in the course of our journey. These include (in no particular order) Matt Foster, Open University; Eamonn Meehan, Catrina Sheridan, Finola Finnan, Karen Kennedy, Sean Farrell, Caoimhe de Barra, Michael Duggan, Fintan Maher, and the team at Trocaire; Paddy Maguinness, Caroline Mulqueen, Maurice Healy, Robert Moodie, and the team and board at Traidlinks; Annemarie Riley, Sean Callahan, Carol Bothwell, Schuyler Thorup, David Orth-Moore, Michele Broemmelsiek, Judson Flanagan, David Palasits, Christina Way, Amy Laroque-Rumano, Chhaya Kapilashrami, and the team at CRS; Marg Mayne; Siobhain McGee and Olga McDonogh, ActionAid Ireland; Tom Arnold, formerly of Concern Worldwide; Chris Jurgens, USAID; Mark Goldring and Karen Brown, Oxfam GB; Ian Anderson, Oxfam Australia; Darius Teter, Oxfam America; John Nduba and Peter Ngatia, AMREF Health Africa; Jo Ensor, the Philanthropy Workshop; Susannah Hares, Ark; Nigel Spence and the team at ChildFund Australia; Brian Doolan, Victoria Morris, Tom White, and the team at the Fred Hollows Foundation; Paul Ronalds and the team at Save the Children Australia; Jane Edge and David Lewis, CBM Australia; Peter Walton, Australian Red Cross; Lord Nigel Crisp, Sightsavers; Robert Glasser, Geneva Centre for Security Policy; Marcy Vigoda, UN Office for the Coordination of Humanitarian Affairs; John Mitchell, Plan International; Kevin Jenkins, Charles Badenoch, and Tim Gray, World Vision International; Mike Penrose, Olivier Longue, Jean-Michel Grand, Andrea Tamburini, Paula Tenaglia, Action Against Hunger; and Ray Jordan, Gorta Self Help Africa.

Special thanks as well to Jim Emerson, formerly of ChildFund Alliance and Plan International; Ian Gray, formerly of World Vision; Christine Allison, formerly of the World Bank; Peter Thompson, formerly of Shell International; Tom Dente and Eric Walker, InsideNGO; Jeremy Hobbs, formerly of Oxfam International; Anna Patton and the team at Devex; Mark Spelman, World Economic Forum; John Hailey, City University London's Cass Business School; Siham Bortcosh and Tim Boyes-Watson, Mango; Tosca Bruno-van Vijfeijken, Transnational NGO Initiative, Syracuse University; George E. Mitchell, Powell School of the City College of New York; Burkhard Gnarig and Peter Christiansen, International Civil Society Centre; Hans Zomer, Dochas; Adrio Bacchetta, Sandstone Consulting and Baobab Associates; and David Spriggs, Marcus Harvey, and the team at Infoxchange.

At Accenture, our appreciation goes to Gib Bulloch (founder of Accenture Development Partnerships), John Downie, Kausar Qazilbash, Vasi Nadarajah, Colin Sloman, Catherine Marsh, Shannon Roper, Florence Micol, Heidi Strawson, Jill Huntley, Yih-Jeh Teen, Dianne Rajaratnam (formerly with Accenture Development Partnerships), and the whole Accenture Development Partnerships team, in particular, Matt Radford, Angela Werrett, Louise James, Roger Ford, Ian Lobo, Dee Jadeja, Ryan Johnson,

Rachel Manton, Mary Woodgate, Lionel Bodin, Natalie Co, Sara Lamb, and Dan Baker.

Certainly not least, a big thank you to Olive Heffernan, Kelly O' Donavan, and Michael Bond for early reviews and editing; to Tony, Katrin, and Elvira Ryan and to Matt and Melika Grantham; to Rebecca Crowley for some of our illustrations; to Aisling Crowley for moral support and a shared passion for international development; and to Deborah Crowley, chief proofreader and jargon detector.

—*James Crowley and Morgana Ryan*

Introduction

Navigating change in any large organization—in any industry or sector—is difficult. There are many kinds and levels of change, and there are many war stories—some good and many less so. Some changes can be fairly tangible—such as reducing costs, moving to a new office, implementing a new IT system, or reallocating responsibilities. Larger, longer-term improvements can sometimes be less precise, such as improving the quality of programs, improving decisionmaking, increasing agility, or bringing in stronger accountability approaches. Particularly when the complexity is greater, there are many things to take into account and a fair number of ways to trip up.

We are strong believers that successful change needs to bring together three important elements: the *content* of the change—what we are trying to achieve and what specific changes that involves; the *context* of the change—the reality of the situation we are working within; and the *approach* to the change—the process of navigating toward the intended destination. Good change leaders have an intuitive understanding of how to balance and integrate these three aspects. This demands a rare combination of analytical rigor, intuition, determination, and resilience.

The approach one takes depends on the content and the context. Sometimes a prescriptive, tightly managed project or program is appropriate. Sometimes it is good to lay out a series of intermediate destination points, each defining a useful degree of progress, but only develop detailed plans to get through the first few steps—knowing that flexibility and redirection may be needed after that. Sometimes, it may be better merely to set a vision of the intended destination, painting as clear a direction as you can, but then letting staff and managers work out the best path to get there.

Why is navigating change so demanding in very large organizations? When addressing this issue, it is instructive to reflect on another curious question: what, actually, *is* an organization? We can see that it has many parts—people (staff, management, and boards), reputation, things offered to customers/beneficiaries, relationships (with partners, donors, supporters, volunteers, suppliers), buildings, values and principles, habits, processes, systems, and policies. All of these have been built up and refined in layers of experience, improvements, experiments, and learning. Each layer builds on the previous, year after year, decade after decade. New management and staff bring fresh ideas that eventually blend with previous layers. When we build the foundations of any major change process, we inevitably dig into some of these previous layers, causing disruption, confusion, and probably resistance. Progress requires analysis, understanding, empathy, and respect as well as rigor, patience, and perseverance.

Before proceeding, we would like to offer a vote of empathy to the leaders of large agencies in this sector. We appreciate that the business of development is complex and sometimes quite difficult. We understand that many agencies are extremely stretched, working in many different countries, in many different contexts, from failed states to large middle-income countries, and tackling a plethora of technically demanding topics. At the same time, the profile of poverty is shifting. The simplistic dividing line between the rich, developed world and poor, developing countries has become blurred. A significant proportion of those living below the poverty line are now in middle-income countries, in places such as India, Nigeria, and Indonesia—where the welcome for international civil society is receding. The increased frequency and duration of major emergencies (from conflict or natural disasters) is also placing enormous pressure on the global humanitarian response system. In many of these situations, security is becoming more problematic—think about the realities on the ground in Afghanistan, Somalia, South Sudan, Syria, and Palestine. To compound all of this, many donors and politicians have suddenly become self-professed experts in the business of development, demanding clear and immediate (and sometimes ridiculously simplistic) evidence of impact—apparently blind to the realities of the situations where NGOs are trying to help.

Access to funding is getting more difficult. Much of the global economy is stuck in an extended period of minimal or zero growth. This is driven by a range of factors, including weak demand, sluggish productivity growth combined with projections of a significant reduction in the working-age population in most developed countries up to 2050—even in emerging economies such as China, Russia, and Mexico.[1] As well as casting a negative shadow on growth opportunities in the developing world, this slowdown is already provoking questioning of the justification and affordability for the levels of aid funding that many aspire to.

Of course there are some areas of progress and encouragement. We have seen impressive progress in reducing poverty levels, particularly in China, parts of Asia, and South America. In a number of developing countries we have seen encouraging levels of economic growth with increasing enterprise and trade, helped along by new sources of external capital—including foreign direct investment and remittances. New technologies in many forms are providing the opportunity for some countries and sectors to leapfrog their way into a better place. However, for every positive sign of hope, there are dark clouds. The battle of cultures, as predicted so clearly by Dominique Moisi in his *The Geopolitics of Emotion: How Cultures of Fear, Humiliation, and Hope Are Reshaping the World,*[2] is raising instability, conflict, and displacement in many parts of both the developing and developed worlds. We know that the effects of climate change, which is finally an accepted trend, will be felt most harshly in the developing world. Despite encouraging progress at the Paris 2015 summit (the UN Climate Change Conference), this will undermine food production, water supplies, and livelihoods, even though developing countries have contributed precious little to the carbon and other harmful emissions that have brought it to bear. Together, these issues are likely to stimulate levels of migration from areas of drought, famine, and conflict far beyond what we have experienced to date.

International NGOs find themselves in a challenging position and unfortunately too often feel that they are on the back foot. As the world around them rapidly evolves, NGOs urgently need to figure out their optimum future role and focus. At the same time, many are striving to catch up with the demands of yesterday, strengthening and professionalizing their systems and processes, improving their decisionmaking in terms of allocation of capital and scarce expertise, reducing duplication and cost, and of course improving the quality and sustainability of their programs. Many are also trying to tighten their scope in terms of where they work and the content issues they seek to contribute to. This requires "complex and brain-hurting" thinking and analysis to reach a deeper understanding of how change really comes about—often discussed under the controversial label *theories of change.*

All of this essential work is ongoing and, unsurprisingly, is taking a considerable amount of time. This is not helped by inordinately complex governance structures, a scarcity of unrestricted funding, and the revolving doors of leaders who come and go. These large international NGOs are complicated, principled, and often stubborn organizations—and can be extraordinarily hard to shift.

Adding all this together, we should not be surprised to find that many NGOs are in a period of instability. They are no longer the small, nimble, independent agencies they were in previous decades. Although they have been doing their best to strengthen their operations to meet yesterday's expectations, they are not yet the high-performance, disciplined, professional organizations they aspire to be.

At this point, you may be thinking it is surprising that turnover and burnout in the ranks of the senior leadership in the sector is not even higher than it is.

This book is intended as a practical handbook for NGO executives, boards, donors, and staff who are seeking to navigating large-scale or complex change to respond to these complex challenges. It follows our earlier work, *Building a Better International NGO: Greater than the Sum of the Parts?*[3] There we argued the need for change and described the kinds of changes agencies need to make to stay relevant over the coming decades. That book was concerned with the why and the what— this new volume centers on how to make change happen. It brings together a broad range of ideas and insights from the world of managing change and seeks to make them directly relevant to NGOs and the international development and humanitarian sectors.

In Chapters 1 and 2, we cover a range of ideas, tools, and advice for navigating organizational change. To make this manageable, we structured these two chapters around four levels of thinking: (1) the basics for any change process, (2) dealing with complexity, (3) getting more insights by questioning context, and (4) bringing in the subtle but critical issue of timing and organizational rhythm.

The remaining chapters tackle five areas that we feel merit particular attention. Chapter 3 looks at the practical aspects of implementing a high-performance organizational model. Chapter 4 looks at the controversial subject of how to develop and implement a serious, agency-level theory of change. Chapter 5 investigates the practical changes required to work more effectively with the private sector. Chapter 6 examines the thorny issue of why NGOs have so much trouble with information technology. The final chapter looks at the rationale for, risks of, and possible approaches to mergers in the sector—respecting that the arguments for consolidation are growing ever stronger and respecting that a merger could be one of the most transformative changes in the life of any agency.

Note

1. United Nations, Population Division, World Population Prospects, 2015 Revision, (medium variant), http://www.un.org/en/development/desa/population.

2. Dominique Moisi, *The Geopolitics of Emotion: How Cultures of Fear, Humiliation, and Hope Are Reshaping the World* (New York: Anchor, 2010).

3. James Crowley and Morgana Ryan, *Building a Better International NGO: Greater than the Sum of the Parts?* (Boulder, CO: Kumarian Press, 2013).

1

The Basics of Navigating Organizational Change

There is an enormous volume of research and literature in circulation on the various aspects of managing change. Some of this material tackles the substantial difficulties associated with delivering on major change initiatives, as typified by the useful *Harvard Business Review* (HBR) article "Why Transformation Efforts Fail" by John Kotter.[1] Another good example is the HBR article by Robert Kegan and Lisa Laskow Lahey, "The Real Reason People Won't Change."[2] Based on the waves of current and historical literature, institutional change is clearly not a subject for the faint of heart. On the other hand, there are some heroic stories describing successful turnarounds and major transformations. Examples include the well-documented turnaround at IBM led by Lou Gerstner in the 1990s, at GE led by Jack Welsh,[3] or at Southwest Airlines.[4] Business schools are well versed in studying these much publicized success stories.

Over time, almost every large organization we know has gone through a major change, improvement, or transformation to respond to changing circumstances. This is often driven by a combination of external and internal pressures as well as ambition for faster growth and better performance. For ambitious organizations, the quest for ongoing improvements is a continuing and everlasting process. One might argue this is even more pressing today, when the pace of technological change and global interconnectedness is driving new opportunities and a range of new problems.

What are the main challenges that organizations face when engaging in a major change initiative?

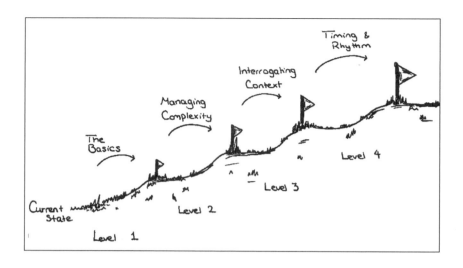

The first challenge relates to the risk that managers seek to look for a silver bullet—raising the risk that they are overly limited in their perspective. In fact, much of the current literature is overly focused on finding a unique secret or formula to explain why some turnarounds are successful. Although this can be instructive, we know that multiple factors contribute to success. It is often the weak link or the forgotten piece of the jigsaw that causes progress to flounder. An interesting analogy is the competitive performance of a Formula 1 racing car. A car is the result of painstaking planning, design, execution, and concentration, building on years of learning and experience. Failure at the track typically occurs due to one specific error or omission somewhere—faulty brakes, the wrong tires, or driver error. Failure can be caused by any one of a hundreds little errors; success requires every link of the chain to perform as intended.

The second challenge is that there is a tendency to speak about strategic change as a single generic thing and the ideas and insights as uniform in applicability. In reality there are many kinds of change in terms of nature, scope, and scale. Upgrading a bathroom should be a relatively simple project, but it has caused much angst to many because it requires the careful coordination of a considerable number of tasks and tradespeople. It requires careful upfront design and planning prior to construction. Steps need to happen in sequence. This can take less than a week if well planned and organized, and up to a year if not. Turning around a failing school is clearly even more complex, as there are less tangible issues to be tackled; even if all goes well, it can take several years. Achieving transformation at an organization like Hewlett Packard or Apple, where there is significant technical, geographic, and operational complexity as well as embedded ways of working, is something quite different.

Achieving change in a large NGO is a nontrivial challenge. It is driven by a wide range of complex factors that are forcing fundamental changes in how NGOs operate, such as the need to strengthen programs, respond to global shifts in donor preferences, embrace new technologies and new types of programs, and work with new kinds of partners. Of course, navigating change for an international NGO follows many of the same basic challenges as for any large organization. There can be added complications, too, for example:

- It can be extremely **difficult to get funding** for internal organization-strengthening initiatives, as donors understandably prefer to channel their funds to front-line programs in the field.
- It can be challenging to get the **time and attention of internal management and staff**, as these individuals are more motivated to devote their limited time to what seem to be more urgent field priorities.
- The **governance and decisionmaking** realities of large NGO families, federations, or confederations can be complex and not always conducive to easy or quick decisionmaking.
- Finally, many international NGOs **are spread very thin**, across a wide array of program domains in many countries and contexts. As a result, the investment and efforts to carry out major organizational strengthening may be daunting in comparison to the available resources.

Because of these challenges, it is essential to be thoughtful in defining what is achievable, diligent in gaining support from relevant groups and stakeholders, and ruthlessly determined in following through initiatives to completion. It is also important to select the best possible approach while recognizing the specific context in a particular agency.

The Aims of Chapters 1 and 2

The primary aim of the first two chapters is to provoke readers to be thoughtful and rigorous in planning and navigating change in their organizations. We seek to demystify the factors and challenges that frequently come into play and offer a way of framing ideas around change that is accessible and, where possible, tailored to the issues that confront NGOs. We cover a number of ideas, tools, and perspectives, and we fully appreciate that not all will be applicable to every situation. Many are drawn from tried-and-tested, referenced sources. However, some are drawn from our practical experience and shared here for the first time. We hope readers will find one or more of the ideas relevant to the changes you are seeking to make.

The material is structured along four levels of thinking, as summarized in Figure 1.1. The levels build on one another. This approach is analogous to the five levels of leadership, described by Jim Collins in his very useful book *Good to Great.*[5]

Level 1 contains some of the basic elements—not because they are easy but because they are the foundational pieces that should apply to all

---

Level 1: The Basics

- Clarity on drivers and benefits
- Authentic leadership
- Clear and consistent communication
- Selection and continuity of the right people
- Acknowledging and overcoming resistance and barriers to change
- Basic project management disciplines

Level 2: Managing Complexity

- A program as a journey rather than a rigid set of projects
- Understanding the interconnected cogs in an integrated organizational system
- Choosing the best change approach
- Aligning disconnected agendas and priorities
- High-impact leadership
- Aligning content, context, and approach

Level 3: A Deeper Investigation and Appreciation of Context

- Understanding and strengthening organizational glue
- Deeper understanding of context: organizational life cycle model
- Deeper understanding of people context: motivation and ability segmentation
- Deeper understanding of people context: Social Style Model

Level 4: The Art of Exploiting Organizational Rhythm

- From static to dynamic thinking: the concept of natural frequency
- Applying dynamic thinking to human structures (organizations)
- Using dynamic thinking to help in navigating change in NGOs

Figure 1.1 The Four Levels of Thinking About Organizational Change

change processes, big and small. We believe that adopting good practice around each of these elements will increase the chances of success in any change process.

Level 2 thinking includes a number of additional ideas that may be useful when the complexity of the change is high. This complexity may be because of geographical reach, the scope of functional disciplines affected by the change, the severity of the change, or a combination of all three.

Level 3 includes a few practical ideas and tools that may be useful when a deeper analysis of internal organizational context could be helpful. Here we seek to understand some more subtle aspects or circumstances that can have an important bearing on how individuals in an organization, or the organization at large, are likely to embrace and adapt to change. These ideas and tools can give us an appreciation of the factors that may need particular attention along the way.

For Level 4, we invite readers to explore the idea of timing and rhythm when planning and navigating change. In doing this, we are moving further into the realms of the art of change rather than the science of change, the latter being more at the fore for Levels 1, 2, and 3. The central thesis here is that making decisions about the choice and timing of actions is a complex art form that rarely gets enough attention in the busy agendas of senior leaders. This level is likely to appeal to more lateral and intuitive thinkers who are deeply interested in the subtle aspects of planning and navigating longer-term change.

In this first chapter, we tackle the basic elements of Level 1 thinking. We also set out some practical hints and tips. We conclude with a few helpful steps for those seeking to initiate and navigate a major strategic change process. However, we stress that we are not proposing a rigid or prescriptive methodology. The variation in contexts and types of change initiative are so diverse that this would be unrealistic.

Of course, the ideal is to have an organization that is constantly striving to reinvent itself from within—without the need for a special transformation initiative. However, for all organizations, from time to time, a major change process may be unavoidable.

Level 1 Thinking: The Basics

Level 1 is what we refer to as the basics of navigating change. We believe implementing good practice around these elements will increase the chances of success for any change process. Too often these foundational pieces are skipped over or taken for granted.

Clarity on Drivers and Benefits

When framing any significant new change initiative, it is important to ask the question, "What problem are we trying to solve?" To answer this question, we need to identify the key factors driving the change and the benefits expected. Although this seems obvious, it rarely gets the attention and rigor it deserves. This is an essential foundation of navigating change because:

1. If done well, it should provide some clear and factual understanding on the reasons the change program is happening in the first place. This should also help strengthen the **alignment and buy-in across senior leadership**, which in turn will be invaluable in communicating to and winning over the organization at large.

2. This investigation provides an **anchor for steering and guiding the change** by linking decisions and choices back to the original drivers and benefits. If external circumstances evolve or new learning is uncovered, it can provide a clear basis for reappraising the future shape and focus of the program.

3. It provides the anchor point or a baseline against which we can **track the actual benefits** and success of the change.

Table 1.1 illustrates some of the kinds of drivers we have observed in a number of large NGOs pursuing ambitious programs to strengthen their organizations. These drivers can be broken down into a number of broad categories, including, for example:

- Responding to the implications of a new strategic direction
- Being able to address the evolving needs of donors
- Responding to concerns around program quality, consistency, and learning
- Exploiting new technology possibilities
- Addressing issues around organizational performance in terms of cost, effectiveness, coherence, or agility
- Mitigating concerns about access and legitimacy that could undermine an agency's license to operate.

These are all understandable areas of concern for any ambitious NGO.

Any major change program can involve a broad and complex range of drivers. However, it is important to identify a handful of the most important ones, rather than a multitude of issues that one could expect to be on the day-to-day agenda of any leadership team.

Table 1.1 Why Change? Common Drivers for NGOs

Category	Example Driver
New Strategy	• Translating a new strategic direction into day-to-day plans and actions
Donor Expectations	• Addressing the **evolving expectations of donors** • Working in long-term partnership with strategic donors
Program Quality, Impact, and Learning	• Increasing **confidence and evidence of program quality and impact** • Ensuring robust and consistent program learning and knowledge management • Encouraging breakthrough innovations and industrial scale solutions • Enhancing capacity to act across borders (regionally/globally) • Being an effective partner in consortia and major partnerships
Organization Performance	• Creating a **high-performance/inspiring environment for talent** • Reducing costs, eliminating duplication • Improving decisionmaking: optimization use of resources, key expertise, and investment • Becoming more agile to respond to new emerging needs • Building vibrant, credible country organizations • Correcting North–South power balance issues • Establishing integrated planning, performance management, and accountability • Harmonizing and strengthening enabling functions, processes, and systems
License to Operate	• Improving long-term legitimacy and access • Addressing issues around reputation, risk, and global coherence

It is better if the change drivers can be articulated in concrete terms, for example:

- "We want to be able to compete for and successfully win the very largest multinational grants—increasing our win ratio to one in two or better."
- "We want to be able to design every project using our best learning from everything available internally or externally."

- "We want to be able to bring every single project up to the standard of our best project."
- "We need to be confident to direct our scarce time, expertise, organizational energy, and of course our private/unrestricted funding to those future programs that have the very best return on investment for impact, irrespective of geography or program area."
- "We want to effectively leverage technology to better deliver on our strategic goals."

When defining change drivers, it can be very useful to articulate a clear, tangible, and ambitious goal, one that indicates clearly what the agency wants to be or what it wants to achieve. Setting a goal (or set of goals) can provide focus and clarity and can help communicate ambition. Within some NGOs, we have seen many vibrant and heated debates about whether setting an audacious goal is indeed possible. Clearly, this is easier to do in the private sector, where one can set goals around revenue, market share, or shareholder value, but it should be possible for NGOs as well. One goal could be to double an agency's measured impact in three or five years. Such a target assumes that you are able to define what impact you are seeking and a means of gathering data to assess it at an agency-wide level. What about goals around income, such as an ambition to be a $1 billion agency by a defined date? This promotes rage among some, who argue that the aim of NGOs should be to work themselves out of a job. We feel that this line of argument is somewhat trite, as there is and will continue to be so much still to do in the fight against poverty and injustice, and to respond to the increasing onslaught of natural and man-made emergencies. If agencies continue to improve their approach and their capacity to help, then growth in income is at least concrete evidence of progress. We feel that financial goals, although useful as part of internal stretch targets, should not be a high-profile item for external audiences. Goals that are firmly anchored around the external impact or change that you want to see in the world are likely to be more powerful and motivating to all.

We warn that singular overarching goals, unless robustly defined, can be detrimental as they will gradually seep into day-to-day priorities, targets, and decisions. An example of a very questionable goal (in our opinion) is the number of beneficiaries helped. This can be criticized for a range of reasons, most notably because it can lead to fairly spurious counting and the risk that it encourages a "mile wide and an inch deep" approach.

> ### NGO Takeaway
>
> *Be crystal clear on your drivers for change as well as the explicit shift desired, in practical terms that all staff can understand and buy into. Try to define a tangible, quantifiable, and inspiring goal—where you want to be at the end of the change or what impact you want to have contributed.*

Authentic Leadership

Professional, positive, and authentic leadership behaviors can be a challenge for many NGOs. There may be many causes for this—including the enormous scope of programs and geographies covered, the difficulty of being confident about impact and value for money, and the inevitable risks involved.

However, when navigating change, leadership is a critical ingredient. For avoidance of doubt, when we refer to *leadership*, we are referring not only to CEOs or members of a senior executive team but to those at a variety of levels and positions who play a leadership role in their day-to-day jobs. Irrespective of the best-laid plans, a significant change process is a voyage into the unknown; hence, trust in leadership is essential. In our view, an important foundation of authentic leadership is building trust that you really care deeply about the organization's mission and about the individuals that make up that organization. This is best highlighted by the quote "people only care how much you know when they know how much you care."

Change is uncomfortable to many and is likely to have difficult or painful implications. Leaders signal by the way they behave, initiate, interact, and communicate information about the intended change process. As well as explaining the vision, drivers, and benefits, leaders should be able to describe the implications of the intended change, providing practical information and as much reassurance as possible.

It is very helpful if different leaders speak in consistent terms about what is driving and implied by the intended change, otherwise staff may be confused and reluctant to embrace what is proposed. Equally important is the tone and style of communication of individual leaders. It needs to be open, be honest, and show empathy but also show commitment and determination. Sometimes it is all right, or even better, to say honestly "we do not know yet, but expect to know by X." This builds credibility. Finally, the approach should be true to each individual leader's personal style—being authentic is essential for longer-term credibility and trust.

Leadership style is a highly researched topic and helpfully explored in a range of useful publications, including the excellent book by Rob Goffee and Gareth Jones, *Why Should Anyone Be Led by You?: What It Takes to Be an Authentic Leader*.[6] Susan Cain's book *Quiet—The Power of Introverts in a World That Can't Stop Talking*[7] explores emerging research considering the different ways extroverts and introverts lead:

> In the modern world there seems to be a natural bias towards extro-verted styles of leadership—the sometimes overwhelming pressure to be a great public speaker, gregarious and outgoing. Introverts of the world fear not, this is not always the case!
>
> The research suggests that "extroverted leaders enhance group per-formance when employees are passive, but that introverted leaders are more effective with proactive employees."[8] This is based on the idea that introverted leaders are inclined to listen and "are more likely to hear and implement suggestions."[9] They are willing to empower oth-ers. Extroverts, "with their natural ability to inspire . . . are better at getting results from more passive workers."[10]
>
> Whether you agree with this or not, it is worth spending some time thinking about your leadership style, your natural bias to extroversion or introversion and how you motivate others to follow your lead and make change.

NGO Takeaway

NGO leaders need to try doubly hard to be positive, be authentic, and build trust for the long term. NGOs are not easy organizations to lead!

Clear and Consistent Communication

Communication is a critical part of any change process. Though it is a very broad subject, we would like to emphasize the following points.

- Communication will be more effective if it is anchored in a clear vision of the targeted benefits and articulated in a consistent way by a unified and committed leadership.
- It's best to capture the vision, drivers, and benefits for the change in a limited number of short, clear messages. If the concept isn't simple and easy to grasp, people will find it hard to embrace.

- As the change progresses, it is important that communication is well planned and at an appropriate tempo and level of detail. Not too little or not too much—keeping a good digestible flow of information throughout. It can be useful to have a complementary set of channels/media, for example, a combination of short emails from senior top executives, cascade briefings, and intranet updates.
- Information needs to be relevant to the day-to-day realities and pressures of management and staff. To this end, it is useful to articulate the new future in a way that is clear and practical in the eyes of the target audience. One very simple technique we find useful is to describe, ideally on one page, the strategic shifts that are intended. This is illustrated by the examples in Table 1.2.
- When you plan a communications program it is essential to recognize the conflicting pressures of staff throughout the organization. Figure 1.2 is a simple pictorial representation of the practical tensions (and sometimes conflicting loyalties) faced by staff as they seek to balance messages and pressures from different directions.

NGO Takeaway

No different than for any organization in any sector: keep it simple and honest. Make it practical and relevant. Don't go overboard at the beginning and then fail to keep up the momentum. Use multiple complementary channels. Underpromise and overdeliver!

Selection and Continuity of the Right People

Although technology, processes, and structures are all important parts of a change journey, ultimately the *people (staff and management)* are the real enablers and adopters of change. They are also the greatest potential source of resistance. Investment in staff is vital to help them embrace, contribute to, and ultimately deliver the changes intended. Making sure that staff members are genuinely engaged is essential. Investing in training and giving people the time to develop their skills can be a powerful way to help them embrace the change, especially where it requires new ways of working.

It is also important to *invest in the individuals who make up the core change team*. Often selected people are asked to contribute part-

Table 1.2 Articulating "Strategic Shifts" as a Practical Way of Aiding Communication

Change Area	Today	Tomorrow
Donors	Several hundred donors managed on an ad hoc country-by-country basis	Focus on five to eight global strategic donors—managed on integrated global basis
Enabling Systems	Separate finance and HR systems in each country —little or no integration	Single global approach, consistent and professional systems and procedures for key designated processes
Organization Performance Management	Inconsistent or nonexistent performance management at organizational level— limited to financial and exception reporting	Integrated planning and performance management approach, embracing all of the key areas—consistently implemented across all countries and departments; provides a foundation for strong individual performance management process
Leadership Behaviors	Variable, and less than inspirational	Consistent, positive, and authentic behaviors, defined and embedded in the individual performance management framework
Knowledge Management	Informal if at all	Clear protocols and process embedded into career development and performance management processes
Private Sector	Private sector seen as "not that relevant" and primarily as a negative force	Carefully selected private sector organizations (local and international) embedded into program planning and execution—regarded as key partners to deliver, sustain, and scale impact
Theory of Change	No explicitly articulated agency-level theory of change—a wide range of implicit assumptions and beliefs based on personal perspectives and history	Alignment on a clearly articulated agency-level theory of change with clearly defined assumptions; integrated into country planning, program design, monitoring and evaluation, and knowledge management processes; a framework for ongoing learning and sharing

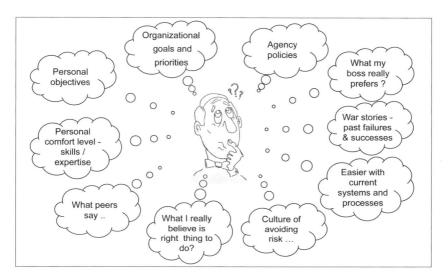

Figure 1.2 How Will Front-Line Staff Respond to Proposed Change?

time on a change project team without any reallocation of their current responsibilities. This can make it hard for them to be successful as they are carrying a 100 percent day-job workload in addition to leading a major change. Often, there is an unhelpful habit for some well-known individuals to get allocated to multiple initiatives in parallel—without fully recognizing that they have little possibility of contributing to each as needed. Getting the right people in the right roles is important, and making sure they have the mandate and the time to dedicate is equally essential.

We emphasize the need for continuity—that is, the importance of keeping key individuals in the change team until the ultimate results are achieved. This is one of the most frequent mistakes we have observed in several organizations. Discontinuity as a result of handovers is a major risk as new individuals rarely have as deep an understanding of the intended vision and the key shifts implied. Additionally, changing key personnel can send a strong message to the wider organization that this particular initiative is no longer a priority.

Finally, as you assign change leadership roles, it is useful to avoid using the obvious choices, that is, selecting individuals who may have done similar roles in previous programs. Where possible, it can be beneficial to give people the opportunity to step up. This can be a good way of showing commitment to those staff members, build their confidence and skills, and show them that leadership sees them as important people for the future.

NGO Takeaway

Pick the change leaders carefully and creatively. Support them, help them, trust them, and let them follow through until the job is 100 percent done!

Acknowledging and Overcoming Resistance and Barriers to Change

When embracing a significant change process, it is important to acknowledge that some resistance will be unavoidable. Much of it is likely to be genuine. It is natural that management and staff, who have had successful results and are comfortable with current ways of working, will be wary of embracing a different way of doing things. Change can be unnerving because it usually takes people outside their comfort zone.

Even in failing organizations, it is not unusual to find people who feel that their performance and contributions are beyond question—others are the problem, they will say, or factors outside of the organization's control. Understanding the kinds of resistance likely to be encountered is an important step in planning any significant change process. Table 1.3 sets out some of the kinds of resistance that can be frequently found.

It can be helpful to distinguish between resistance to change on one hand and barriers on the other. Resistance to change is mainly related to people's concerns or discomfort with the prospect of the change process. Barriers to change go beyond the human aspects and include elements such as suitability of current assets, skills, reputation, or existing networks of relationships. Both are real challenges and often manifest as interconnected sets of issues.

NGO Takeaway

NGOs are typically populated with many spirited, committed, and deeply opinionated people who have their own domains of influence. Understanding and recognizing resistance is probably more important for NGOs than for organizations in other sectors.

Table 1.3 Overcoming Resistance to Change

Resistance	Examples
No Need	• I just don't like too much change. • We are doing grand the way we are; why do we need to do anything different? • I do not understand the real drivers or where the real benefits will come from.
Wrong Time	• The change will absorb too much effort and our day-to-day operations will suffer too much. • Not just now . . .
Wrong Answer	• You are too optimistic about the benefits—you always think the grass is greener—it will take too long and cost far more than you think—the risks are too high. • Your proposed solution is wrong—I know a different and better answer!
Wrong People	• I was not involved in the analysis of the problem or the formulation of future solution or vision, hence I am not going to get involved. • I don't like the people who are shaping this, or the process is wrong.
Never Happen	• You do not understand what its really like—the solution on the table is not practical or realistic. • This will never happen in my lifetime . . . why should I waste time engaging in the process?
Not Good for Me	• This could negatively affect my job, job security, pay, pension, place of employment, or my progression expectations.
Competing Commitments	• Commitment to idea, people, and historic approach.

Basic Project Management Disciplines

Good project management is an essential tool for supporting any good change initiative. Though it is not feasible to completely describe all of the disciplines of project management here, we briefly summarize the key elements in the box below. For those who wish to delve deeper, we recommend the book *The Definitive Guide to Project Management* by Nokes et al.,[11] which is a very practical and useful guide.

In broad terms, we believe there are twelve important disciplines of project management.

1. Developing a robust business case and securing necessary approval
2. Structuring and phasing the overall change process
3. Governance and steering arrangements
4. Project and program team selection, orientation, training, and support
5. Planning, milestones, critical path analysis, and dependencies
6. Resource planning
7. Stakeholder analysis and management
8. Communication planning and management
9. Budgeting and cost management
10. Risk management and contingency planning
11. Progress reporting
12. Benefits tracking

1. Developing a Robust Business Case and Securing Necessary Approval

This is an essential first step before beginning any change project or program. Many projects run into difficulty down the road because of a lack of clarity and agreement at the outset as to the anticipated benefits and costs and what was involved, including the level of effort or disruption. Although every attempt should be made to quantify benefits, in reality, good business cases could accommodate qualitative and quantitative benefits.

2. Structuring and Phasing the Overall Change Process

Working out the overall structure of a change program is something that requires a lot of thought and experience, careful planning, and a bit of intuition. It needs to take account of the organizational context, the openness to change of the organization, and potential barriers plus consideration of what might be the optimum sequencing of the change, based on the scope and objectives of a program. The key issue is to work out how much to bite off at each stage, taking into account the effort and disruption involved.

It can be helpful to clarify the difference between a "project" and a "program." When we first started working in the sector, we were surprised that the key concepts of project (and program) management were not as well understood as we had expected, and the terms were used in many different ways.

- In broad terms, a project is "a temporary endeavour undertaken to create a unique product, service or result." Project management is "the application of knowledge, skills, tools and techniques to project activities to meet the project requirement."[12]

- A program is "a group of related projects, subprograms, and program activities that are managed in a coordinated way to obtain benefits not available from managing them individually."[13]

It is not always possible to have a clear view from the outset of all the activities and steps required to achieve a change. This can vary depending on the nature and scope of the change in question. For example, IT changes are often easier to plan for because methodologies exist and can be reused. Organizational change can be harder. Either way, it is useful to create an initial project structure at the outset, even if it may need to be adjusted along the way.

3. Governance and Steering Arrangements

It is essential to establish a clear governance structure to oversee and steer a change process. Whether you use an existing governance body or set up a specially designed steering committee, it is vital that the roles and responsibilities are defined at the beginning. Given the geographically dispersed nature of NGOs and their unique structures, it is also important to consider the politics of who is represented on the governance team both to ensure the right knowledge and input and also to help buy-in across the agency.

4. Project and Program Team Selection, Orientation, Training, and Support

Even when there is considerable uncertainty at the start of a change process, it is important to identify the right people with the appropriate skills. Putting together teams for each project provides an opportunity to bring together groups of people with complementary skills and knowledge, who may not previously have worked together. When selecting the team and team structure for more complex change processes, it may be useful to include a management layer to coordinate and supervise the various change projects; this is especially the case for change spanning multiple functions and/or geographies.

5. Planning, Milestones, Critical Path Analysis, and Dependencies

Once the project team and governance arrangements are in place, it is essential to plan the change process properly. Ensure that it does not last any longer than necessary. The quicker you get to the anticipated results and benefits, the higher the chance of success. It is useful to identify some important milestones. It is also important to identify and plan for any important dependencies where they are known.

6. Resource Planning

When carrying out detailed project planning, it is important to identify the funding, skills, and other resources that are necessary to enable the project or program to get to 100 percent completion.

7. Stakeholder Analysis and Management

All significant change programs are likely to affect a number of internal and external stakeholders whose support and participation will be essential for the success of the initiative. A thorough stakeholder mapping process is a useful early step. It should be reviewed and updated throughout the life cycle of the project/program.

8. Communication Planning and Management

Communication to the organization at large, and in particular to all key stakeholders (internal and external), is one of the most essential success factors for any change process. This was introduced earlier, in the discussion on Level 1 thinking.

9. Budgeting and Cost Management

All significant change initiatives are likely to have substantial cost implications, in terms of staff and management time as well as other direct and external costs. It is essential that all costs are properly estimated up front and carefully monitored and managed throughout.

10. Risk Management and Contingency Planning

Conducting a practical assessment of the significant risks or potential unintended consequences is an important part of good project planning. It can often help management head off unwanted events before they happen. In addition, having thoughtful risk mitigation strategies in place can be enormously helpful in reducing negative consequences should some of these risks actually come to pass.

11. Progress Reporting

Good progress reporting is a vital step in project management. Reporting should be at a sufficiently high level to enable the management and steering groups to keep a strategic perspective but at the same time grounded in enough detail to help highlight potential issues or blockages that might emerge in the future.

12. Benefits Tracking

Benefits tracking, often forgotten, is an important part of good project management. One common reason for its omission is that benefits may not have been properly articulated in the original business case. Sometimes there might not be sufficient effort invested to effectively establish a robust baseline. If benefits tracking is not properly set up at the outset, there may be a temptation to skim over this aspect down the road, either because it is too hard or management prefers not to face the reality that the anticipated results may have not been fully achieved.

There are at least two important implications of such a deficiency. It can result in (1) insufficient attention and determination to attend to all of the key requirements of the project that are essential for the full set of benefits to be realized; and (2) a lack of learning for future projects—for example, because assumptions made in the original business case have proven incorrect or overly optimistic.

NGO Takeaway

Basic project management disciplines should be followed in organizations for whom delivering projects and programs is their core business. However, applying these disciplines internally to achieve internal change can sometimes require considerable focus and resolve!

Practical Hints and Tips for Navigating Change

The following are some practical suggestions that we feel are applicable to both the not-for-profit and the for-profit sectors when embarking on a large-scale change process.

Tip 1: Underpromise, Overdeliver: Build Trust and Confidence for the Long Haul

People are fundamentally nervous about change, and therefore all communications must be carefully considered to ensure they are going to have the required impact and will not cause unnecessary uncertainty, concern, or fear. There is also a delicate balance between communicating too early (when the plans are poorly formulated) and communicating too late (when people feel the solution is already predetermined and they have had insufficient input). If there are hard messages that need to be understood, it may be better that these are communicated earlier rather than later. This is a challenge for all change processes in all sectors. As noted in the section on Drivers and Benefits in Level 1 thinking, it is important to be very clear on the reasons you are making the change and the expected benefits. Be realistic about what can be achieved and the timeframe required to achieve it. A key message we emphasize is that it is far better to underpromise and overdeliver than the other way around.

Tip 2: Don't Shy Away from the Hard Conversations

Organizational change often requires hard decisions to be made. In our experience, some large NGOs, with their complex governance structures, decisionmaking, and culture can find it difficult to have the hard conversations. Decisions can become highly consensus-driven, based on the lowest common denominator of what people will agree with rather than what is actually best for the agency. Leaders are sometimes guilty of using old arguments, for example, about each entity being unique or having a special local operating context, that mandate things be done in different and inconsistent ways. To be effective, NGOs need to be willing to embrace change. They need to adopt new, consistent, interconnected, and interdependent ways of working and in many cases need to move beyond historical politics and power bases so they can make the most of the benefits of being part of a global family.

Tip 3: Some People May Not Like the Changes Proposed, So Accept Casualties

To make significant change happen, it may be inevitable that some people will not agree with the direction being taken and the specifics of what needs to be done. This may result in upset, disengagement, and ultimately people leaving. Although this is clearly undesirable, it is perhaps better for the organization as a whole to lose a few people (including maybe some very good people) rather than prevaricate a key change decision resulting in a half-hearted change that does not take the organization in the new direction.

Tip 4: Anticipate the Journey, and Don't Declare Victory Too Soon

Change journeys rarely run smoothly from beginning to end. The "Valley of Despair"[14] is a model often used to illustrate this. Searching online reveals a number of different versions of this model, all with similar shapes and broad themes. Figure 1.3 shows one simplified version.

The basic concept here is that most change journeys will experience a period when organizational performance declines before eventually rising out of the slump as the benefits of the change process are realized. The depth of the decline and its duration (weeks, months, years) is

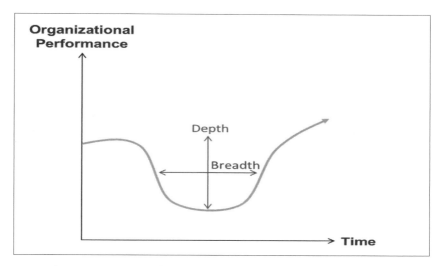

Figure 1.3 Valley of Despair During a Typical Change Process

something that can often be predicted and partly mitigated. The message is simple. The change journey is going to cause bumps along the way, but if you anticipate that and put in place mitigating actions, you can significantly reduce the depth and the breadth of the disruption.

Tip 5: Communicate Concrete Evidence of Progress and Acknowledge Success and Heroes

Having a practical framework to track the progress and success of change is important. In particular, it can be very useful for leadership to publicly acknowledge concrete evidence of success and highlight the work of groups or individuals who have made a particularly important contribution. This can be a powerful motivation tool in its own right.

Tip 6: Pace Can Be Very Important

Once an NGO is aligned on the need to make significant improvements, a quick pace can be effective. When the change is announced, staff across the organization will soon expect demonstrable evidence of progress in terms of benefits for the served constituencies, improved operational efficiency, and benefits for their own roles and careers. It is all too easy to underestimate the ability of staff to embrace change. One important benefit of a quick pace is to minimize the fear or uncertainty created when a new change process is announced. This can be helped by early and decisive steps that allow staff and managers to move quickly into the new world—avoiding the risk of becoming "frozen in uncertainty" as they wait for information to emerge.

Tip 7: Acknowledge Resistance and Expect Multiple Waves

Resistance can be a natural reaction, particularly from those who believe that the current approach or practices are strong and effective. Acknowledge resistance as genuine. Listen carefully to concerns, and seek to address them as best and honestly as you can. Often, resistance is because of inaccurate or incomplete information. Sometimes it can be due to very specific concerns, such as anticipated changes in power and decisionmaking control, changes in working habits, or changes in compensation. An honest conversation often helps, and will rarely do any harm. We have often found that the best champions of change started out as the strongest opponents.

Expect resistance to come in waves. Initially, resistance may be tepid, and the resisters may decide not to get involved on the assumption that this is a new and passing idea or fad and is unlikely to be implemented. The second wave may be slightly more active, when resisters come to the view that this new change may occur after all, and a stiffer response in terms of objections and barriers may be required to bring this new initiative to a halt. The third wave may come after the resisters realize the change is happening and they seek to modify the details of the proposed solution to suit their specific views or preferences.

Tip 8: Build Change Goals into Day-to-Day Goals and Targets

One of the easy temptations of new executive teams with lofty ambitions is to put in place a plethora of new one-off initiatives or programs, which layer on top of existing business activities and other change initiatives. This layering of demands can sometimes be detrimental to progress as staff are overstretched and potentially confused by the multitude of conflicting priorities.

We believe that in some situations achieving the change the organization desires can be done better with a stronger articulation of the future desired state and by building the desired improvements into the organizational and individual goals of management teams and individual staff. Management and staff can, in their own way, find the quickest and easiest way of achieving the desired direction. This point is closely aligned to the "pull" rather than "push" approach to change, which we will discuss in the next chapter.

Tip 9: Take the Time to Get the Governance Right
There are a number of common pitfalls to be aware of when designing the governance structure for different types of change. We emphasize the following points.

- When the change spans more than one function or geography, we strongly recommend that the governance is designed to reflect this.
- Consider what other lower levels of governance may be helpful to guide the change process. This may be in the form of reference groups, process owner groups, or other midlevel steering groups.
- One pitfall is to have insufficient meaningful involvement of field staff in the governance process. Too often change efforts fall into the trap of developing an overly headquarters-oriented design of a "perfect" solution without enough meaningful engagement with field staff. This has the potential to disenfranchise a significant portion of staff globally. NGOs are a fascinating mix of hierarchy and consensus. If people feel they haven't had ample opportunity to engage directly or be represented by someone who mirrors their thinking, they will at best switch off or at worst obstruct the change intended.

Pointers for NGO Leaders Contemplating a Change Process

To reiterate what was stated at the outset of this chapter: the ideal is to have an organization that is constantly striving to reinvent itself from within, without the need for the mega-special transformation initiative necessary to catch up with new demands and changing external pressures. History has shown that over-reliance on a large strategic transformation initiative is a risky route—and not always a guaranteed route to long-term success. Creating a culture of constant reinvention from within is where leading organizations strive to be.

However, for all organizations a major change process may be inevitable from time to time. We indicated at the beginning of this chapter that we are not setting out to present an overly prescriptive, step-by-step guide. The variation of contexts and types of change initiatives are so diverse that this would simply be unrealistic. However, if you find yourself in a situation that demands a major strategic change in your organization, the following are a few pointers that we hope might be helpful.

Articulate the drivers and benefits in simple, practical language
- What are the key drivers or reasons we are embarking on the change?
- What are the targeted benefits?
- What, in practical terms, are the key shifts that are implied by the change?
- What are the costs and other important implications?
- Make sure the senior executive team all understand and are aligned behind all of the above.

Rigorously appraise current internal (and external) context
- Conduct a thoughtful review of context: organizational context? Staff context? External stakeholder context?
- What does this tell us? Is it still a good idea? Is this the right time? How fast?

Think through the best approach to making the change
- Can we build the intended change into performance management targets at organization and individual levels?
- Do we need a special, one-off initiative?
- Overall timeframe: when to start? How long overall? How much in the first stage?
- Develop a high-level roadmap.

Identify the overall project structure and key team members
- Governance structure and membership.
- Project/program managers.
- Key technical experts.
- Champions and reference groups.

Develop a well-thought-out roadmap (or super plan)
- How much to bite off at each stage? Think through the main stages in more detail.
- Review key interdependencies.
- Define a small number of important interim milestones.

Identify and analyze the key barriers and blockages and prepare to respond
- Anticipate the resistance to change and any other important barriers.
- Prepare mitigation actions.

Prepare a practical communications approach and plan
- Who are the stakeholders?
- When to say what?
- How? email, conference calls, brown bag lunches, cascade briefings, blogs?
- Work out the right rhythm of communications.

Begin regular governance/review process and basic project management disciplines
- Steering meetings.
- Progress reporting.
- Risk and issue management.
- Benefit tracking.

Good luck!

Notes

1. John P. Kotter, "Leading Change: Why Transformation Efforts Fail," *Harvard Business Review* (March–April 1995).

2. Robert Kegan and Lisa Laskow Lahey, "The Real Reason People Won't Change," *Harvard Business Review* (November 2001).

3. Pier A. Abetti, "Jack Welch's Creative Revolutionary Transformation of General Electric and the Thermidorean Reaction (1981–2004)," *Creativity and Innovation Management*, 15, no. 1 (2006): 71–84.

4. Charles A. O'Reilly and Jeffrey Pfeffer, "Southwest Airlines—Case Study," *Harvard Business Review* (January 1995).

5. Jim Collins, *Good to Great: Why Some Companies Make the Leap . . . and Others Don't* (New York: Collins Business, 2001).

6. Rob Goffee and Gareth Jones, *Why Should Anyone Be Led by You?: What It Takes To Be An Authentic Leader* (Cambridge, MA: Harvard Business School Press, 2006).

7. Susan Cain, *Quiet—The Power of Introverts in a World That Can't Stop Talking* (London: Penguin, 2012), 56–57.

8. Ibid., p. 56.

9. Ibid., p. 57.

10. Ibid., p. 57.

11. Sebastian Nokes, Ian Major, Alan Greenwood, and Mark Goodyear, *The Definitive Guide to Project Management: The Fast Track to Getting the Job Done on Time and on Budget* (London: FT Prentice Hall, 2003).

12. PMI Lexicon of Project Management Terms, Version 2.0, Project Management Institute (2012), p. 12.

13. Ibid.

14. See http://www.mindtools.com, based on original work by Elizabeth Kübler-Ross, *On Death and Dying* (New York: Routledge, 1969).

2

The Art and Science of Complex Organizational Change

Now that we have explored the basics of navigating organizational change, we can investigate some additional ideas and tools that are relevant when the proposed change is more complex and where more profound analysis and reflection can be useful. The material in this chapter is structured into three further levels of thinking, building directly on the Level 1 thinking discussed in Chapter 1. These additional levels are:

- Level 2: managing complexity
- Level 3: a deeper investigation and appreciation of context
- Level 4: the art of exploiting organizational rhythm

Level 2 Thinking: Managing Complexity

A Program as a Journey Rather Than a Rigid Set of Projects

Sometimes, the direction and shape of the future vision an organization aspires to is clear. However, the details and precise steps to get there may be less obvious. In this situation, when it is not possible to prepare a complete program plan—setting out all the discrete projects in detail, it is necessary to take it step by step, embarking on specific projects or programs and then planning subsequent steps based on what is achieved and learned. We refer to this broadly as *journey management*, which is illustrated in Figure 2.1. In summary (building from what was introduced in Level 1):

- **A project** is "a temporary endeavour undertaken to create a unique product, service or result."[1]
- **A program** is "a group of related projects, subprograms, and program activities that are managed in a coordinated way to obtain benefits not available from managing them individually."[2]
- **A journey** is a flexible combination of projects and programs toward a longer-term strategic goal or vision.

Journey management is more flexible and dynamic, requiring strategic vision and the ability to deal with ongoing replanning and ambiguity. Typically, it requires change leaders with a more strategic approach and a deep understanding of an agency's programs, structure, culture, and enabling functions.

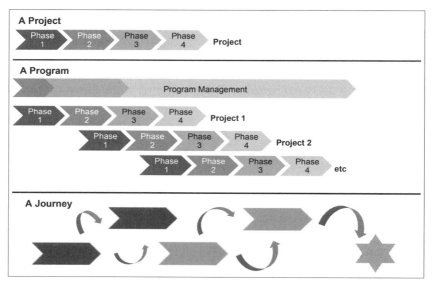

Figure 2.1 Project, Program, and Journey

NGO Takeaway

The scope and complexity of the changes that many NGOs are tackling is more akin to a journey than a neatly defined project or program. Continuity of leadership and strong teamwork throughout the distributed leadership team are essential to navigate this journey successfully.

Understanding the Interconnected Cogs in an Integrated Organizational System

Although a major change program may be centered on a particular aspect of an organization (such as new systems, ways of working, or structure), it will often involve a variety of pieces of the organizational puzzle. Some of these factors are illustrated in Figure 2.2. This illustration was originally introduced in *Building a Better International NGO*.[3] It depicts some of the areas we believe are particularly important when planning the journey to becoming a more effective international NGO. They are:

- Strengthening the **governance, board, and decisionmaking** processes,
- Refining and strengthening the **organization model/structure**,
- Building a more effective relationship with strategic donors and dealing with **donor pressures and preferences**,
- Reviewing and strengthening an agency's **theory of change**— with increased clarity and focus on the specific change the agency is trying to bring about in the world (see Chapter 4),
- Aligning or strengthening **global processes and systems**,
- Improving and aligning **leadership style, behaviors, and capacity**, and
- Developing or strengthening an agency's international approach to **organizational planning and accountability**.

We appreciate that for most agencies, implementing wholesale changes across all of these important and interconnected dimensions may be neither affordable nor realistic. Hence, careful prioritization and sequencing of change is essential.

Figure 2.2 illustrates the interconnected nature of these different components. The positioning of the planning and accountability cog in the center is intentional and indicates that this is a critical piece at the heart of any high-performing organization.

In what order should the various components of change be tackled? A number of the required changes may, by their nature, take some considerable time to bear fruit. Changes that harmonize policies and standards can take several months to implement, even years in some cases. Work to harmonize processes and systems can take even longer, sometimes up to two or three years.

What about changes to leadership style, behaviors, and capacity? Most agree that this may be an absolutely critical contributor to the

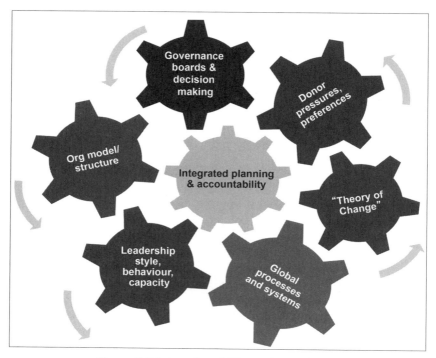

Figure 2.2 Interrelated Dimensions of Progress

change that needs to take place. We believe that leadership issues can be heavily influenced by context—they are a result of the natural stresses and characteristics of the environment within large NGOs. Some early and deliberate action may be advisable, for example, defining and communicating the kinds of leadership behaviors that are expected. This can be a very useful and visible first step, signaling a new direction, which should be welcomed by staff across the organization as well as external stakeholders.

When we consider all of the above, we believe it makes sense to start with those changes that (1) are quickest to do and are the most visible throughout the organization and (2) can help facilitate other improvements that otherwise might take longer. If necessary, we advise making changes to the organizational model and structure at an early stage, since they can often be implemented quickly; they also signify important changes in responsibility, priority, and power. Potentially, this could make it easier to make tougher decisions later.

Changes in governance structures and formal decisionmaking rights link closely with changes in structure, and by their nature can sometimes take time to achieve. However, if boards are serious about leading and supporting the changes that are needed, why not start with early, decisive, and demonstrable changes at this level at the earliest opportunity?

NGO Takeaway

Pursuing wall-to-wall transformation across all the pieces of an NGO system in parallel is neither practical nor affordable. However, almost any major change will have implications for all parts of an organizational system. The key is to be disciplined and determined—making sure what you tackle is achieved. Our advice: Keep the focus on the long-term journey, but in the short term, for each successive step, underpromise and overdeliver!

Choosing the Best Change Approach

What is the best way to get a large, complex organization to embrace change, especially one that may not be universally popular and may cause considerable disruption and resistance? What is the right balance between change that is initiated and owned at executive levels, versus "bottom-up" change that is initiated from below? One way of addressing these questions is to follow a framework that has been used extensively for hundreds of projects supported by Accenture.[4] The framework involves thinking through choices in two dimensions, as illustrated in Figure 2.3.

First, to what degree do we emphasize **push** versus **pull** when implementing change? Push-style change uses well-defined, formal initiatives that are managed in a strong and deterministic manner. This is the classic approach that we have seen attempted in many different organizations, often with tremendous initial expectation—and also too often with somewhat disappointing results. Pull-style change, on the other hand, happens when the demand for change is created at staff and executive levels responding to a shared set of goals or ambitions. This can be facilitated by empowered local action teams or by building stretching goals and targets into a strong performance management framework.

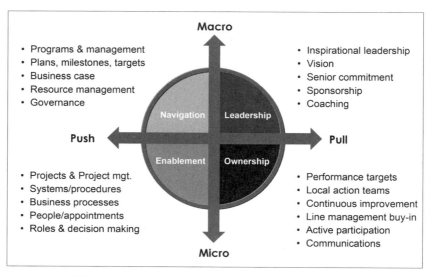

Figure 2.3 Balancing Push and Pull, Macro and Micro

The other dimension to this framework is **macro versus micro**. By this we mean the balance between efforts at senior executive levels to encourage, drive, or lead the change versus efforts in the rank-and-file throughout the organization to embrace and own the change process from within. There is plenty of evidence that top-down change is less successful, often failing to take root and deliver the rich harvest that was first intended. In our experience, this is particularly the case for change driven by external benchmarking, often using scores of expensive external experts. Best practices are hard to duplicate, even if there is a genuine appetite to do so, and externally imposed solutions are often rejected by an organization, almost like an "immune system response." If an organization's rank-and-file really want and own the improvements sought, it will have a much higher chance of success. The ultimate goal is to create an environment where every single member of an organization, at every level, is working to improve performance each and every day.

All four segments of this model—push, pull, macro, and micro—have their place. Success comes from choosing the right mix of tools, depending on the change in question and the organizational context at that time. This thought process is illustrated in Table 2.1.

NGO Takeaway

Choosing the correct change approach can be one of the most important choices an executive will make. In our experience, these choices rarely get the attention or space they deserve. Often organizations are too quick to embrace a high profile, one off change initiative – when there may be other and more effective ways of achieving the same end.

Table 2.1 Selecting the Right Mix of Approaches

Examples of Types of Change	Push		Pull	
	Navigation	Enablement	Leadership	Ownership
Creating a culture of innovation	O	O	●	●
Improving leadership behaviors and capacity	O	O	●	●
Strengthening the technical development capacity as well as ability to do effective monitoring and evaluation	O	●	●	●
Improving interface with key strategic donors	O	●	●	●
Utilizing information communication technology for development for reinventing program approaches	O	●	●	●
Aligning and strengthening enabling processes and systems: e.g., implementing a new global, unified finance/HR system	●	●	●	●
Implementing a new organization model or structure	●	●	●	●
Implementing a new planning, performance management, and accountability framework	●	●	●	●

Aligning Disconnected Agendas and Priorities

Ambitious and impatient executive teams, as one might expect, evolve their agendas and priorities year after year. Often each new agenda and associated priorities are followed by one or more major change initiatives. These inevitably take time to get organized, approved, planned, and implemented, assuming they survive that long. Typically, they work their way through the organization, as they evolve through concept, design, and implementation, feeding through to changes on the ground with field staff and hopefully one day to the benefit of customers or beneficiaries. This flow is illustrated in Figure 2.4.

The result is a potential disconnect between the agendas of senior executives—who are naturally excited about their new priorities and related initiatives—and the priorities of lower-level management and staff, who are already struggling to implement previously initiated programs. This is what happens when an organization doesn't wait for one change program to fully take effect before kicking off the next one.

Finally, a common mistake is to think that the change journey is finished well before the results are fully embedded. This is especially problematic for change that spans multiple levels and geographies of an organization. Don't forget to plan for the final phase of the journey, the post-implementation support phase. This is too often forgotten and consequently under-resourced.

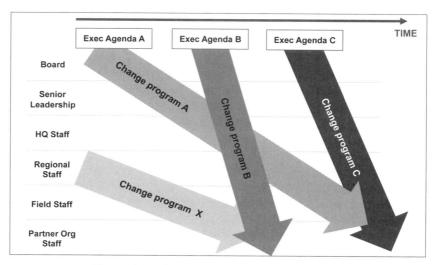

Figure 2.4 Disconnected Agendas and Priorities

> ### NGO Takeaway
>
> *Like most large complex organizations in other sectors, NGOs are often quick to launch new major, top-down change initiatives. However, it is what you finish, not what you start, that really matters!*

High-Impact Leadership

Good leadership can strongly influence the success of large-scale and challenging change initiatives. The basic requirements of leadership have already been included as a key component in Level 1 thinking. Level 2 thinking on leadership raises the bar of what good leadership might look like or could potentially contribute. We refer to this as **high-impact leadership**.[5] The key components are outlined in Table 2.2.

Desired leadership behaviors should ideally be embedded in the individual performance management processes, as discussed elsewhere.[6] This can be helped by the introduction of, for example, a 360-degree feedback survey, allowing leaders throughout the organization to get honest and helpful feedback.

Table 2.2 High-Impact Leadership

Imposes Context	• Lifts people's sights • Makes clear where the business is heading
Makes and Takes Risks	• Encourages "differences" and risks • Demands new ideas and perspectives
Has Conviction	• Articulates strong beliefs and ideals • Builds pride and trust
Is Unpredictable	• Imparts adventure/excitement • Experiments and challenges people
Creates Critical Mass	• Generates energy and urgency • Sustains impatience to achieve more

NGO Takeaway

The ideas of high-impact leadership are particularly important for large NGOs. Because of the breadth, scope, and complexity of such organizations, they are not easy to lead. Creating future leaders from within should be encouraged. Our view is that the chance of achieving high-impact leadership will be better for internal candidates who already have the breadth and depth of understanding and a legacy of trust and respect from the rank and file.

Aligning Content, Context, and Approach

Balancing content, context, and approach, as illustrated by Figure 2.5, is a careful design consideration of any major change process. We raised this idea in the introduction, and we expand on what we mean here.

First, one needs to take careful account of the kind of change being tackled (**the content**). There are many different types of change:

- Strengthening the technical capacity of an organization around a unified development approach
- Implementing a new performance management/accountability framework
- Implementing a new IT system, for example, for finance, human resources, customer relationship management, or grants management
- Putting in place a different structure, for example, moving from a simple, geographical structure to a high-performance flatter matrix approach (the topic of Chapter 3)
- Building new capacities into an organization, for example, to enhance innovation and agility
- Reducing costs to address declining income levels

These changes vary enormously in terms of the content that needs to be handled. It is important to design **an approach** consistent with the content—recognizing that there can and often will be several different routes to the same end. Even for the same kind of project, for example, implementing a new organizational structure or model, there can be a range of different options.

We can illustrate two very contrasting approaches to such a change. When putting in place a new organizational structure/model, one option is to plan meticulously, taking account of all possible details in advance of implementation, with a long lead time before real change occurs on the ground. We refer to this as the **PLAN+PLAN+PLAN-IMPLE-MENT** approach. This is the more top-down, preplanned option. A very different option is what we call the **PLAN-IMPLEMENT-FIX+REFINE** approach. In this option, there is much less detailed planning in advance, and the rank-and-file have more flexibility in working out some of the detail for themselves based on a broader and more flexible template.

Clearly, there are pros and cons to these options. The *approach* you choose needs to take into account the particular **context** of the organization, for example, the cultural context in particular geographies, the current atmosphere or appetite for embracing the change in question, or lessons and memories from what worked well (or less well) in the past.

However, the relationship between these three elements (content, context, and approach) is circular rather than linear. Sometimes, having reflected carefully on the context and approach, experienced leaders might decide to adjust the detailed content (or scope) of what is planned.

This concept will take on deeper meaning when we get to Level 3 thinking in the next section, when we take the opportunity to bring to life a few selected tools to help investigate and appreciate context in a bit more depth.

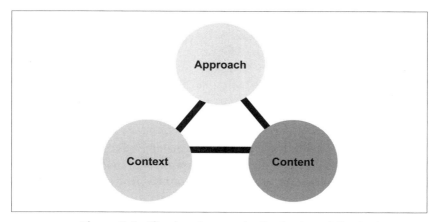

Figure 2.5 Aligning Approach, Context, and Content

NGO Takeaway

This step does take time and effort—likely to be measured in days or weeks. However, the implication of a poorly conceived change process, which does not align content, context, and approach, can be measured in several lost years!

Level 3 Thinking: A Deeper Investigation and Appreciation of Context

While Level 1 provides the basics and Level 2 provides ideas for managing complexity, Level 3 encourages the exploration of some additional ideas that might help us to appreciate context at a deeper level. This should encourage thoroughness and thoughtfulness in designing some of the more subtle aspects of change, such as approach, timing, and pace, and as a result could help increase the likelihood of success.

Understanding and Strengthening Organizational Glue

Here we return to the idea of organizational glue—first introduced in *Building a Better International NGO*. There are two aspects to this glue, which we labeled as "motivating and enabling glue."[7] This concept is presented in Figure 2.6. *Motivating glue* is the essence of what excites people to be part of the organization, inspired by the mission, the development impact, and being part of an international community for improving the world. The *enabling glue* is what makes the organization work, the less exciting facets such as standards, processes, and systems.

The core message is that when designing and executing big changes, we should be careful to at least preserve and ideally strengthen the glue that binds the organization together. This is what ultimately ensures that the whole is more than the sum of the parts.

A well-designed change process needs to have a reasonable balance between strengthening the enabling glue of the organization on one hand, and at the same time nurturing the motivating glue that is so essential to the morale and the performance of an NGO workforce. This is especially the case for changes that are often perceived internally as being very dry—a good example might include projects to implement IT enhancements.

Motivating Glue

- Quality programs and impact in the field
- Mission and identity
- Camaraderie with like-minded, high-caliber, loyal staff
- Part of international community/civil society

Enabling Glue

- Program design standards, guidelines, and methodology
- Monitoring and evaluation (processes, systems, and expertise)
- Financial processes and systems
- HR processes and systems
- Talent management
- Knowledge management tools, processes, and systems
- Business planning and performance management

Figure 2.6 Concept of Organizational Glue

NGO Takeaway

We believe the glue concept is particularly important for NGOs because the motivating glue is such an important aspect of why individuals commit their careers to a particular organization— working long hours, sometimes with considerable personal risk and disruption to their lives, and with very modest financial rewards.

Deeper Understanding of Context: Organizational Life Cycle Model

We discussed the importance of taking account of context (internal and external) in the design of major change programs, in terms of the content or goals sought and the approach to be taken. There are many ways of conducting this assessment.

Sometimes it is useful to stand well back from the current framing of ambitions, weaknesses, challenges, or opportunities that are prompting a proposed change and try to see the bigger picture of where an organization is in its evolution. One tool that we find very insightful is the Organizational Life Cycle Model, generally credited to Mason Haire.[8] This uses the analogy of the human life cycle to illustrate the aging process of all organizations, from infancy through maturity and ultimate decline. One adaption of this model, as developed by Ichak Adizes (see http://www.adizes.com), uses four dimensions referred to as PAEI to trace the journey of a typical organization over its life cycle. This is illustrated in Figure 2.7.

The dimensions are:

P = Productive capacity: the ability to make or produce a product or service.

A = Administrative capacity: the ability to administer, be consistent, efficient, and organized.

E = Entrepreneurial capacity: the ability to develop new ideas or products.

I = Intrepreneurial bias: the bias to reflect on own internal make-up, structure, and culture.

Very briefly, this is how the logic flows. At Infancy, organizations have a small **e**, and definitely no **a** or **i**. From Go-Go through Adolescence, the entrepreneurial bias rapidly grows, followed afterward by **p**, the capacity to make or produce. At Adolescence the model

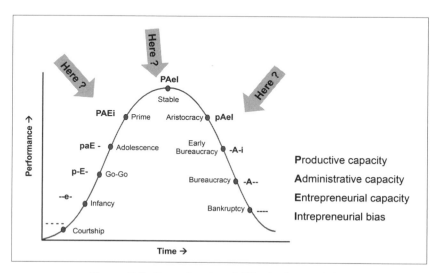

Figure 2.7 Organizational Life Cycle Model—PAEI

shows a large **E**, a small **p**, and still little or no **a** or **i**. At Prime, we see the development of a larger **P** and **A**, still a large **E**, and still little sign of **i**.

At the Stable phase we see the first sign of difficulty. This creeps up slowly. The large **A** makes life difficult for entrepreneurial flair to flourish, and creative talent may leave to seek a less constricted environment. Hence the large **A** kills the big **E**. As growth slows or stalls, the bias to turn inwardly grows and the **i** appears, first as a small **i**, and ultimately a big **I** at Aristocracy—with the added consequence of drowning out whatever **e** that still remains. Very soon, the lack of innovation and bureaucracy causes the **P** to be less powerful than before—production methods become out of date, and we now have a small **p** relative to what the current market demands.

What does this tell us? First, one of the most dangerous stages of an organization's life cycle is when it is approaching its Prime through the Stable stage at maturity. Yes, administrative rigor (the **A**) is required, and this needs constant investment to ensure consistent quality and the service levels at industrial scale that customers demand from mature professional organizations. However, it is essential to re-create the entrepreneurial flair that is needed to stay relevant in a changing external context. At Aristocracy, with a small **p**, a very small **e**, an enormous **A** and **I**, it may be too late.

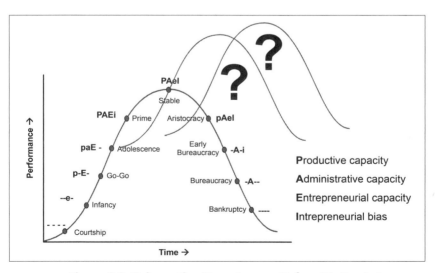

Figure 2.8 Reinventing Your Agency Before It's Too Late

NGO Takeaway

There are several lessons (really questions) in this model for the large and well-established NGOs.

- *Where is your agency on this life cycle?*
- *What are the implications of your position in the life cycle model?*
- *What are the short- and long-term responses you should consider?*
- *How do you harmonize different life cycle positions in different parts of your organization to deliver a transformational change?*
- *What is the position of your key competitors, and what is the impact of this on your priorities?*
- *Is there a way of switching life cycle curves to allow your agency to break ranks?*

The more challenging question is to explore what is required to create a new cycle, essentially reinventing an organization's offering, positioning, approach, and makeup, before the existing organization goes into decline. This is illustrated in the revised life cycle diagram in Figure 2.8.

Deeper Understanding of People Context: Motivation and Ability Segmentation

When thinking deeply about organizational context, sometimes less sophisticated approaches can be useful. One of our favorites is a simple but revealing segmentation we first designed during a change program for a large energy client in Eastern Europe, just after the fall of the Berlin Wall in the early 1990s. In the course of internal context analysis, we sought to understand the mind-set and motivations of the broader workforce. Using a very simple framework, we simply divided a 15,000-member workforce into four intuitive segments based on **ability** (low to high) and **motivation** (also low to high). This simple framework is illustrated in Figure 2.9.

Those in the high/high quadrant were clearly the potential *stars* and were easy to work with though relatively few in number. They became invaluable in planning the journey to become a higher-performing, effective, and sustainable organization, capable of dealing

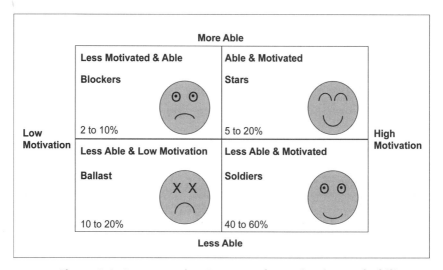

Figure 2.9 Segmentation Framework: Motivation and Ability

with the new commercial realities following the disintegration of the communist system.

Those in the high motivation/low ability quadrant were also valuable in navigating the change process, as long as they were usefully involved and allocated appropriate roles and tasks. We referred to this segment as *good soldiers*.

We realized those in the low motivation quadrants were somewhat more tricky. The low/low quadrant needed careful consideration. Though the numbers were fairly significant and they were a drag on progress, they typically did not present enormous blockages or resistance to change—hence we labelled these *the ballast*.

The most challenging were those who were highly able but poorly motivated. Though relatively few in number, they held up progress considerably. We referred to this group as *the blockers*. Sometimes this resistance was explicit, but more often and even more challenging was implicit resistance, which was difficult to identify and address. In this case, we put a great deal of effort to move some of the able but poorly motivated staff over the line into the able and motivated quadrant. However, in some cases it was necessary to move these blockers to a part of the organization where they would cause the least difficulty, or in some cases move them out of the organization completely.

NGO Takeaway

It can be helpful to take a variety of approaches to investigate and appreciate the mind-set, capability, and perspectives of the various segments of an agency. Exploring a variety of practical investigative tools can be useful. Success requires that you engage with all segments—even those that initially may not be supportive.

Deeper Understanding of People Context: Social Style Model

Another segmentation that is extremely useful in a variety of situations is the Social Style Model. This is a well known tool, and further information can be found at a variety of useful sources, such as the TRACOM Group (http://www.tracomcorp.com). Social style theory is based on work originated by David Merrill and Roger Reid,[9] who used factor analysis to identify three very important style dimensions: **assertiveness**, **responsiveness**, and **adaptability**. This is a practical tool to help us understand the preferences of different kinds of people in terms of how they think, analyze, communicate, and make decisions. This can be used to help engage key individuals whose involvement and support is important for the success of a change process. By understanding people's social style, we can adjust our communications and arguments to achieve the best effect.

The first two dimensions are assertiveness (ask versus tell) and responsiveness (emotive versus controlled). The third is adaptability. Mapping the first two dimensions in a two-by-two grid results in a model with four quadrants, representing four broad social styles. This is illustrated in Figure 2.10.

This seems to imply there are only four types of people. However, we know that there will be a great deal of variation in styles within each quadrant. We should also emphasize that each style has pros and cons, and there are plenty of examples of very successful people in each quadrant.

Driver: With high assertiveness and low emotional response to others, drivers are less worried by how others react and hence are more independent and candid. With less concern about people, they have a greater concern for results and are quite pragmatic. They may be poor

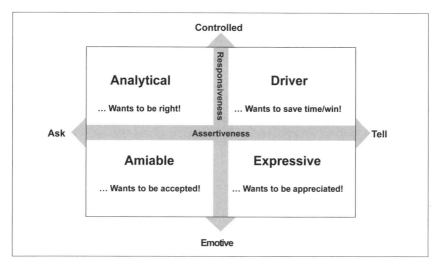

Figure 2.10 Social Style Model

collaborators and upset others with their focus on results and potential for inconsiderate words and actions.

Expressive: Expressive people have higher assertiveness and greater responsiveness to others. They can come across as articulate, quick, and visionary. On the down side, their assertiveness may make them poor listeners, with a tendency to get distracted. This can also lead them to be impractical and impatient.

Amiable: People with higher responsiveness and lower assertiveness are typically regarded as people-oriented and sociable. They may avoid conflict and be perceived as rather passive, sometimes as lacking drive and urgency. There is a risk that they will verbally express agreement to avoid conflict even when at heart they disagree.

Analytical: Analytical people are less assertive and less responsive to others. They tend to focus more on tasks than people, be less interested in leading, and can also be very comfortable working alone. They may be prudent, systematic, and analytic at work. A downside is that they can sometimes be seen to pay excessive attention to detail in ways that can slow down progress and delay decisions.

How can the Social Style Model be used in navigating change?
This is a relatively simple model, making it fairly easy to assess and classify people from everyday interactions and predict (to some extent)

how they may react to new ideas. By understanding individual styles, you can also customize the way you influence, negotiate, and persuade, for example, by adapting your style to be closer to others (and thus seem more "reasonable"). It can also be useful in diagnosing team dynamics, understanding differences and the natural tensions that can sometimes occur between individuals with different styles.

With a deeper understanding of styles, you can make some adjustments in how you seek to inform, engage, or convince others on the merits of new ideas or possibilities.

- Leading with solutions and carefully selected evidence for drivers and expressives, but with details on process, approach, and consultation/involvement for analyticals and amiables.
- Adjusting the pace and level of detail in your arguments—slower for analyticals and amiables (more patient), faster and more precise for expressives and drivers (less patient).
- Adjusting the sequence of your communications—for example, leading with process and facts for analyticals, solution choices for drivers, vision for expressives.
- Using inductive logic for drivers and deductive logic for analyticals.

How can the styles model help us understand some specific issues for NGOs? What does this mean for the international development and humanitarian sector? NGOs can have an interesting blend of styles, which we believe can cast some light on some of the behavioral challenges that we sometimes grapple with in this sector.

Slow decisionmaking: In some NGOs there is a strong bias toward consensus-based decisionmaking. If we layer on top of this context a situation with a disproportionately high number of amiables, there is a risk that decisions take forever to make or are made but never implemented. Amiables like to avoid conflict and will often employ less direct forms of resistance to change, rather than stating their concerns outright. This can mean that consensus is seemingly reached, but in reality it is not.

Tensions between field, regional, and headquarters leaders: In some organizations there can be natural tensions between directors at field, regional, and headquarters levels. Although there are a variety of factors behind this, the level of tension can be enhanced where there is a high proportion of drivers or expressive types, characters who place a high value on autonomy and control in key leadership positions.

Tension between doers and technical advisers: In some cases, field directors and field project managers are dominated by driver or expressive types, with a strong bias to getting going, moving at a quick pace, and making things happen. In contrast, technical staff are more likely to have analytical styles with a strong emphasis on detail, facts, and proper process. This clash can present challenges in program design, day-to-day communication, and learning. For example, it may be necessary to ensure that field project managers have the patience and rigor to do thorough and robust monitoring and evaluation, including solid baselining at the outset of each new project. Similarly, some field managers may regard the important task of developing an agency-level theory of change as an esoteric or academic exercise.

NGO Takeaway

As for any organization, the major learning from this social style analysis is to realize that all styles have particular strengths to contribute as well as weaknesses to be aware of. Mutual awareness can help mitigate tensions as individuals are aware of their own and other natural social styles. This understanding can also provide the basis for helping improve the dynamics of some leadership teams.

Level 4 Thinking: The Art of Exploiting Organizational Rhythm

We are all influenced by an endless number of cyclical rhythms that are an important part of our lives—the times of the day, the days of the week, the seasons of the year, the ebb and flow of the tides.[10] We are also affected by other, less regular cycles, such as the continuous evolution of preferences in fashion, our appetite for physical exercise, the build-up to a holiday, and sometimes the almost equal relief when it is all over. When selecting and timing actions in our lives, we instinctively take account of these multiple cycles or rhythms. Some people know that they are at their best in the early morning, when they will try to do some of their most creative and demanding work. For others, the morning is a time to wake up, and they will be at their best later in the day.

The art of timing and rhythm has an important bearing on success in many arenas. In sports, we understand that the difference between supremely gifted athletes and hard-working players can be quite small in absolute terms. However, these gifted individuals have a knack when it comes to the precise timing of key moves. This can be the difference between winning and losing.

When we reflect on the major changes in society and industry, we can notice that times of major change are often followed by periods of stability. This allows society and organizations to assimilate the change before the next wave arrives. Understanding of the importance of timing and natural cycles is not completely new. To some degree, this idea has come into play in the research and writing of a range of business academics such as Peter Drucker,[11] Gary Hamel,[12] Derek Abell,[13] and more recently Malcolm Gladwell.[14]

We invite readers to explore the idea of timing and natural rhythm as it relates to navigating significant change initiatives in large, complex organizations. Level 4 thinking is centered around the idea that subtle decisionmaking in terms of timing of actions is an intuitive art form that can have a significant impact on the likelihood of success. Here we are placing a stronger emphasis on the "art" of change as distinct to the more rational "science" of change, which was more to the fore in Levels 1, 2, and 3.

What problem are we trying to solve? Let's start with some honest reflection. Sometimes we are surprised at how an organization takes to an idea, an opportunity, or a change—how quickly things fall into place, with rapid success, and sometimes even with minimal effort. But too often we are disappointed at how resistant organizations are to good new ideas or opportunities. Have you ever noticed, for example, that some very well-executed programs that started with broad support, excitement, enthusiasm, and outstanding business cases have gradually faded and the intended improvements seem to have become pipe dreams? Indeed, it may seem like the organization is determined to revert to its old ways and habits. Too often, despite considerable efforts to implement seemingly well-designed and well-executed change initiatives, we find that little lasting progress is achieved.

Our thesis in Level 4 is that part of the response to these kinds of questions is related to misguided decisions on the precise timing of change initiatives and not paying sufficient attention to the natural cycles or rhythms within a particular organization. We believe that "dynamic" rather than "static" thinking will offer leaders a window to a better understanding of when to roll out important new changes into an organizational system.

From Static to Dynamic Thinking: The Concept of Natural Rhythm

To introduce the idea of dynamic thinking, we invite you to take a little detour into the fields of physics and engineering. In the field of structural engineering, dynamic thinking and analysis became widely used in the design of some complex structures in the 1970s and 1980s, in response to some high-profile and sometimes spectacular engineering failures that were a direct result of the limitations of static thinking. In engineering, static thinking is not sufficient in a dynamic world because it ignores the fact that structures resonate at their natural frequencies. Some well-publicized examples include the severe oscillations of the Severn Bridge between England and Wales and the excessive and frightening movements of the new Millennium Bridge in London when it was first opened. The summary explanation for these and other cases was the coincidence of one or more of the natural frequencies of these structures combined with the frequency of outside forces—typically waves or wind gusts—often resulting in what is referred to as *resonance.*

What do we really mean by "natural frequency" and "resonance?" The simplest representation of this phenomenon is in the motion of a basic pendulum, and a good example is a child's swing. Curiously, a swing will oscillate (move back and forth) at a constant frequency no matter how hard you try to change it. If you observe the time taken for one full swing, you will find that it is constant. If you push at the correct time, aligning with the natural frequency of the swing, you will manage to swing it higher with little effort. Gradually, we instinctively learn to push and pull at exactly the optimum time. If we push at the wrong time, the extra force will act to slow down the motion of the swing—generally accompanied by a bit of a shudder or disturbance—since we have disturbed the natural rhythm of the swing.

The reason for this is fairly straightforward in terms of physics. The swing is a simple pendulum with a natural frequency depending on mass and stiffness. The *mass* is the weight of the child in the swing. The *stiffness* is the natural force trying to get back to equilibrium, which in the case of a swing is the force of gravity. A mass at the end of a simple cantilever (such as a diver on a diver board) is another example.

For advanced analytical types with an appetite for more detail on natural frequencies and how the concept could be applied to organizations, refer to the box on natural frequency.

Natural Frequency from Physics and Structural Engineering

To introduce you to the idea in a little more detail, we take a foray into the world of physics and structural engineering and reflect on the dynamics of long bridges, very tall buildings, or offshore engineering structures that protrude through the surface of the oceans. In static thinking, a load (w) applied to a point of a structure will produce a displacement (Δ). For example, a load of 1 nanonewton, applied to the end of a simple cantilever, will produce a displacement of Δ mm. Where the stiffness or strength of the cantilever is higher, the displacement will be less, and where the stiffness is less, the displacement will be more.

When we move from static to dynamic thinking, we find that the prediction of the resulting displacement is not so simple. Physical structures (tall buildings, towers, offshore structures) have natural frequencies at which they can be very sensitive to dynamic loading. By *dynamic* we mean loading that is oscillating, as is the case with wind gusts or ocean waves. These waves or gusts typically repeat at regular intervals. Where the frequency of the loading matches the natural frequency of the structure, the response or displacement can be 20 or often 100 times more than for static loading or for loading at any other frequency. This is referred to as *resonance*. The general formula for the natural frequency function (f) of a single-degree-of-freedom system (e.g., a simple cantilever with a mass at the end of a beam) with stiffness (k) can be expressed as:

$$f\,(\text{hz}) = 1 \,/\, 2 \text{ frequency of the oscillations/second}$$

If you prefer, this can be expressed in terms of natural period (λ), or the time in seconds for one oscillation ($\lambda = 1/f$). Of course, complex structures can move or oscillate in many different ways (referred to as degrees of freedom); hence, there will be many different natural frequencies, one for each degree of freedom.

Static thinking is not sufficient in a dynamic world because it ignores the fact that structures resonate at their natural frequency, as illustrated by some high-profile problem cases that experienced extreme and unexpected oscillations. The response to a dynamic load is partly driven by its magnitude, but more important by the match of the frequency of the load with one or more of the natural frequencies of the structure. In the 1960s and 1970s, relying on static thinking, engineers reacted to structural failures in major offshore structures in the North Sea and Bass Straits by making them stronger and heavier, only to find that the problems became more severe. They discovered their apparent reinforcement measures shifted the natural frequency of the structures to coincide more closely with the frequency of the wave loading, thus making the problem more severe. The correct but counterintuitive solution was to make the structures weaker (less stiff), moving the natural frequency the other way.

If we translate the concept of dynamic thinking to organizations, we can hypothesize that organizations (we could think of them as human structures) are also complex mechanisms with inherent natural frequencies that are comparable to physical structures. As for physical structures, we can imagine that responses will be significantly more pronounced when the natural frequency of the external stimulus coincides with one of the natural frequencies (or natural rhythm) of the organization.

In theory, it could be possible to alter the natural frequency of an organization to ensure that it responds better or potentially resonates with the external stimuli (new pressures, new opportunities). This would require a thorough understanding of the size and stiffness relationship for different aspects of an organization and for the organization as a whole. It is possible (but not always easy) to model physical structures to establish the main natural frequencies, even when these structures are large and complex. In reality, this is a job for a 'brainy' computer to model and analyze the makeup of the various parts. For human structures, modelling the natural frequencies for parts or the totality of an organization structure is probably just not possible.

We can simplify our analogy and consider the basic influencers of the two key factors—the mass (m) and stiffness (resistance to movement) (k) for an organization. If we push the analogy to its absolute limits (probably beyond!), following from the formula of a simple pendulum, increasing the mass will increase the natural period and reduce the natural frequency. Increasing the stiffness will reduce the natural period or increase the natural frequency.

However, we are not proposing the exact translation of the laws of dynamics to organizations. The point we are really encouraging the reader to consider is that organizations may have a natural rhythm that may influence the likelihood of success of new change initiatives or new opportunities. We are asking leaders of change to move beyond the limitations of static thinking and analysis.

Applying Dynamic Thinking to Human Structures (Organizations)

If we translate the concept of dynamic thinking, we can imagine organizations as complex mechanisms with inherent natural frequencies. As for physical structures, responses will be significantly more pronounced when the natural frequency of the external stimulus coincides with one of the natural frequencies (or natural rhythm) of the organization.

How does all of this relate to the art of navigating change for NGOs? The point of this section is *not* to propose the precise translation of the idea of natural frequency. Instead we encourage the reader to think more deeply about the idea of organizational rhythm and start to have a more thoughtful approach when navigating change—particularly of the timing of new significant initiatives.

Using Dynamic Thinking Can Help in Navigating Change in NGOs

We offer the following five broad hypotheses.

1. We believe that **dynamic thinking, embracing some deeper reflection on organizational rhythm, can provide a deeper understanding of organizational context.** Essentially, it can help us make better decisions in the timing of change initiatives and guide us in how much change to tackle at a particular time. The timing of decisions on change can be a very important determinant of success—what might work this year may not work one year later. Stretching our thinking to include a sense of dynamics can put a bit more science behind what we normally think of as intuition. Truly good leaders will have an intuitive feel for these matters, whereas the average competent manager may not.

2. **Different organizations, because of their contrasting focus and history, may have very different rhythms.** That is neither good nor bad. The point is to appreciate the differences and the implications for the kinds of opportunities and change that might resonate easily or be resisted. Using dynamic thinking, even at a conceptual level, can be helpful in understanding how organizations are likely to respond.

The experiences of large companies during the first wave of the dotcom revolution offers a practical illustration. Early opportunities initially appealed only to small, start-up companies, where decision times were fast, risk adversity was low, technology was flexible and scalable, and capital was readily available. It was not surprising that most major corporations found it harder to grasp these sorts of opportunities because they were more likely to be slow in making decisions, had a high adversity to risk, and had a long-term and prescriptive attitude to the adoption of new technology. They were less dynamic—their natural rhythm was not suited to the opportunities available, and hence, there was little resonance.

In this sector, we expect that the natural rhythms of emergency or humanitarian organizations are very different from agencies that have a stronger development value at their core. Emergency organizations, such as Médecins Sans Frontières or the International Red Cross, have shorter cycles, often thinking in days and months to react, engage, and then disengage when the worst of the emergency has passed. Development-centered organizations have a much longer cycle of planning and action—often measured in years.

3. For large NGOs, **different organizational parts** (e.g., affiliates; members; national, regional, and country offices; or international headquarters) **may all have their own different rhythms.** Hence, what works well for one part may be less effective for another. Being aware of this and trying to design and navigate the change based on where the individual organizational parts are in their natural cycle can be a challenge and be very instructive.

4. Many of the **management tools commonly used are predominantly static in their nature** and reinforce a static way of thinking. Although they are clearly useful and can provide excellent insights and ways of framing and simplifying complex forces and factors, they have some limitations in a truly dynamic world. Examples of the popular frameworks include Porter's Five Forces,[15] which is a snapshot at a point in time; BCG's Growth Share Matrix (http://www.bcgperspectives.com), a snapshot of the fit of one's own products within the market in which they sit at that point; and McKinsey's 7-S Framework (http://www.mckinsey.com), a snapshot of the linkages and fit between a broader set of factors. Arguably, these tools can be manipulated to reflect time (and dynamics) to some degree, for example, through thoughtful scenario analysis.

5. As we look to the future, we can imagine that the Internet economy and its associated new technologies are having a significant impact on the natural rhythm(s) of some modern, high-performance, and agile organizations. To be successful and stay relevant, traditional agencies may need to consider **a deliberate change in their organizational**

rhythm—requiring fundamental changes to skills, structures, cultures, and ways of working. They might need to adapt their approaches, organization models, and decisionmaking to survive and stay relevant. This point links directly to the question posed at the end of the organization life cycle section: can organizations move on to a new life cycle curve while they are successful and still have the resources and energy to change? This is one of the key questions we want readers to ponder.

In the world of organizational structures, as in physical structures, static thinking has important limitations. History has shown that when the nature of the environment is truly dynamic, a static approach can often be counterproductive. As engineers discovered, this kind of thinking encouraged bigger, stiffer physical structures, which just fell down faster. The analogy for human structures might play out with similarly disappointing results.

NGO Takeaway

NGOs can be regarded as human structures with a set of natural rhythms that have a major impact on how the organization will respond to new opportunities and change initiatives. Change efforts that are significantly out of sync with the natural rhythm of the target organization will probably not result in the intended benefits. More likely the energy expended will be wasted. Just like the playground swing, after initial shudders, the organization will return to its natural rhythm probably even before the project team has disbanded.

Notes

1. PMI Lexicon of Project Management Terms, Version 2.0, Project Management Institute (2012), 12.
2. Ibid.
3. James Crowley and Morgana Ryan, *Building a Better International NGO: Greater than the Sum of the Parts?* (Boulder, CO: Kumarian Press, 2013), 189–191.
4. Accenture journey management research, 1990–95.
5. Accenture research and publication on high-impact leadership.
6. Crowley and Ryan, *Building a Better International NGO*, 163.
7. Ibid., 83–84.
8. Mason Haire, *Modern Organizational Theory* (New York: John Wiley & Sons, 1959).

9. David W. Merrill and Roger H. Reid, *Personal Styles and Effective Performance* (New York: CRC Press, 1981).

10. Original research from James Crowley, see http://www.thecrowleyinstitute.com.

11. Peter F. Drucker, *Age of Discontinuity: Guidelines to Our Changing Society* (London: Heinemann, 1969).

12. Gary Hamel, *Leading the Revolution* (New York: Plume, 2002).

13. Derek Abell, "Strategic Windows," *Journal of Marketing*, 42 (July 1978): 21–28.

14. Malcolm Gladwell, *The Tipping Point* (New York: Little, Brown, 2000).

15. Michael E. Porter, *Competitive Advantage: Creating and Sustaining Superior Performance* (New York: Free Press, 1985).

3

The Essential Components of a High-Performance Organization

The search for a higher-performance organization model or structure has been on the minds of many leaders of international NGOs. Growing external demands and expectations, coupled with a general consensus on the need for internal improvements, are provoking a desire to significantly strengthen organizational models and structures. These pressures and forces have already been discussed in *Building a Better International NGO*.

Since that book was first published, we have had numerous follow-up questions from senior agency staff and curious board members, typically phrased as:

- "What would this new high-performance matrix structure look like in practice?"
- "How can we ensure that the benefits of moving to such a model outweigh the risks?"
- "How would we tackle the changes involved?"

This chapter is intended to address these kinds of questions and build directly on the ideas and recommendations from the earlier book.

To advance this debate, we find it helpful to reduce the emphasis on the words *structure* or *matrix* and start with the fundamental goal we are seeking to accomplish. This could loosely be described as the desire to create "a high-performance international organization," with a very high degree of confidence that this can contribute to good projects, selected, designed, and implemented in the best possible way.

A High-Performance Organization

If you are a CEO or senior executive in an international agency, ask yourself the following question. Where do you honestly feel your agency sits on the continuum shown in Figure 3.1? Where would you feel you could get to in the next two to three years?

What are the components of a high-performance agency? In the world of humanitarian and international development work, there are a number of responses to this question, but essentially we believe there are four leading components.

1. We are clear and aligned on what we are trying to achieve in the external world, with
- Real clarity and alignment on concrete external goals pursued, and
- A robust approach to "how" we plan to contribute to these external goals, with transparent assumptions articulated in a clear theory of change and with continuous reflection and learning.

2. We are able to attract, develop, and use the right talent, so that
- Staff skills and experience match the goals and needs of our agency,
- We optimize the deployment of all key staff against the most productive/demanding jobs,
- There are strong career development and growth opportunities for all staff (national and international), and
- There is a robust and professional performance management process.

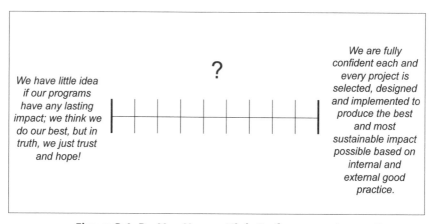

Figure 3.1 Do You Have a High-Performance Agency?

3. We have a high-performance environment with strong planning, decisionmaking, and accountability, with

- Thoughtful, timely, and disciplined decisionmaking,
- Agreement on what good performance looks like for all parts of the agency,
- An integrated and consistent planning and accountability framework and related processes, and
- An environment that encourages innovation and learning.

4. We run strong and vibrant country programs and country teams, that

- Are carefully designed to respond to local context and needs,
- Promote long-term local ownership and commitment, and
- Use the best of the agency's global know-how and resources.

These four components are easy to list, but they do not happen by accident. To implement them, it is essential to have an *organizational model or structure that is fit for the purpose*. This is the subject of this chapter.

There are, of course, other factors that contribute to organizational effectiveness, for example:

- Good **processes and systems,** so staff can focus on maximizing contribution and impact—rather than merely surviving basic operational day-to-day demands of donors, stakeholders, and staff.

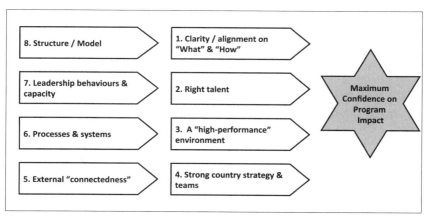

Figure 3.2 Interlinked Factors that Contribute to a High-Performance Agency

- Strong **leadership behaviors and capacity** at every level of the organization that is forward-looking, inspiring, inclusive, and authentic.
- External **connectedness** and participation in broader networks, partnerships, consortia, coalitions in the pursuit of the longer-term goals and impact sought.

All of these components interconnect in a dynamic way, as illustrated in Figure 3.2.

Case for Change

So where do we start? How do we go about developing and strengthening an organization model or structure so that it is truly fit for purpose? As we begin our efforts to strengthen an organizational model, we believe it is essential to stand back and candidly ask ourselves a few fundamental questions.

Question 1: *What have been the most significant barriers to delivering on our goals in the past?*

This is an essential starting point because often some of these barriers or blockages may be largely independent of structure, and hence may not be helped by moving to a different structural model.

Question 2: *What are the additional demands that will come into play from changes in external context or from a new strategic direction with new goals or priorities?*

Some issues or challenges may become less important, others more so.

Question 3: *What are the pros and cons of alternative organizational options that one could conceivably adopt in the future?*

Organization redesign, in simple terms, is the careful selection of the best organizational structure or construct to support the key goals or priorities of an organization over the coming years (typically three to five). Every option will have pros and cons, and some of the cons may need to be addressed in ways other than structure. It can be useful to note the pros and cons of the current organizational structure or model. Too often, we may not fully appreciate many of the advantages of the existing structure, while at the same time being (understandably) very agitated about its weaknesses.

As we continue this analysis, we build on the suggestions found in Chapters 1 and 3 of *Building a Better International NGO*.[1] Our thesis was (and still is) that a simple line structure, based primarily on geography and with a command-and-control management philosophy, is unlikely to meet the demands of today's world. We believe that if well designed and implemented, a high-performance matrix approach has many advantages, as summarized in Table 3.1.

For avoidance of doubt, we do not recommend a complex matrix approach in every single situation. However, for large NGOs that have had significant growth in scale and complexity in recent years, we believe this can be a powerful approach that will help deliver more sustainable impact in the years ahead.

What Are the Key Benefits?

The targeted benefits of a new stronger and more explicit matrix approach include the following:

• Stronger standardization of approaches, more effective sharing and learning, resulting in higher-quality and more consistent programs.
• Improved decisionmaking in prioritizing use of scarce investment resources.
• Improved decisionmaking in prioritizing the allocation of scarce technical staff to the most productive global opportunities.
• More career development opportunities for all staff throughout the agency, allowing their careers to develop in multiple ways. This will increase the attractiveness of the agency as a place to work for the most talented staff (existing and potential new recruits).
• A more transparent and joined-up accountability framework, setting out the complementary goals, targets, and associated review process. (Designing and making this work will be a key ingredient of the implementation process.)
• Stronger feeling of "glue" and camaraderie across the entire agency as horizontal goals and accountability complement geographical accountability.

In the next section we describe in practical terms what we mean by a high-performance matrix organization.

Architecture of a High-Performance Matrix Organization

Working in a matrix management model is not entirely a new phenomenon for most international NGOs. Many agencies already have a number of informal, horizontal communities of practice that span multiple countries and regions that get together to share learning, encourage standardization,

Table 3.1 Comparing a Simple Structure with a High-Performance Matrix Model

Components of a High-Performance Organization	Simple Line Structure			High-Performance Matrix Approach			Comment
	No	Partly	Yes	−	Same	+	
1. Clarity and alignment on what we are trying to achieve in external world and also on the how							
• Clarity on concrete external goals	✓						
• A transparent theory of change with clear assumptions—with continuous learning		✓				✓	Stronger horizontal alignment on desired impact as well as on learning, best practices
2. An environment to attract and nurture the right talent							
• Staff skills/experience matching goals and needs of agency		✓				✓	More opportunity to use key skills where they can contribute most
• Best use/application of key staff against needs of agency	✓					✓	More opportunity to grow skills and contribute to knowledge
• Career development and growth opportunities	✓	✓				✓	
• Professional individual performance management					✓		
3. A high-performance environment with strong planning, decisionmaking, and accountability							
• Decisionmaking quality, speed, and disciplined follow-through		✓				✓	Be rigorous in selecting the right programs and opportunities
• Clarity on what good performance looks like		✓				✓	
• Consistent planning and accountability framework	✓						
• An environment that encourages innovation and learning	✓					✓	Better sharing among peers in different locations
4. Strong and vibrant country programs and country teams							
• Fully adapted to local context and needs		✓				✓	
• Long-term local ownership, long-term local perspective and commitment		✓				✓	
• Bring to bear the best of the agency's global know-how and resources	✓					✓	

and deal with day-to-day issues. Examples of this can be found in some program domains (such as emergency, education, or health), finance, and human resources. Indeed, for these important enabling functions, there have been considerable efforts to standardize processes and systems across all geographies. Many staff in these functions already report to their regional or country lead in the field as well as the international lead.

The organizational model advocated here involves taking a further step in *strengthening these horizontal dimensions*, to drive increased consistency, improve decisionmaking, and improve opportunities for skilled/experienced staff to contribute beyond their home country. We refer to these horizontal dimensions as "lines of expertise" (although they could be labelled differently, e.g., lines of service or lines of responsibility, depending on what resonates best).

What Do We Mean by Horizontal "Lines of Expertise"?

These are new or strengthened horizontal dimensions and will complement the country/geography (vertical) lines of management that will, of course, continue to be important. Lines of expertise have explicit budgets and targets at a global level and can be responsible (fully or partially) for aspects such as career development, methods and tools, and allocation of scarce resources/expertise. They can also have an important input into key decisions, for example go/no-go decisions on new opportunities, in tandem with the appropriate country or regional leads.

What might be the likely candidates for lines of expertise? There are three broad categories that one could anticipate, which could be loosely grouped under the labels of *program, resource acquisition*, and *enablement* (similar to the horizontal dimensions introduced in Chapter 1 of *Building a Better International NGO*), shown in Table 3.2. It is important to recognize

Table 3.2 Potential Lines of Expertise

Running Operations		Supporting Operations
Program	Resource Acquisition	Enablement
• Emergency/humanitarian • Health • Education • Agriculture/livelihoods • Enterprise and trade • Gender • Climate	• International institutions • Public fundraising • Corporate/Private Sector	• Finance • HR and talent • Information Communication Technology (ICT) • Communications • Risk

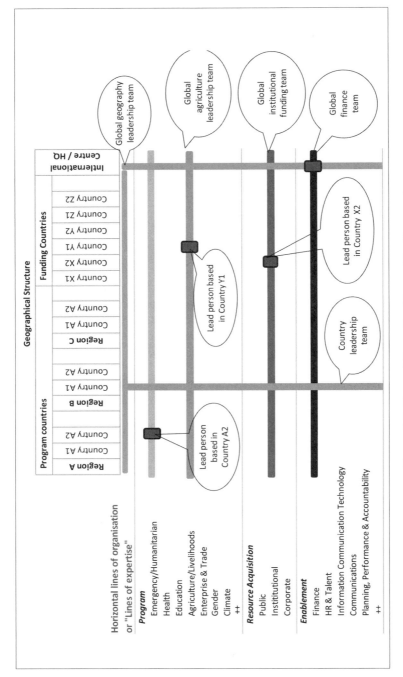

Figure 3.3 Lines of Expertise Mapped to Geography

that each candidate may have its own particular characteristics in terms of its remit around decisionmaking power, responsibility, and accountability.

Figure 3.3 is a practical illustration of the matrix model approach. The columns relate to the traditional geographical structure, divided by regions and countries. The rows relate to the potential horizontal lines of expertise under the three broad groupings of program, resource acquisition, and enablement. All staff will be within the matrix, with the allocation of their time between geography and lines of expertise varying depending on a range of factors, such as their levels of experience and stage of their career. Although one would expect that the leader for each geography will reside in that location, the lead for a line of expertise could be based wherever it makes practical sense.

Some staff (the majority) will continue to be primarily "owned" (for pay and rations) by the geography dimension. However, a proportion may have some formal alignment with a specific line of expertise (for part or all of their time) or in certain cases be deployed in full to that line of expertise for a part of their careers. Other staff may be primarily owned by a line of expertise but may be deployed with a particular geography (again, for part of or all of their time). This may appear more complex than is the case in actual practice. An illustrative case study of the day-to-day career of a development professional (Joy) in a high-performance matrix organization is described in the box at the end of this chapter. This contrasts with the parallel and somewhat different story of Jack (also featured in the box), who developed his career within a more traditional geographical structure.

It is important to stress that we are not advocating a greater centralization of power at headquarters. The goal is the opposite, in fact. The intent is to allow the best people across the entire organization, wherever they are, to contribute to and where appropriate to take leadership roles, often in addition to their country or regional responsibilities. The intent is to create a unified, cohesive, flatter "global leadership approach," where many key staff act as dual citizens—active in their local department or country as well as contributing to the global horizontal dimensions (lines of expertise). The ultimate goal is to find a way to develop and use the best talent, wherever it is located.

Remit for Lines of Expertise

The specific remit of each line of expertise can vary considerably in terms of role, decisionmaking power, and accountability. It can vary from nothing at one extreme to being a globally managed function in the other. In summary, any line of expertise could:

1. Be a *community of practice* that meets informally (either virtually or face to face) to share experiences and create a sense of horizontal community.
2. Lead the development of *policies, standards, and protocols* (which could be for guidance only or be mandatory).
3. Lead the development of *common processes and systems.*
4. Lead the process of *knowledge capture and learning.*
5. Lead or contribute to *staff recruitment, training, mentoring, and career development.*
6. Lead or contribute to the process of *individual performance management and career development.*
7. Lead or participate in key decisions either in *go/no-go for new opportunities.*
8. Lead or participate in key decisions in terms of the *scheduling/allocation of key staff* to conflicting demands.
9. Take full *operational responsibility* for delivery of particular programs because of their nature or scale—an example could include major emergency missions that span multiple countries.

As you map the potential candidates for lines of expertise against these roles, it is possible to see a dispersed picture, and one that could evolve over time as the experience and confidence with this model develops. This is illustrated in Figure 3.4. It is likely that decisionmaking in a number of areas will be highly collaborative between geography and lines of expertise. For example, performance feedback, promotion, and career progression decisions should be made collaboratively between country/geography and line of expertise leadership at the appropriate levels.

Key Differences and Implementation Choices

How Is This Kind of Model Fundamentally Different?
This model differs in a number of fundamental ways from the more traditional simple line structures. The differences lie in planning, decision-making, knowledge management, career development, standardization, and importantly, leadership structures.

1. Leadership teams and approach: Leadership teams need to be redesigned to embrace both the horizontal and vertical dimensions. As there will be more recognized global leadership roles, this will likely result in an extended global leadership team (or teams) embracing geography and lines

Figure 3.4 Remit and Levels of Decisionmaking for Lines of Expertise

Horizontal Lines of Expertise	NONE	Community of practice	Policy, standards, protocols for this dimension of organisation	Common processes and systems	Knowledge capture & learning	Staff recruitment training, development (skills and expertise)	Individual performance management	GO/NO-GO decisions re new opportuinities	Scheduling/ Allocation of staff to conflicting demands	Operations management responsibility
Leadership										
Program										
Emergency/Humanitarian		Mandatory	Lead	Lead	Lead	Lead	Collaborative	Collaborative	Collaborative	Selected cases
Health		Mandatory	Lead	Lead	Lead	Input to	Collaborative	Collaborative	Collaborative	
Education		Mandatory	Lead	Lead	Lead	Input to	Collaborative	Collaborative	Collaborative	
Agriculture/Livelihoods		Mandatory	Lead	Lead	Lead	Input to	Collaborative	Collaborative	Collaborative	
Enterprise & Trade		Optional		Lead	Lead	Input to	Collaborative	Collaborative	Collaborative	
Gender		Optional			Lead					
Micro-Finance		Optional			Lead					
Climate		Optional			Lead					
International advocacy		Optional	Lead	Lead	Lead	Input to	Collaborative	Collaborative	Collaborative	
++										
Resource Acquisition										
Public		Optional	Lead	Lead	Lead	Input to	Collaborative	Collaborative	Collaborative	
Institutional		Optional	Lead	Lead	Lead	Input to	Collaborative	Collaborative	Collaborative	
Corporate		Optional	Lead	Lead	Lead	Input to	Collaborative	Collaborative	Collaborative	
Enablement										
Finance		Optional	Lead	Lead	Lead	Input to	Collaborative	Collaborative	Collaborative	
HR & Talent		Optional	Lead	Lead	Lead	Input to	Collaborative	Collaborative	Collaborative	
Information Communication Tech		Optional	Lead	Lead	Lead	Input to	Collaborative	Collaborative	Collaborative	
Communications		Optional	Lead	Lead	Lead	Input to	Collaborative	Collaborative	Collaborative	

of expertise. However, it is possible and likely that certain individual leaders can take on more than one lead role, which is a manifestation of the dual citizenship concept. It is key to emphasize that this model may require some important changes in leadership behaviors—moving further toward a more collegial and interdependent approach rather than the more siloed or territorial behaviors evident in some agencies.

2. Career development: As staff members move through their careers, they can become aligned or sometimes deployed to horizontal lines of expertise. This provides additional opportunities for broadening and deepening their expertise and allowing them to take on supplementary responsibility for roles within these horizontal dimensions of an agency. At some periods during an individual's career, their focus will be 100 percent on their country or program role. At other times, it will make sense for them to take on additional responsibility for aspects of a particular line of expertise—and in some cases be fully deployed to that line. In such a situation, the line of expertise will be the main determinant of their day-to-day scheduling/deployment. This approach can provide significant avenues for staff development. In particular, it can be very beneficial for national staff in program countries who do not want to relocate but have the ambition and capacity to contribute at an international level (see the example of Joy in the box later in this chapter).

3. Decisionmaking in selection of new programs and partners: New substantial opportunities, which will take up a significant amount of investment and time, will need consideration from the relevant geographical leadership, as well as the relevant lines of expertise leadership in terms of important go/no-go decisions. Decisionmaking processes will have to be significantly modified to ensure that the right people are involved in a timely manner.

4. Decisionmaking regarding scheduling of staff: When programs are approved, scheduling key staff to meet various demands needs to be carried out by geographical and line of expertise leadership working together. This will ensure that key capability is not underutilized or suboptimized.

5. Knowledge capture, use, and ongoing learning: This is a priority area for many agencies, one where lines of expertise can play a very valuable role through their global communities. This is often the first role for lines of expertise and can provide a great opportunity for younger staff to take on early leadership roles on behalf of the global agency.

6. Standardization and professionalization of processes and systems: Communities of like-minded professionals can play a vital role in identifying areas where processes and systems could be standardized across different geographies. They can also play a key role in helping deliver this new standardization, in a way that is useful and accepted by their peers across the agency.

7. Planning and accountability—horizontal and vertical alignment: One of the essential requirements of the high-performance approach is a strong, joined-up planning and accountability framework, with a plan of key goals and targets for all the different dimensions of the organization. This topic is discussed in more detail in *Building a Better International NGO*. An associated part of this is a robust process for tracking all costs, particularly time spent by all staff, and allocating these costs to the relevant activities and projects.

8. Culture and team-based environment: In time, this organizational model will foster a very different atmosphere—one that is much more collaborative, interdependent, and team-based and, importantly, has greater individual and collective accountability for the overall contribution of the agency.

9. End of HQ as a physical place: Implicit in all this is the end of the road for the notion of a headquarters as a physical center or place. This is a major bridge to cross for many international NGOs, as they will need to unwind many engrained habits and traditions.

Across all of these aspects, it is important to emphasize the roles technology can play in facilitating a modern global organizational model. For example, technology may not completely eliminate travel, but it can reduce it dramatically.

Implementation Choices and Considerations

So how might one approach implementation? Which lines of expertise might be implemented and when? Migrating to this kind of organizational model involves a number of key shifts. Table 3.3 is an organizational strengthening template, to help leaders consider the elements of a high-performance agency both in terms of where they are placed today and where they might aim to be in 3 to 5 years. Examples of key shifts include moving to new and different roles: some individuals will probably take on two or more parallel roles in this new high-performance, flatter organizational form. There will be important shifts in decisionmaking processes, as well as changes to the structure of the leadership team(s). CEOs may begin to recognize the need for an expanded leadership team (or teams), as it makes increasingly little sense to rely on a few leaders on every issue. There will be changes in budget structure and cost management. A very practical implication is the need for a more disciplined approach to capturing time spent by all management and staff on different projects and activities. Yes, this probably implies adoption of time sheets! Arguably this is already a requirement irrespective of organizational structure, as the need to recover overhead costs against every project becomes more important for financial sustainability.

In practice, lines of expertise can be implemented in a phased process, as an agency gains experience and confidence with the matrix approach.

Examples of Careers in a Modern, High-Performance Matrix Organization

Joy, Joined Save the Planet in 2020

Joy grew up in Kenya and, after earning a medical degree in Nairobi, decided to take some time out and volunteer with Voluntary Services Overseas, completing a two-year assignment in nearby South Sudan to help with the long-running nutrition crisis. This inspired her to continue her studies. She completed her postgraduate degree in international development at the Institute of Development Studies in the United Kingdom. After graduating, she immediately joined Save the Planet (STP), the world's largest development agency, in 2020. She was attracted to STP by the wide range of programs she could get involved in, the well-organized career structure and options, as well as the obvious professionalism she experienced in her early interactions.

After joining, she completed a one-month induction and intensive training in South Africa, along with all of the other graduates and experienced hires of that year. She returned to the Kenyan branch of STP, which was her formal place of employment. Her first role was as a field project assistant in northern Kenya, close to the border with South Sudan, where she spent her first two and a half years. This was a highly insecure environment, and although the program was focused on addressing widespread and severe acute malnutrition challenges, a good deal of her work was with the local institutions to help build their internal skills and capacity.

During the early months of her placement, she was encouraged by her project manager to sign up to be a member of the interest group of the global nutrition line of expertise (LOE), one of twelve such dimensions of STP's global organization. This was a vibrant virtual global community, which interacted on an online Q&A forum. Interesting case examples were shared and discussed and online questions could be reviewed by participants across the world. However, in the early years, Joy was a very informal participant—

devoting a few hours each month to this community to help her own learning and development.

For the first four years of her career, her main connection with STP was with the Kenyan Country Office, which organized all of her scheduling (project allocation), training, and objective-setting and conducted her performance assessment, with the main input coming from the project leads to whom she reported for each assignment. She completed weekly time sheets online—though with the exception of training and a few other assignments, close to 100 percent of her time was dedicated to her field projects.

At the end of her fourth year, having completed three significant assignments in the nutrition arena, she was asked to take on a new and additional role—one of a team of the four global leads for knowledge management on behalf of the nutrition LOE. There was a small allocated budget for this task, which took up on average between 5 and 10 percent of her time. The cost was allocated in her time sheet to a global LOE cost code. All global LOEs have a small preplanned budget to allow them to carry out their remit in areas such as training, knowledge and learning, and policy development. The size of the budget depended on the specific remit. This was already planned in the rolling annual financial planning processes, which was set up so that fully loaded cost of all staff, charged to individual projects, was designed to recoup global costs incurred for agreed roles performed by LOEs as well as related management overhead. Joy greatly enjoyed this new dimension of her work, and it allowed her to have a growing involvement for the global contribution STP was making in the world.

As one of the emerging experts in the area of nutrition, she knew that she wanted to increase her global contribution and responsibility.

Luckily, she was contacted to see if she was willing to become part of the global pool of key talent for the nutrition LOE. This was a very difficult decision in her career, and though her loyalty to Kenya was extraordinarily strong, in conjunction with her country director, she knew the right thing for her career and her contribution to the area she was passionate about was to make this shift. This meant that her scheduling now moved from the country to the global LOE scheduling process. This was supported by a dynamic online system, facilitated by short biweekly calls to discuss priorities and expected availability of key staff. These discussions had to deal with the allocation of staff to cover short-term high-priority grant proposals, as well as allocating key staff to strategic programs both in Africa and across the world.

Joy continued to stay in Nairobi as her home, and her pay and rations were looked after by the Kenyan office. However, as the Kenyan CD particularly valued her contribution to local activities, she retained the right to use 20 to 30 percent of her time over any year to support and advise on projects in Kenya and also help with recruitment, mentoring, and training of local staff. All of her time was charged to the relevant activity through the time sheet process, so that time charged to activities outside Kenya or on behalf of the LOE was recouped through the global financial management processes. Her annual performance management process changed from the Kenya office and was led by the global LOE, though it remained a collaborative exercise with input from the global LOE leadership, the project leads where she contributed, and the country management in Kenya.

At the age of thirty-four, Joy was delighted to be offered the role as the African leader of the nutrition LOE and shortly after the full global role. This meant she was the leader of 175 professionals who were either 100 percent or had a significant proportion of their time deployed to this LOE. She advised on a number of the most strategic global projects and was deeply involved in resolving conflicting demands on key individuals. She was also the convenor of the decisionmaking go/no-go calls on strategic nutrition opportunities, which were rigorously reviewed according to a standard set of criteria around impact and risk. These calls were held biweekly and participants were invited from the leaders of the country and regions involved as well as from other LOE representatives that were relevant to each specific opportunity. All investment funds more than $10,000 had to be approved by the new opportunity process, irrespective of where the funds originated. In addition, Joy was becoming one of the key representatives of STP externally and her opinion was sought widely on her area of expertise. She was part of the STP extended global leadership team, formally reporting to the head of programs and policy, in addition to her ongoing but now small responsibility with her local Kenyan office.

She loved her work, but began to tire of the travel and the increasing administrative aspects. However, a new and very different kind of opportunity arose: a request through a combined government initiative by the governments of Ethopia, Kenya, and South Sudan for a partnership for capacity building to finally eliminate acute malnutrition in the East African Economic Community by 2035. This was a very senior secondment role, in many ways very different from what she had done in the past and involving regular dialogue with senior government ministers. It built directly on her technical expertise as well as her experience in local capacity building and influencing that had been an important strand in almost every project she had contributed.

Jack, Joined STP, 1971

Aged thirty-three, Jack joined STP in the 1970s as an experienced English and geography teacher. He never really enjoyed being in the classroom and had a deep longing for travel, to roll up his sleeves and help those in need. He initially volunteered to teach for six months in Ghana and immediately discovered that his real vocation was in helping in the remotest and most demanding corners of Africa. At the end of his volunteering stint, he applied to a number of international agencies and was soon offered a role as field program manager for Save the Planet in Malawi. Although he had no formal induction or training, he adored the work, the early responsibility, and the practical experience he gained, primarily using his own ingenuity and that of his local national staff.

Jack built a strong local team and demonstrated that he could supervise a portfolio of projects across a range of domains: education, health, livlihoods, and microfinance in southern Malawi. After two and a half years when the previous country director was approaching the end of his five-year term (the maximum allowed as an expatriate), Jack was offered and accepted the role of country director. He enjoyed a very warm and trusting relationship with the regional director, who visited at least twice a year, and was always impressed at how Jack was in control of the programs in the field and had the respect of his growing team. However, as he managed to always stay out of the project problem lists, as evidenced by the various audit evaluations, and because he always spent the funds allocated to his projects on time, it was not surprising that the visits from the regional director became shorter and less frequent. Jack enjoyed the autonomy and respect that was clearly implied.

Before the end of his first five-year term, a gap emerged for a deputy regional director, and Jack took the opportunity and moved to Asia. After just two more years he was appointed to the regional director position in Asia. Jack disliked too much intrusion in his area of control, valued the loyalty of his directors and staff, and felt proud that he looked after his people and knew them all personally. He disliked formal processes or global procedures, feeling that they got in the way of his flexibility and ability to respond to local needs.

He continued as a regional director for eighteen years, alternating among the six global regions every five years. Though this clearly caused disruption to his family and children's education, he enjoyed the novelty of living in new countries and bringing his unique way of managing, particularly his unique approach to development, to each new country.

When STP decided to adopt what they referred to as their new flat interdependent global organizational model, Jack's love affair with the agency quickly receded, and shortly afterward he left to find a role in a smaller NGO with a more conventional organizational model.

Table 3.3 Organization Strengthening Self-Evaluation Template

Components of a High-Performance Organization	Well Equipped to Meet Current Goals and Priorities?					Fit with New Goals and Priorities (3 to 5 yrs.)?			Priority (top three)
	Very Weak	Weak	OK-ish	Strong	Very Strong	Less Important	Same	More Important	
1. Clarity and alignment on what we are trying to achieve in external world and also on the how									
• Clarity on concrete external goals									
• A transparent theory of change with clear assumptions—with continuous learning									
• Capacity to measure outcomes and impact									
2. An environment to attract and nurture the right talent									
• Staff skills/experience matching goals and needs of agency									
• Best use/application of key staff against needs of agency									
• Career development and growth opportunities									
• Professional individual performance management									
3. A high-performance environment with strong planning, decisionmaking, and accountability									
• Decisionmaking quality, speed, and disciplined follow-through									
• Clarity on what good performance looks like									
• Consistent planning and accountability framework									
• An environment that encourages innovation and learning									
4. Strong and vibrant country programs and country teams									
• Fully adapted to local context and needs									
• Bring to bear the best of the agency's global know-how and resources									

- Well-selected local partner portfolio
- A strong and vibrant local team with requisite skills and experience

5. Align and connect with others in strategic way
- Strategic relationships with key donors; strategically managed
- Active in relevant global and local networks
- Partnering with other complementary agencies and stakeholders
- Part of global consortia toward common external goals

6. Strong and clear external identity and reputation
- Brand/identity in North
- Brand/identity in South
- Brand/identity internationally

7. Strong enabling process and systems— international consistency where needed
- Finance management
- HR and talent management
- IT/ICT
- Internal communication
- Risk management

8. Management and leadership capacity and behaviors
- Authentic
- Collaborative/team oriented
- Professional, positive, and inspiring
- Forward-looking, constructive coaching

9. Organization structure/model—fit for purpose
- Clarity of accountability
- Well-functioning leadership teams at all levels
- Consistent planning and accountability framework
- Important dimensions of expertise/responsibility embraced

Note

1. James Crowley and Morgana Ryan, *Building a Better International NGO: Greater than the Sum of the Parts?* (Boulder, CO: Kumarian Press, 2013).

4

Getting Serious About an Agency-Level Theory of Change

A theory of change! Should we really bother? Is it possible for an NGO to have a single theory of change that will (1) make any sense, (2) be vaguely correct, and (3) be practically useful? Is the world of development too complex to be represented in a statement or diagram? Are we better off with best endeavors achieving pockets of good, working with poor communities, in the well-intentioned hope that it will help and not getting distracted with the development of some master logic showing, through a torturous and complex map, how our tiny interventions are likely to result in lasting reduction in poverty or injustice?

I [coauthor James Crowley] have come across these types of concerns many times in the past decade. During a coffee break from one of my first projects with a large international agency, I found myself scribbling a kind of "causal-loop" map to help my novice brain plot out how the money channelled from well-meaning donors translated into improvements in education, health, and ultimately long-term progress in poverty reduction. From my previous career in the commercial sector, I was already a dedicated disciple of the value of a systems thinking approach, which we used frequently and to very useful effect across a range of situations, often with the ultimate goal of maximizing long-term shareholder value. I was keen to see if I could apply this kind of approach for the development sector. One of the senior executives from the NGO walked by and inquired with some curiosity what I was doing. When I explained, he replied that I was the first person he had ever seen attempting such a task. I was puzzled, to say the least. My line of curiosity continued as I worked on a number of subsequent assignments with a number of other large agencies, often with leading questions such as

A Collection of Personal Perspectives on the Question of How Change Really Happens

"Go out there, find the poorest people we can find, and just help them in any way we can."
    —Aengus Finocune, Concern

"Keep children alive, until they are five
Then make it the rule, that they all go to school
Protect them from abuse, and give them a choice
Listen to them, and recognise their voice
Because their future vocation, and the success of the nation
Will most certainly flow, from what they learn while they grow."
    —Jim Emerson, Plan International

"It's all about education, education, education—everything else should follow eventually."
    —Unattributed

"Close the gap between the formal and informal health systems in Africa."
    —Dr. Michael Smalley, AMREF International

"More trade and enterprise will take more people out of poverty sustainably than any other approach."
    —Paddy Maguinness, Traidlinks

"It's about the infrastructure—if I was starting with a clean sheet of paper, I would invest everything in infrastructure—that is what the Marshall Plan demonstrated to us over 60 years ago. The Chinese have studied this history and implemented it themselves with good success."
    —Senior executive of a major insitutional fund

"The definition of insanity is to keep trying the same thing over and over again and expecting different results."
    —Albert Einstein

"where would I find your agency insight or logic to help me understand how the interventions you support lead to lasting change?" After a while, I am embarrassed to say—I stopped asking.

I am encouraged to say that this debate seems to have reappeared with some gusto in the past few years, usually under the broad label "theory of change." With the growing emphasis on value for money and results-based approaches, the need to articulate an agency-level theory of change has moved, somewhat belatedly, to center stage. Agencies suddenly want to be able to articulate their own particular theory or logic. This is inserted as an important part of funding applications to institutional donors; increasingly it also tends to be included, often with some apprehension, into an agency's strategic planning document.

Whatever it includes or looks like, for many agencies a theory of change is still not at the heart of planning, decisionmaking, and learning in the way it should be. I often get the feeling that for every 1,000 staff members, there is one lonely and ignored person sitting in the corner of the head office thinking about how change really happens (theory of change), and 999 others getting on with making the agency work, trying to overcome the day-to-day, practical, administrative challenges that arise.

This chapter has two broad objectives. First we want to demystify the subject and break it into its component parts; second, we propose a way forward that would like to make a theory of change a central and integrated part of agencies' fabric. We begin by focusing on the problem we are trying to solve. We then explore what a theory of change is really for. We try to define what it is and is not. Later on we set out some steps—indicating how one could begin to develop an agency-level theory of change.

In broad terms, international agencies are in the business of making significant and lasting changes to the lives of the poor and disadvantaged. This is a nightmarishly complex affair. Let us start by recognizing what we know of the situation we are working in (some basic observations) and then review some of the core problems caused by that situation. These are summarized in Figure 4.1.

The Situation

Eight Important Context Factors

1. The process of development is extraordinarily difficult. Intervening in local poverty situations is more complex than one might think, as there are multiple social, political, cultural, economic, and infrastructure dimensions that need to be understood. When we intervene, even with the best endeavours, there can be some unintended con-

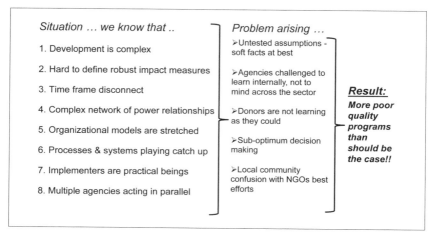

Figure 4.1 The Problem We Are Trying to Solve

sequences. Without a broad and thoughtful approach to help us under-stand the local context and the various interrelated factors that come into play, we can make many mistakes. In the worst-case scenario, we end up doing more harm than good.

2. It is often challenging to define meaningful measures of impact at local, country, or international levels, beyond simplistic output measures like the number of people helped or dollars spent. Hence, we can some-times miss the benefit of a unifying, stretching, and robust metric of impact at an organizational level—akin, for example, to profit or share-holder value in the private sector. However, we are not implying that this is impossible to do in all situations.

3. We have to recognize that there is a very complex network of power relationships between local governments, NGOs, donors (and their governments), local citizens, private sector firms, academia, and community-based organizations (CBOs). As a specific example, one of the unfortunate consequences of the power relationship between donors and implementing NGOs is that there can be a reluctance to fully share the complexity of the local situation. There can also be bias toward not fully acknowledging failures and learning—"declare success some-how"—for fear of getting in the way of future funding opportunities.

4. We appreciate that there is a fundamental timeframe disconnect between the duration of typical programs (often between one and three years) and the time it takes to make meaningful progress. Practically,

very few agencies have the resources to track long-term impact, looking five, ten, or even twenty years hence.

5. Organizational models and capacity of international NGOs are stretched—they are still attempting to catch up to the ever-growing demands of their work. A contributory factor is that agencies are often spread far and wide, arguably "stretched far too thin" to be able to join the dots of thinking and learning. As we discussed in Chapter 3, the simple structural form of an organization risks being out of tune with the sophistication required for joined-up sharing, learning, decisionmaking, and accountability. These simple line structures, with a strong command-and-control ethos and with a risk-averse, relational style of management, are poorly equipped to meet current needs.

6. Processes and systems within many agencies have been struggling to catch up with the growing demands of their own ambitions as well as the expectations of external stakeholders. A good example is the increasing demands from donors, who are anxious to demonstrate clear, early results and value for money to maintain a political and public support base for their aid investments. The drive for a "results-based agenda" is the recent manifestation of this trend. Unfortunately, despite even the best intentions, there is a risk that this encourages an overly simplistic, linear, cause-and-effect type of mentality and a bias to counting short-term outputs. As more sophisticated agencies are beginning to embrace the complexity, nonlinearity, and the long-term timeframes involved in the development process, many staff members and systems are still catching up with yesterday's demands.

7. Program implementers and their local support staff are typically practical and pragmatic beings. As one might expect, they are guided by their experiences, past successes and failures, and the views of their peers. Furthermore, the types of individuals who are attracted to field implementation roles often appreciate autonomy, which has been a strong feature of these roles in the past. They may not be great fans of slavishly following a consistent agency-wide approach, which they might perceive as limiting their flexibility to respond to specific local conditions and needs.

8. Finally, we know that in many poor areas, we can find multiple agencies contributing, often in parallel, all with their own very good intentions, assisting the same or overlapping communities. What on Earth must the local population make of all this? This is their community, their country, their long-term futures we are dealing with. This is indeed a most troubling topic, one we revisit later in this chapter.

If we look across all of these important issues, we should ask ourselves: what are the key implications? In summary, as Craig Valters usefully pointed out: "there are considerable practical, organisational, and
bureaucratic constraints to the promotion of learning throughout the sector."[1] Duncan Green, a very experienced Oxfam adviser, is another valuable and stimulating contributor to the discussion on many aspects of
this topic and we recommend his various blogs and writing on the subject.[2]

Problems Arising from this Situation

In summary, we believe there are at least five specific problems that
arise from this set of contextural issues.

• There are many untested assumptions; many projects are implemented on logic that is based on very soft facts, may be completely
untested, or have already proven unsuccessful in other comparable situations. Result: more poor-quality programs than should be the case!
• There is insufficient learning within the walls of a particular
agency, between an agency and its funding partners, and across agencies
contributing to the same areas. Result: more poor-quality programs than
should be the case!
• The basis for decisionmaking, particularly in terms of where to
invest funds to maximum effect, is too weak or subjective. This means
that funds may not be invested to maximum effect. Result: more poor-
quality programs than should be the case!
• Beyond the walls of a particular organization, when different
agencies come together in partnerships or consortia, there is inevitable
friction and inefficiency as these myriad beliefs and assumptions get
in the way of designing and implementing cohesive, large-scale combined programs. Result: more poor-quality programs than should be
the case!
• Finally, there is a risk that local communities, CBOs, and local
institutions are somewhat bewildered by the plethora of theories,
approaches, and activities and become unwelcoming and even hostile to
best endeavours by different international agencies. Result: more poor-
quality programs than should be the case!

These challenges and problems need a response from the NGO
community at an agency level and at a sector level. A good agency-level
theory of change is a way to start to make progress.

What Is A Theory of Change For?

Before describing specifically what an agency-level theory of change might include, let's briefly summarize what exactly it can be used for. At its simplest, we believe there are at least seven basic uses for an organizational theory of change:

1. For internal learning: It should provide a platform for the best experts of the organization to share learning on how positive change happens in various development contexts and build from previous learning where possible.

2. For decisionmaking: Why would we invest in any project we do not believe will deliver the best return on investment in terms of long-term impact? Agencies have endless opportunities to apply their scarce skills and resources.

3. For training: To support the induction and training of all staff, not only so there is a shared understanding of how positive change happens but also to ensure that the work of every department and function is aligned with the goals.

4. For stakeholder communication: Given that there are a very broad range of stakeholders, contributing, affected, or benefiting in different ways, a good theory of change provides a basis for more effective communication and learning between NGOs, donors, and other key stakeholders.

5. For program selection, shaping, and design: A theory of change can provide a foundation for selecting and shaping the best interventions, as well as a starter kit for developing more specific theories of change for each individual program.

6. For collaboration and partnering: How can you collaborate effectively with others unless you have a transparent and shared articulation of your own logic and assumptions?

7. For fundraising: A good theory of change is a useful and increasingly an expected part of fundraising applications. If done well, it could provide a basis for much more effective communication, alignment, and shared learning between implementing agencies and supporting donors.

What a Theory of Change Is Not

The corollary of the above may be useful to emphasize what we mean. Here we present what a theory of change is not (in our view).

It is *not* a completely new idea. All agencies already have a theory of change (or in most cases several theories of change) that are implicit, deep in the heads of key people. Although the language may be new to some, the concept of a theory of change is not new. What is kind of new is the idea of making these theories explicit, stronger, and more connected across an entire agency, so it can learn better and support better and more consistent programs.

It is *not* a single, horrendously complex chart indicating cause and effect that is uniformly applicable at global, country, and local levels. Change is too complex and the number of moving parts are just too many. It is not linear, and of course the systems we are trying to influence are dynamic, not static. Charts might be a useful way of capturing one's understanding and logic at a certain level, but are not the end of the story.

It is *not* a convenient wrap-around for existing interventions, targeted outputs, outcomes, and impact without any meaningful critical reflection/challenge or little regard to the many other factors or outcome areas that relate to the end goals.

It is *not* a top-down dictate—something that can be designed as a dogma from headquarters and merely rolled out for implementation in program countries.

It is *not* a separate thing but part of the broader fabric and know-how of any agency. It should be integrated into policies, approaches, tools, systems, and training and should be reflected within an agency's management process.

Hierarchies of Theories of Change

This chapter primarily speaks to the idea of an agency-level theory of change. We recognize that there can be theories of change at different levels, potentially within some form of coherent hierarchy, with lower levels containing more detail as well as being designed to respond more specifically to the relevant local contexts and goals. For example, underneath an overarching, agency-level theory of change, we could imagine a sector-level theory of change (for example, around education or health) and then develop that theory and adapt it for a country or specific program context. This idea is illustrated in Table 4.1, which also seeks to illustrate the important point that these theories are not independent of other external theories or plans and are ideally developed collaboratively, not just across an international NGO family but with other civil society and local government bodies.

Table 4.1 Hierarchy of Theories of Change

Theory of Change Level		External Linkages
Agency	Collective wisdom of how change happens in developing world	Combined civil society joined up thinking on development
Sector	Agency Theory of Change developed more specifically for sector work (health, education, etc.)	Combined civil society joined up thinking on development related to this sector
Country	Components adapted following thorough analysis of country social, political, and economic context	National development plans of local countries as well as combined civil society joined up thinking on development related to this country
Program	Components adapted following thorough analysis of program content	National and local district development plans as well as combined civil society joined up thinking on development related to this locality

The Architecture of an Agency-Level Theory of Change

In the previous section, we discussed the issues we are trying to tackle, the problems arising, and the potential uses of a good theory of change at an agency level. Now we describe some of the key components of a theory of change. There seems to be a good deal of debate and confusion in the sector at the moment as to what a theory of change really is and what it should include.

Let's put our cards on the table. We believe that an agency-level theory of change is a central piece of the fabric of any forward-thinking and learning agency in the twenty-first century. This is not a single thing, chart, or diagram but an intertwined collection of different components. These are living rather than static as the organization learns from internal and external evidence of what works best. These form part of the joined-up fabric of the ideas, knowledge, policies, and approaches of any agency.

Although there are many different ways to represent a theory of change, we believe the components could encompass the following.

1. **A synthesis of learning**, lessons, mistakes, and successes from the best people inside and outside the agency, which will help inform the next component.

2. A set of **explicit beliefs and assumptions** on how change happens in general and specifically in an agency's area of contribution.

3. A **stretching goal** that is achievable as well as inspiring for all stakeholders.

4. An **outcome map (or change canvas)** to describe different outcomes or interim destinations (or intermediate metrics) that are important stepping-stones or indicators of progress toward the ultimate goal. This should embrace all of the most important outcome areas, not just those directly related to your interventions or within the limitations of your own agency's particular contribution.

5. An insightful **lens or framework for analyzing local context**, respecting that this will be valuable in the work to formulate theories of change at local country or program level.

6. A set of potential **interventions** which we, as an agency, believe we could bring to bear to deliver specific outcomes, to contribute to the ultimate goal being pursued.

7. Last and by no means least, an **easy-to-understand summary** that sits on top of all of the above, which is clear, insightful, and free of jargon and speaks to multiple audiences, both internal and external.

These components are illustrated and summarized in Figure 4.2 and Table 4.2.

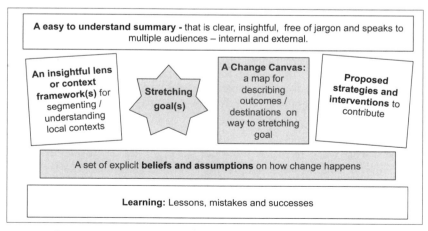

Figure 4.2 Components of an Agency-Level Theory of Change

Table 4.2 Summary of Components of an Agency-Level Theory of Change

Component	Description	Comments
Summary	An easy to understand synthesis that is clear, insightful, and free of jargon and speaks to multiple audiences—internal and external	• Sounds easy but in practice is very hard • Coulld be phrase, paragraph, picture, simple diagram
Assumptions and Beliefs	A set of explicit assumptions/beliefs on how change happens	• Living and growing over time • Relevant to agency specific area of contribution
Change Canvas or Outcome Map	A map for describing outcomes/destinations on way to ultimate goals	• Embraces all important outcome areas; not just those within the capacity of a particular agency to address • Relevant to agency specific area of contribution • To be interpreted and adapted to each local context—as a tool in the selection and design of local programs
"Stretching" Goal	Stretching and ambitious goal(s) that speaks to all key stakeholders	• Speaks to local stakeholders and partners • Inspiring, may be long term • May take contributions from many actors to achieve
Interventions	Proposed strategies and interventions to contribute	• Based on our skills, experience, or core competence • What specifically do we bring? • List of possible programs—selected and tailored depending on local context and needs
Context Analysis Framework	An insightful lens or framework for segmenting and interrogating local context	• A tool for local context analysis using a consistent framework • Insight and learning as to what is really going on • Forward thinking
Learning	Lessons and insight (what did and what did not work?)	• Collective insight of best brains from hands on learning (internal and external)—not a job for a junior officer at HQ • Solid evidence, if possible from robust baselining and monitoring • Living and growing over time

This sounds like a lot of pieces and is by no means prescriptive; it is merely a way of framing or thinking about the challenge. A good theory of change is not a separate, isolated thing. Each of the components are nested within and often interwoven with some of the more familiar parts of an agency. In reality, the development of these components is an iterative rather than a sequential process, requiring successive iterations to gain increasing clarity and insight. It will also be important to make sure that day-to-day approaches, tools, training, and actions are properly aligned.

Let's explore what we mean by these suggested components.

Synthesis of Learning

The key foundation of a theory of change is the collective wisdom of the best practitioners across the agency and particularly from the field, in terms of what has worked well and what has not worked in the past. The best practitioners will have a strong view of good and bad developmental practice and good interventions and appropriate contexts. It is vital that there is an opportunity to share, debate, and challenge these views and beliefs based on concrete evidence and experience to strengthen the combined wisdom. These key people (often low in number) may not be the most senior in an organization. However, they often have a cadre of dedicated followers who are strongly influenced by their views and advice, relying on them for guidance in decisionmaking around project selection, scoping, design, and implementation approaches.

As an aside, it is worth noting that many agencies are beginning to adopt the rigor of building a specific research question into the design of each field program to ensure some targeted learning from every project. This is to be encouraged, and it demands discipline and investment.

Explicit Beliefs and Assumptions

This is the core of an agency level theory of change. Building on past experience and learning, any theory of change is likely to include a set of clear assumptions or beliefs that capture an agency's views on how change actually happens. Some of these may be well tested and reinforced by hard evidence over decades of experience. Others may be beliefs that are based on project learning, though not yet fully validated. Others may be mere hypotheses that need to be developed and tested through future work. This is an important aspect of any learning organization.

Ambitious Goals

We believe that the definition of a tangible goal or goals is a very useful discipline to anchor and guide the work of an agency. Ideally, these should:

- Be recognizable and meaningful to beneficiaries and key local stakeholders.
- Have external profile and traction and, if possible, be shared by a range of other agencies working in the same broad area.
- Be inspiring and genuinely stretching.
- Be tangible and quantifiable, providing clarity and a basis for monitoring progress.

What should these goals look like in practice? The following are three indicative examples (from different agencies in three different sectors) that we feel are useful illustrative examples.

- Universal access to WASH (water, sanitation, and hygiene) by 2030
- Reducing the number of people suffering from acute malnutrition in a defined region from 20 percent to 0 percent by 2030
- Increasing the agriculture capacity of a developing country or region so it can meet 75 percent of its needs by 2030 instead of 10 percent today

Framework for Analyzing Local Contexts

It is important that an agency-level theory of change recognize the wider variety of contexts where poverty exists: from (a) extremely poor, unstable, and insecure countries to (b) poor but stable developing countries to (c) pockets of poverty in emerging middle income countries or (d) pockets of poverty in the more developed affluent countries. A useful component of a good theory of change is a broad and thorough framework to help analyze the different contexts and to drive rigor and insight in the preparation of local plans and interventions. As indicated earlier, we expect that agencies will develop more precise theories of change at sector, country, or program level, responding to particular local contexts and needs.

This should look at a broad range of factors such as security, education, health, social norms, institutional capacity, enterprise and trade, governance, human capacity, industrial policy and plans, governance and national plans, rule of law, and corruption, tackling questions such as:

- What is really going on?
- What has hindered change over the previous decades?
- What are the views and habits at individual, community, and national levels that affect the pace of progress?
- Who holds the real power and why?
- Where positive change has occurred, what has been the key ingredient?
- What major historical events (good or bad) flavor beliefs and perceptions? What can be learned from previous attempts by other agencies?
- Who else is trying to help? What are they doing and seeking to achieve? How are they getting on?

Too often, when we see a clear area of need—be it levels of acute malnutrition or instances of extreme injustice—the temptation is to dive in and apply our preferred interventions based on familiar approaches, using our principles, with some rudimentary consultation—and hence without properly understanding the context and existing plans and momentum on the ground. A telling illustration of the risks of not understanding local context is set out in the following quote. This example shows how best endeavors by external agencies in the fight against Ebola ran foul of local beliefs and customs.

> The Acholi people called it gemo—a bad spirit that arrived suddenly, like an ill wind—and they had strict protocols to deal with the deadly sickness that followed. Patients were quarantined at home, and cared for by a gemo survivor. Two poles of elephant grass were erected outside, as a warning to other villagers to stay away. Dancing, arguing and sex were forbidden, rotten meat was to be scrupulously avoided, and those recovering had to remain isolated for a lunar month. Those who succumbed were buried at the edge of the village.
>
> It took the skills of a trailblazing anthropologist, Professor Barry Hewlett from Washington State University, to discover that the Acholi, an ethnic group in northern Uganda, had their own rather effective method of dealing with Ebola. . . . Ebola may be classed as an emerging disease but the Acholi, he found, may well have been battling it for a century.
>
> Recently, Professor Hewlett revealed his dismay at how current outbreaks in Guinea, Liberia and Sierra Leone were being handled by the international fraternity, whose urgent, well-meaning containment

efforts were leaving scant room for the beliefs, customs and sensitivities of locals. . . . Professor Melissa Leach, from Sussex University, has pointed out that remote communities associate past epidemics with the sudden arrival of masked white foreigners bearing syringes and body bags.

Strangers in space suits came to take the blood of sick children — then the children died. Corpses were zipped up, kept behind curtains and then burnt before relatives could check that their loved ones were passing intact to the afterlife. Lurid rumours arose of Western trade in body parts; efforts at disinfecting villages were misconstrued as deliberate contamination.

Such misunderstandings explain why Ebola containment teams, lacking the peace offering of a cure, have been met with hostility — and worse. Tragically, eight healthcare workers, officials and journalists were murdered a fortnight ago in Guinea, their bodies thrown into a septic tank. Even when outsiders are welcomed, a slender grasp of cultural norms can lead to perilous knowledge gaps.[3]

Change Canvas (or Outcome Map)

As we design programs, it is essential that we understand the range of factors that might affect or contribute to the longer-term goal. These could be factors that benefit from direct intervention, or alternatively interim destination points, where we can gauge progress toward the larger goal. As indicated earlier, contributing to lasting impact can sometimes take considerable time.

Part of the response to this is the idea of an outcome map or what we call a *change canvas*. This would set out the outcome areas (for example, changes in attitude or behaviors) likely to be most important in the journey to the long-term goal. It would reflect changes of different kinds and at different levels (for example, at individual, community, institution, and national government levels).

The idea of an outcome map is not new, and it was very usefully introduced in a paper by Organizational Research Services for the Annie E. Casey foundation back in 2004.[4] That publication described three broad categories of outcome areas: **impact, influencers,** and **leverage**, summarized in Table 4.3. Impact outcome areas are core areas of progress, for example, around household income, economic growth, or educational attainment levels. Influencing outcome areas are important factors that could either help or impede progress, including political will, the strength of national strategies and plans, and institutional capacity. Leverage outcome areas could be useful to facilitate growth, for example, capital access through banks and institutions, accessibility

Table 4.3 Change Canvas: Illustrative Outcome Areas for Navigating and Tracking Change

Impact Outcome Areas	Influence Outcome Areas	Leverage Outcome Areas
Changes in attitudes (e.g., perceptions and beliefs)	Changes of visibility of issue	Changes in public funds
Changes in knowledge	Changes in community norms	Changes in philanthropy
Changes in awareness	Changes in partnerships	Changes in resources available to a community
Changes in skills	Changes in public will	Changes in private investment
Changes in behavior	Changes in political will	
Changes in health	Changes in policies	
Changes in family stability	Changes in regulations	
Changes in financial status	Changes in service practices	
Changes in education	Changes in business practices	
Changes in social norms		
Changes in economic conditions		
Changes in safety		

Source: Adapted from Organizational Research Services, "Theory of Change: A Practical Tool for Action, Results & Learning," Annie E. Casey Foundation (2004).

of public funding, availability of private investment, and even private sector participation. Figure 4.3 shows an actual example of a change canvas for an agency—with a focus on supporting trade and enterprise in east Africa.

At an agency level, it is likely that attempts to precisely map the interrelationships between all outcome areas will lead to an overly complicated map because inevitably there will be an endless set of causal loops and interrelationships. However, at the level of an individual program or intervention, when the focus is a small subset of outcome areas, it may be possible to map some of the most important of these interrelationships. This will be illustrated further in the case study at the end of this chapter.

In the design of specific programs, it can be useful to define a small number of outcome statements for each area as a way to articulate, as clearly as possible, the change we are trying to bring about. Hence, this approach can help identify useful interim metrics of progress to provide some reassurance and confidence to key stakeholders and donors and, where necessary, to steer or refine interventions as needed.

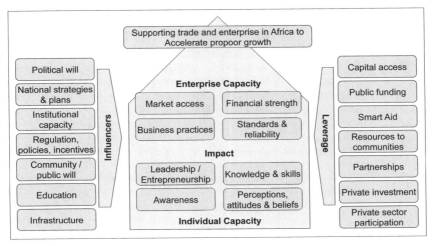

Figure 4.3 Example of Strategic Change Canvas

To summarize, a change canvas (or outcome map) has four broad uses:

1. Provides a consistent language or map for communicating (internally and externally) the range of factors or intermediate outcomes that may need to be considered in individual programs in relation to the longer-term goal being pursued.

2. Provides a template to help with the scoping and design of individual programs, showing in an understandable way how each program contributes to the broader change canvas.

3. Helps identify key metrics that can be tracked to gauge interim progress.

4. Provides a unifying framework for learning as an agency gathers the lessons from individual programs.

A Set of Strategies or Interventions and Principles

How does an agency actually contribute? It is now appropriate to discuss the set of interventions a particular agency feels it is well positioned to support, depending on the particular situation or context. All agencies will have a set of preferred interventions where they have deep skills, experience, and credibility. Much of the capacity of any agency will be heavily invested in these particular areas of intervention.

These should be mapped on the change canvas, describing which change areas are affected directly or indirectly. This mapping allows a clear articulation of how any specific intervention fits into the broader efforts of an agency, as well as providing guidance for the selection of intermediate-level metrics to gauge progress toward the larger goal.

For avoidance of doubt, these interventions may well be implemented with or through other local partners.

An Easy-to-Understand Summary

Finally, once the seven components are worked through, a very useful step is to articulate a summary description of an NGO's insight, logic, and intended contribution. This could be a few words, a few sentences, and/or a simple diagram that communicates meaning and focus to a range of audiences.

A very good example is the theory of change developed a number of years back by AMREF Africa (http://amref.org/silo/fites/amref-business-plan.pdf; at that point they did not use the theory of change language).[5] They were able to summarize their theory into just a few simple words: "closing the gap between the formal and informal health systems in Africa." This statement was the summit of a well-thought-through strategy document and was derived from months of robust reflection and debate on the key issues and challenges in health in Africa, building from internal and external learning. Not only did this represent the apex of their insight in their new strategy, it became the fulcrum of their new program focus and resulted in a major shift in emphasis in the mix of their work.

How a Theory of Change Fits Within the Broader Architecture of an Agency

Finally, we revisit how the ingredients that we have described under agency-level theory of change fit into the broader components of any NGO. As mentioned earlier, a theory of change is not a separate thing, but is intertwined with most of the essential parts or fabric of any agency. For example, an agency-level theory of change is likely to dovetail closely with:

- The program policy and methodology the agency uses to design and implement its programs;

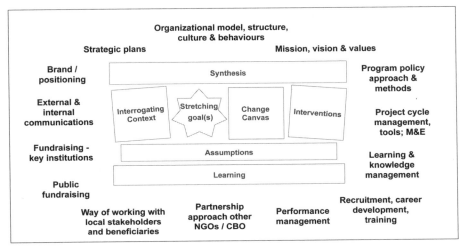

Figure 4.4 How a Theory of Change Permeates the Key Pieces of Any Agency

- The systems and tools to support day-to-day programs, for example, project life cycle management and monitoring and evaluation; and
- The enabling systems and processes around finance, and particularly HR—specifically, the performance appraisal approach needs to support and encourage the intent of the theory of change as a learning tool.

This interconnectivity is illustrated in Figure 4.4.

Organizational Resistance: Overcoming Barriers and Blockages

What are the key challenges that NGOs need to overcome to embrace the core idea of an agency-level theory of change? What are the barriers and blockages? How do we overcome them? Despite the efforts of many NGOs to strengthen their organizations, professionalize their program approaches, and strengthen their processes and systems, when it comes to theory of change, there can be considerable obstacles. These are summarized in Table 4.4.

Table 4.4 Possible Barriers and Blockages to an Agency-Level Theory of Change

Barriers and Blockages	Response
It's just too difficult!	A good theory of change approach is a way of navigating through something that is truly difficult, building and learning over time.
Facing up to failures	Failure is how we learn the most!
Donors don't want to know	They can't know if we are not open. Be honest with them—involve them as full partners in the change process.
Senior leadership just doesn't get it	We may need to rethink our approach to selecting boards and senior leadership, perhaps with more emphasis on bringing through and promoting more of the best people from within.
Command-and-control style of management and lack of forward-thinking planning and accountability approach	This is not necessarily a conundrum as progress can be made across both of these areas in a synergistic way.
Weak practices and habits around baselining, research, and learning	We just have to get better and fast!
Misunderstanding about what real innovation really means	A good theory of change can be a catalyst for more effective and productive innovation.

It's Just So Difficult!

The logic around helping respond to immediate needs as a result of a famine or emergency seems to be fairly straightforward on the surface. However, contributing to lasting long-term development progress in local contexts with a variety of urgent needs and complex combination of social norms, tribal politics, and weak infrastructure can be extraordinarily difficult. This could be regarded as high-risk social investment, with some parallels to high-risk venture capital. Just like venture capital, we know that only a modest proportion of social investments are likely to achieve substantial returns and many might fail to achieve the outcomes intended. We need to apply the best collective and historical learning to ensure the percentage that meet and exceed their impact expectations is as large as possible.

This is where an agency-level theory of change comes into its own. With a strong theory of change, NGOs can make a better attempt to optimize learning and improve decisionmaking in the selection and prioritization of social investments.

Facing Up to Failures

For a variety of understandable reasons, there is sometimes a lack of openness in respect to program failures. All agencies are eager to report the positive progress to their donors. However, we know that often, we learn the most from cases where it went horribly wrong.

Unfortunately, a chain of pressures can result in a temptation not to look failure in the eye but instead to declare success somehow. This can be a direct result of the growing pressures of donors for evidence of positive and consistent results. It can also arise as a result of unproductive or unhelpful performance and reporting pressures on front-line staff.

Donors Don't Want to Know

We believe that donors *do* want to know and in many cases are making good progress in improving their understanding of the realities of the development process. Yes, some donors do not have the time and patience to think through in full detail the fiendishly complex process of development. This is an understandable issue, and one that can be made worse by poor two-way communication between donors and NGOs.

In some cases donors are dependent on implementation agencies to keep them informed of progress and learning along the way. However, communication can sometimes be undermined, for example, when agencies specify metrics of targeted outputs, outcomes, or impacts that are overly simplistic, optimistic, and sometimes contingent on several factors far beyond the scope of the project in question.

On the other hand, it is also not surprising that at certain times the leadership of some government donor aid agencies can find themselves pressured to act on the whim of their current political leaders. These officials have a responsibility to understand and take account of the views of politicians and of the general public. This is why all international NGOs have a secondary role of helping these officials strengthen the political and public support for international development and humanitarian investments. We believe a clearly articulated, agency-level theory of change can be very valuable in strengthening this communication process.

Organizational Inertia

All large organizations in any industry can have considerable inertia. Similarly, NGOs are invested in the traditional ways of thinking and acting, in their program policies, methodologies and tools, career development and training, fundraising approaches, and performance management habits, to mention a few. Many of these are illustrated in Figure 4.4. Implementing a clear and unified theory of change might well demand changes in many of these areas and disturb the natural inertia of an international agency. Changing the inertia in a large NGO can be particularly challenging. This is because, as mentioned elsewhere,[6] many agencies are spread very thin over many program countries, in a wide range of contexts, covering many different topics.

However, we firmly believe that a good theory of change provides a great opportunity to strengthen and align all the different parts of the fabric of any agency.

Senior Leadership Just Doesn't Get It

One of the challenges in this sector is the gap in understanding that can sometimes exist between development and humanitarian staff on one hand and senior leadership and board members on the other. Board members serve with good intent and do their best to bring their specific skills to bear. However, too often they are just not equipped in terms of their backgrounds, skills, and experience to fully appreciate the complexities, challenges, and the risks of the development process. Some boards, in our humble opinion, are also too large and cumbersome to be able to intimately engage with the key choices and decisions that come into play in the leadership of a large agency.

This gap in understanding applies not just to board members but also to senior-level (often talented) executives who come from outside the development and humanitarian sectors. This is hardly surprising when much of the rank-and-file is made up from a cadre of committed development practitioners, with advanced degrees and decades of practical experience.

Conducting a thoughtful and patient process to gain deep alignment on a meaningful and compelling agency-level theory of change can be a considerable challenge. This is not to say that outside experience and thinking cannot be useful. In fact, we believe it can be invaluable. However, it does require that those from outside have the interest and time and are given the opportunity to understand the real dynamics and realities of the development process.

Command-and-Control Management Approach and Lack of Effective Planning and Accountability

In chapter 1 of *Building a Better International NGO*,[7] we suggested ten requirements that an NGO should have to give it a fair chance of being "more than the sum of the parts." One of the aspects we particularly emphasized was the need to move away from what we referred to as a relational, line of sight, or command-and-control style of management. This can often be accompanied by a low-risk culture as well as a fairly basic approach (if any) to organizational planning, performance, and accountability.

This is somewhat of a "chicken and egg" conundrum. On one hand, deficiencies in these areas can impede efforts to develop a forward-thinking and powerful theory of change approach. On the other hand, a good theory of change could be extremely useful as a foundation in the development of a more mature and sophisticated performance management framework.

Weak Practices and Habits in Research and Learning

As the NGO sector becomes more adept at understanding and effecting positive change, it needs to get better at research and learning. Building very clear research questions into field programs, although it is becoming common for many agencies, is still a relatively new practice. This is not always simple, for example, many international agencies work through local partners, who may in turn work through smaller local entities such as CBOs.

However, the historic weakness in these areas is a considerable impediment to developing and strengthening an agency-level theory of change, particularly one that is based on sound, evidence-based sharing and learning. One of the other unfortunate implications of this weakness is that there is an insufficient link between policy and advocacy efforts and practical learning from fieldwork.

Misunderstanding about What Real Innovation Involves

There can be some confusion over what good innovation really means. The desire for flexibility and the space for trying out new ideas and approaches are useful, but these are just part of a productive innovation process. Productive innovation also demands that agencies are extremely disciplined and do not diffuse energy across too many ideas and topics, in too many places, using too many inconsistent approaches. It requires ruthless focus and follow-through to ensure that the best ideas get the attention and investment they need and build on the knowledge and experience of the whole agency.

We believe that a good theory of change approach should be an anchor for focused and productive innovation, providing a framework to position and prioritize good ideas, as well as helping weed out questionable initiatives.

An Approach to Developing a Theory of Change

The following is a rough outline of the steps one could follow in developing a theory of change at an agency level. Although the steps appear sequential and complete, in practice an iterative approach will be necessary to arrive at a theory of change that is clear, robust, and a foundation for future learning, planning, and decisionmaking.

Step 1: Best Brains to Reflect on and Summarize Past Learning, Successes, and Failures

- Gather a small group of (say, three to six) experienced program staff members, and ask them to reflect and recount their individual learning; develop a process for a broader selection of staff to contribute their ideas and learning.
- Similarly collect the views of key staff involved with monitoring and evaluations (M&E) and post project appraisals.
- Get hard data to support insights and learning.
- Note any areas of divergence; these are important as a backdrop to future research and learning.
- Summarize the findings and learnings in as simple a format as makes sense.
  Note: This is not a job for an inexperienced person sitting in the corner of the head office!

Step 2: Develop a Clear Set of Assumptions and Beliefs on How Change Happens

- Summarize where there is alignment.
- Take time to consult with stakeholders who know your agency well.
- Gather and include insights from peer organizations and academic research.

Step 3: Develop a First Hypothesis to Articulate the Ultimate Goal of Your Agency

- The more stretching and inspiring the better, but it also needs to be as tangible and measurable if at all possible.
- Should ideally be a goal that all key stakeholders would recognize and see as highly desirable.

Step 4: Develop Draft of Change Canvas, Mapping Important Outcome Areas, Interim Destination, Longer-Term Impact/Outcome Areas

- Seek to create a broad canvas, using the kind of template described in Table 4.3, with impact, influencing, and leverage outcome areas that are most relevant to the ultimate goal from the previous step.
- Include all outcome areas that are important in the achievement of that ultimate goal, not just the areas where your agency feels equipped to contribute.
- Although it may be useful to indicate how the outcome areas flow through to the ultimate goal, avoid the temptation to do the detailed causal loops at an overall level; this can be more usefully done at an individual program level.

Step 5: Develop and Agree on an Insightful Framework to Help Assess and Understand Local Contexts

- Although detailed analysis of context will happen at a local program level, it will be helpful to have an agency-wide tool or framework that will drive consistency and rigor.
- It can be helpful to segment context types depending on level of need, risk, or political situation so that an agency can have some guidelines on the kinds of interventions that are most likely to be most useful in each context.
- It can also be useful to create a shared language for describing and analyzing different situations, as well as being an aid for more effective learning.
- Reflect on what common threads can be learned from what is really going on in different contexts in relation to the defined ultimate goal.

Step 6: Summarize the Intervention Types or Programs Your Agency Feels it Can Support

- Be very clear on the particular strengths, assets, or competencies your agency is bringing to the table.
- Create an indicative mapping how each program maps on to the change canvas, both directly and indirectly. (Illustrative example shown later in this chapter in the case study.)

Step 7: Create a Clear Synthesis That Is Understandable to All Stakeholders

- Using a few paragraphs in plain language, perhaps including a clear and insightful diagram, of all the above items.
- This could form the front overview part of your theory of change document.

Step 8: Consult Widely Internally and Externally to Challenge, Gain Feedback, Refine, and Improve

- Consult internally with all key departments, including as many field staff as possible and program, M&E, fundraising, HR, and other key departments.
- Select a handful of external respected specialists to gather outside feedback.
- Socialize and test with some of your key institutional donors.
- Wherever possible, seek opportunities to align your theory of change to those of your peers—having a similar or ideally unified approach should be encouraged!

Step 9: Check and Address Misalignment with Other Key Parts of the Agency

- Test and see what needs to be done to align key parts of agency program functions and tools—including program policy, program methodology, supporting tools, and M&E systems.
- Check to make sure the enabling functions and activities are aligned, especially in the area of talent management (e.g., HR strategies and plans, staff induction and training, career development, performance management).
- Review the broader organizational planning, performance management, and accountability frameworks at organizational (rather than at individual) level.

Step 10: Repeat Steps 8 and 9 on a Systematic Basis
- This needs to be a serious process, building on previous progress and refining in light of new learning internally and externally.
- In addition, some NGOs now find that a more in-depth reevaluation of an agency-level theory of change can be very useful as part of the agency-wide strategic planning process.

Stretch Ideas and Disruptive Thinking

Despite the implied systematic approach set out in previous sections and illustrated in the case study at the end of this chapter, we know that an agency-level theory of change may not be enough. We need to constantly strive for deeper insight, seek out those rare and precious windows of opportunity for large scale or "mega" breakthroughs. We refer to these as stretch ideas or disruptive thinking. These build on the platform we described in the previous sections. What is set out below is not expected to be a complete or prescriptive list, and we fully respect that some of the ideas may come across as provocative or controversial for some, although for others they may just be a reflection of good practice. The intent is to provoke the reader to think more deeply about what is required in the search for major breakthroughs in the battle against poverty and injustice.

There are ten ideas that group into three broad themes, stretching our ambition and contribution (Theme A), improving our connection and building trust (Theme B), and shifting our program focus (Theme C).

Stretching Our Ambition (Theme A)
1. Spotting the windows of opportunity for mega breakthroughs
2. Selecting the best intervention in a given context and at a particular time
3. Using return on social investment (ROSI) as a useful discipline

Improving Our Connection and Building Trust (Theme B)
4. Truly seeing the world as locals do: the "you-you" conversation
5. Becoming a trusted friend and adviser—the soft factors, "the elephant in the room"
6. Acknowledging our own legacies

Shifting Our Program Focus (Theme C)

7. Justice, not charity
8. Encouraging trade, enterprise, and the private sector
9. Infrastructure—the hard stuff
10. Helping create an atmosphere of hope and momentum

Theme A: Stretching Our Ambition

1. Spotting the Windows of Opportunity for Mega Breakthroughs

If we analyze some of the major change events in our time, we know that at certain moments an opportunity presents itself to make a step change and do much more. For example, a major epidemic can present an opportunity to effect a step change in the formal and informal health systems in a country or region. A crisis or famine can present an opportunity to address policies or regulations in the developed world that are hampering progress in the developing world. An outbreak of war can draw attention to long-term injustices.

International development and humanitarian agencies should be exceptionally well positioned to spot these windows of opportunity for breakthroughs and work with others to ensure the flames of desperation can be reframed to flames of hope and progress. That should not just be an opportunity—it should be a *responsibility* for international NGOs. When we look at recent history, we can see a number of situations where windows opened for a limited period—for example, the recent escalation of conflict in Palestine, or the search for a vaccine for Ebola in West Africa. In the latter case, Médecins Sans Frontières showed tremendous leadership in bringing the world's attention to a globally threatening epidemic.

2. Selecting the Best Intervention in a Given Context and at a Particular Time

One of the important benefits of having a well-thought-through change canvas, as described earlier, is that NGOs can have a more thoughtful debate on which specific areas are most productive in different contexts and at different times. This removes the limitations of a more rigid or static theory that says "we do this, that contributes to that, and will help achieve XYZ."

In practice, we know that the political will, the public mood, and practical day-to-day needs will have a major influence on the best course of action to ensure the best impact for a given investment. Sometimes investment in education is the best; sometimes it may be better to refurbish a disused water well; sometimes it is better to work side by side with ministry staff and help them achieve their objectives, building their skills and experience along the way. In other cases investment should be closer to home, persuading richer governments to change their policies/subsidies, for example, in fishing and agriculture or pricing levels of essential medicines.

3. Using Return on Social Investment (ROSI) as a Useful Discipline
There have been considerable efforts to think more robustly and more dispassionately about how and where international NGOs invest scarce resources for the most impact. The idea of return on social investment has been usefully used by organizations such as UNICEF,[8] CARE International, and a number of others in recent years. What it means is that you make a calculation of the social return, in dollar terms, that $1 of investment contributes through different specific programs and program types and in different contexts. This approach necessitates the quantification of a range of intangible factors. Yes, it results in a simple answer that inevitably will not be precise; for example, $1 investment in education in India returns, say, $43 in social return, while the same dollar invested in a program in Malawi may only return $0.50. Despite its challenges, this approach has a range of benefits in terms of comparative assessment and more thoughtful decisionmaking. In addition, the emphasis on capturing and analyzing the returns provides the opportunity for enormous learning and sharing among peers.

This kind of approach is likely to get renewed emphasis as the growing popularity of "Social Impact Bonds" builds momentum. Essentially, these can be expected to use private equity approaches to produce both quantifiable business and social returns as part of the same investment.

Theme B: Improving Our Connection and Building Trust

4. Truly Seeing the World as Locals Do: The "You-You" Conversation
Too often, the approach of Western, developed country governments, as well as some NGOs, to helping poorer, developing countries is characterized by what we call the "me-me" conversation. This is when I see their problems through my own lens, using my frame of reference, my methodology, and my values. To have a more meaningful "me-you" conversation—and try to see the problems through the other party's lens—it can be helpful to properly understand and appreciate the "you-you" conversation. This may often be hard and uncomfortable.

We came across a very different and somewhat controversial example of the you-you conversation in an article in the *Observer*, which shone a light on the views and insights of Philippe-Joseph Salazar,[9] on the crisis around Islamic State, which has been seeking to establish a caliphate in Iraq and Syria. This was difficult and uncomfortable reading. However, Salazar's discipline, patience, and approach were based on spending two years watching, reading, and viewing Islamic State prose and propaganda. This is a good example of the lengths that are required to fully understand the you-you conversation. As Western governments plan their responses to this crisis, responding to the political moods and biases of their support base at home, it is really challenging to take the time to deeply understand the "you-you" conversation, identify the best response, and sell that approach to the media and the general public at home.

As a simple illustration, consider the rights-based organizations that place considerable emphasis on helping individuals and communities demand their rights while being vociferous in holding institutions, such as government bodies, to account. This is likely to include well-meaning demands on government ministries on various issues. This approach can be a bit like throwing stones at the windows from the outside. We have to ask what it is like or feels like from inside that window. We may find that there are few staff and very limited resources. Some may not have been there very long, may not fully understand the brief of their department, or may not have been properly inducted or trained. In some cases staff may not have been paid for several months. In this scenario, throwing stones from outside at the window is unlikely to do much good.

These examples illustrate the importance of appreciating the you-you conversation. Unfortunately this might be challenging for political leaders in some Western democratic governments. It should be a core competence of international NGOs because they typically do understand these contexts deeply.

5. Becoming a Trusted Friend and Advisor:
"The Elephant in the Room"
There is a growing discourse in the sector on the importance of local partnerships and local capacity-building. Unfortunately, there is a risk of lots of empty words without much deep reflection and candidness on these important issues. We wonder if, as the old saying goes—there is an elephant in the room.

The truth is this: many development and humanitarian organizations are often barely tolerated, and in some cases severely disliked, by host governments and local institutions. How much does it matter? We know it absolutely does. Human nature dictates that we are more likely to listen to and heed advice from those we respect and like. If NGOs want to provide helpful support and advice, the ultimate value of this support will depend on how they are respected and accepted by local governments, local leaders, and local communities in host countries.

Why do some host governments often have such negative views of development agencies? Here are some of the issues that are sometimes raised. There are complaints about the high salaries of senior expatriate NGO staff, which are often many times the local norm and consume far too much of the aid budgets. Some complain that these international NGOs pay scant respect for local plans and other initiatives already in place. There is a view that some organizations simply do what they like. Some complain about the unhelpful practices of paying local people to attend workshops or providing free food, resulting in a band of freeloaders who are disincentivized to participate in other local government or community-organized initiatives which lack the budget for such incentives. Some complain that ambitious programs create lofty expectations and result in deemphasizing other local efforts, only to leave behind a population that is cynical and despondent when the grant money runs out. All of this is seen as propagating the hand-out culture that is unhelpful for strengthening local capacity, essential to meaningful long-term progress. There are many NGOs, and in some areas we can find several working in parallel on overlapping issues. Unfortunately this presents a complex and sometimes chaotic picture for local leaders, and as a result, the good, the bad, and the indifferent all risk getting tarred with the same brush. Although this can be regarded as a fairly biased set of views, we know that there is at least some truth behind these criticisms.

Adding to all of this is the natural human emotions of local leaders and politicians, who can easily grow to despise the hand that feeds them, irrespective of the quality and value of the programs on offer. This can come about for several reasons, for example, the conditions and requirements that come with the help or because it is a visible reminder of their own shortcomings; perhaps they blame the helpers or those the helpers represent for their current state or misfortune. This kind of resentment may be as true of direct budget support at government level as for support that is channelled through international or local agencies.

So what are NGOs to do? There are a number of implications that sound like "just good practice," but which we think deserve to be taken to a deeper level.

- Being willing to listen more carefully, learn, understand the local context to a much broader, deeper, and more meaningful level.
- Being around for the long haul, building trust in small steps; underplaying promises, exceeding expectations.
- Being willing to contribute to local agendas and projects that make good sense—not making up new or separate initiatives.
- Being willing to exit when the conditions of progress are not there, and being honest with donors rather than somehow declaring success on some questionable metrics.

Of course all of this cuts across the trend toward larger institutional grants and the growing importance of institutional funding in the overall funding mix. Making progress in becoming a long-term trusted adviser does require independence of thought and action—raising the stakes in the need for sensible proportions of private or unrestricted funding.

6. Acknowledging Our Own Legacy

As we approach the complex work of tackling poverty and injustice, it is important to recognize that all agencies come with their own legacy or baggage. Some of this baggage has to do with past programs that may not have gone as hoped and may have left a bitter taste in the minds of important local stakeholders. Some of this baggage may be related to the historic policies and actions of the governments of our own countries—what they have done, not done, or how they have reacted to particular events.

The baggage of the past is explored at a very strategic level in Dominique Moisi's insightful book the *Geopolitics of Emotion*,[10] in which he divides the world into three parts or cultures: **the culture of fear** (the old wealthy "North" including Western Europe and North America), **the culture of hope** (parts of Asia and some new emerging economies), and **the culture of humiliation** (including many parts of the Middle East and the Muslim world). These three cultures are an interesting illustration of how our past actions and interactions cast a long shadow on the world around us. Although this book was released long before the more recent upsurge in crises related to the Islamic State, its analysis and insight can help us appreciate some of the key factors fueling this crisis. The key point is this: as we approach our dealings with the range of stakeholders we want to engage with in the course of our work, it is important that we acknowledge the impressions and the legacies of the past and work to create future trust through honesty, openness, and transparency.

Theme C: Shifting Our Program Focus

7. *Justice, Not Charity*

We are taken by the approach of a number of forward-thinking agencies, for whom development and humanitarian work is not a matter of charity but a matter of justice: economic justice, social justice, or climate justice. This is an important reframing of the challenges of the developing world, which we believe could provide some potential seeds for breakthrough thinking. As an example, this philosophy is a central part of the mandate of Trocaire, an Ireland-based agency that works exclusively through local partners in twenty countries throughout Africa, Asia, the Middle East, and South America.

The shift in mind-set implied by this approach might sound subtle, but it could be fundamental. It could help reposition international NGOs from the traditional, noble, charitable helpers from the enlightened/well-off North to equals in a global network of local and international stakeholders seeking to tackle the challenges of poverty and injustice. Such a shift might also encourage a much stronger emphasis in tackling the root causes of poverty and injustice in all parts of an interconnected world.

8. *Encouraging Trade, Enterprise, and the Private Sector*

Ultimately, the tendency to despise or bite the hand that feeds it will continue to be an understandable emotion in the aid industry. Where there is a more explicit win-win relationship, for example, based on trade, enterprise, and investment, the emotion can be very different. This is an uncomfortable space for many agencies. The idea of giving and helping is natural. The idea of earning profit from activities with the poor is not. But we know the latter is of potentially more value and more sustainable. These countries need investment, jobs, trade, at a large scale and with longevity. This means attracting and encouraging the private sector, both local and international. As William Easterly remarked candidly, "The reason that poor countries are poor, is that their incomes are low—and hence they cannot afford the investment in health and education that is needed."[11] This sounds very obvious, but is a salient point that often seems not to be front of mind in the aid sector, or at least as much as one might expect.

9. *Bringing Infrastructure Back to Center Stage*

For a number of decades, international agencies have focused more and more on the softer issues of social and economic development—empowerment, capacity building, rights, governance, and inclusion—and have been pulling back from direct provision of education and health systems. This has been a result of ongoing learning and discovery in the development process, as well as pragmatism in the application of scarce funding. Where government/institutional funds have not been channelled to direct budget support (an unconvincing logic in our view) it has been directed to fund projects on many of these softer issues.

We wonder if the spotlight has been taken away too much from the hard, physical infrastructure opportunities such as roads, ports, dams, railways, and power systems. These are the scaffolding on which economic progress develops, and hence on which sustainable social progress can also build. Infrastructure investments are projects that no individual or company can justify on their own, and which governments in poor countries cannot easily organize or afford. It is worth reflecting if too many NGOs have restricted their thinking on change to the topics they are comfortable with themselves, rather than seeing the bigger picture of what is really needed.

10. Creating an Atmosphere of Hope and Momentum
To conclude this set of ideas and suggestions, we would like to make the following remark. Despite the recent momentum toward measuring impact, a results-based agenda, and payment by results, it is important to be realistic and perhaps a little humble. It may not be the concrete results we can identify that matter most in the long run. Sometimes what really matters is to do what we can to help create an atmosphere of hope, confidence, and momentum, respecting the outputs and outcomes that local communities feel are most important.

Summary

The following is a summary of our nine main conclusions from this chapter.

1. We believe that an agency-level theory of change is a **central piece of the fabric of any forward thinking and learning agency** in the twenty-first century. A theory of change is not a single thing, chart, or diagram but an intertwined collection of different components. These are living rather than static, as an organization learns from internal and external evidence of what works best. These form part of the joined-up fabric of the ideas, knowledge, and processes of any agency.

2. All **agencies already have a theory of change** (or in most cases several theories of change), that are implicit and deeply held in the

minds of a range of key staff. Although the language may be new to some, the concept of a theory of change is not new. What is kind of new is the idea of making these theories explicit, stronger, and more joined up across an entire agency so it can learn better and support better programs and decisionmaking.

3. A good theory of change needs to be owned by the **best minds of the organization** and reflect the insight and historic learning from previous decades of experience, especially from the field. It is definitely not something separate, to be developed by a recently recruited, junior program staff member sitting in a corner at HQ.

4. The scope of factors or outcome areas taken into account should **not be limited to an agency's own areas of contribution**. This would inevitably lead to too narrow an understanding of what is going on in a broader context. A good theory of change should recognize all of the most important contributing factors—accepting that many may well be beyond the direct influence of one agency.

5. An agency-level theory of change can be useful in at least seven ways: in **learning, decisionmaking, training, communication** (internally and externally), **program selection and design, collaboration and partnering,** and **fundraising.**

6. There is **not a single correct format** for what a theory of change should look like or include. What seems to be useful is a short (three- to four-page) accessible document. We identified seven potential components: (a) a short summary, easily understandable to internal and external audiences; (b) summary of learning and lessons from the past; (c) key assumptions and beliefs; (d) an outcome map (or change canvas); (d) an insightful lens to help analyze local contexts; (e) an ambitious or stretching goal that has meaning and traction internally and externally; and (f) a summary of the strategies and interventions the agency feels it is equipped to support. As an aside, our guidance is to avoid the temptation to put all of the know-how and insight that an agency wants to communicate into a single, horrendously complex chart; though a clear chart of some form might be helpful.

7. A good theory of change is **not something separate** but is intertwined with many other parts of the normal fabric of a good agency, such as program policy, approaches, tools, fundraising, career development and training, learning, and knowledge management to name a few. Hence, there is not a clear division between what is within the scope of a theory of change and what is covered in other parts of an agency.

8. A good theory of change can be **a unifying force** among these different parts of the fabric of an agency. This could be a source of con-

siderable value, helping in alignment, cohesion, and better agency-wide learning. It can also ensure that an agency presents a clear picture to outside stakeholders—be they beneficiaries, partners, donors, or other stakeholders in the developed world.

9. A good theory of change is the beginning, a foundation—not the end of the story. We need to constantly strive to seek better insight, look harder and deeper, seeking out those rare and precious **windows of opportunity for large-scale or mega breakthroughs**. We refer to this as stretch or disruptive thinking.

Case Study

Supporting Trade and Enterprise in Africa to Accelerate Pro-poor Growth

Let's bring these components to life through a case example. Traidlinks is a very small and young agency, based in east Africa and Ireland, which has developed a new agency-wide theory of change using the broad approach outlined in this chapter (http://traidlinks.ie/about-us). The components were developed in an iterative manner over several months. This is a brief description and includes selected and edited extracts for illustration purposes.

An Easy-to-Understand Summary

The understandable summary was a few short paragraphs as well as one high-level diagram, as shown in Figure 4.5.

> Our ultimate goal is to help accelerate the growth of economic activity in the countries where we work, in a manner that is pro-poor. This means higher value added commercial activity from the most important sectors such as agriculture and also from the increasingly important natural resource opportunities. Micro, Small and Medium Enterprises will be key to economic development. Developing these areas should result in more jobs and higher GDP. . . . We believe that economic growth is fundamental to poverty eradication. Growing economies can help create more jobs and supply the finances for better public services in health, education and other social sectors. The combined effect of these impacts can lift many more people out of poverty.
>   There are three important components that we believe are central to drive economic growth. These are; Institutional capacity building of key government and semi state organizations; enterprise development and the expansion of agricultural value chains. We call this a

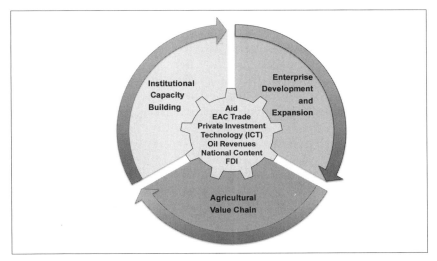

Figure 4.5 Flywheel Approach to Economic Development and Pro-Poor Growth

"Flywheel" approach to economic development. We understand that they are not the only components but they are significant ones in which we think we can add value.

The cog at the centre of the flywheel we call accelerators. These consist of factors such as private sector investment, foreign direct investment (FDI), government investment, aid, technology, trade facilitation, natural resource tax revenues and local content from emerging natural resource opportunities. Over time these accelerators will change. For example, in East Africa in the coming years, revenues from the extractive industries is likely to displace aid. What happens in this sector will be critical for the development of many countries in Africa.

Stretching Ambitious Goal

"The stretching goal is that, by 2030, the countries where we work are able to produce 50% of the food they need for their own population, and 85% by 2050."

Now let's try and illustrate the other main components of their theory of change for this case example.

Synthesis of Learning

This agency recognized that it is a small and relatively new organization in an innovative area. As it developed its theory of change, team members felt it was important to identify the learning from a number of early programs in east Africa. There were many lessons—from what did and did not work. For example, early attempts to build export links from local east African producers into European markets proved difficult, despite significant investments in a new and very innovative brand "Heart of Africa," and despite the positive support of major retailers in Europe. They soon learned that there are many interim steps that made much more commercial sense for local firms, for example, dipping their toes in the water by exporting into local markets in their own and neighbouring countries. Most local producers were nowhere near ready for the expectations of European markets.

They identified a range of other important learning areas, for example:

- There is a massive opportunity in agriculture, but many cultural /understanding/behavioral blockages; for example, that profit is an alien concept to many, and the idea of farming as a subsistence activity rather than a potential business is heavily embedded in the local norms.
- There is a necessity to move from supply-driven to demand-driven approaches, creating sustainable industries that connect markets to producers.
- It is necessary to work at multiple levels in parallel—at both an industry and political level.
- A hand-out culture is well embedded among a range of key stakeholders.
- The potential opportunity of future oil has already adjusted/distorted expectations.

Explicit Assumptions

They articulated some important assumptions or beliefs that underpinned Traidlink's philosophy and approach. Many of these assumptions built directly from past learning, as well as from in-depth discussions with stakeholders.

Some of the key assumptions are set out here (edited extract):

1. Commercialisation and value addition in the agriculture sector will be essential for the growth of the economy and job creation. Shifts need to be made to move from livelihoods assistance to the creation of sustainable food industries.
2. Encouraging micro, small and medium enterprises will be essential ingredient to pro-poor growth. Very many people in East Africa are entrepreneurs by nature and necessity. But while they

generate economic activity they do not develop many businesses that are sustainable.

3. Working alongside key bodies is the most effective mode of capacity building—not just running workshops or preaching from the roof-tops. State and other important institutions need to be strengthened so that they can become enablers to the development of agricultural industries and to the development of local enterprises.

4. The natural resource opportunity could be a "positive" catalyst in the development of national economies—however, there is a considerable risk that it could also be an enormously destructive force.

5. Operating with a commercial approach will be essential to everything we do—e.g. charging for services provided—not following in the footsteps of the actions that created a hand-out culture.

Framework for Analyzing Local Context

Traidlinks developed a broad framework, embracing all of the various components that needed to be taken into account when analyzing local context wherever it worked. A brief overview of this framework is set out in Figure 4.6.

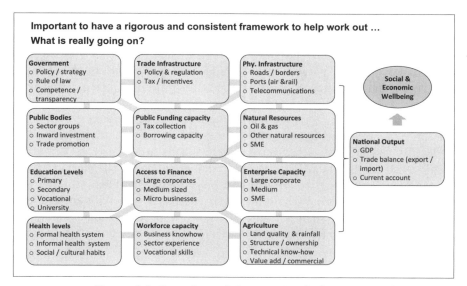

Figure 4.6 Overview of Context-Analysis Framework

A Strategic Change Canvas

One of the challenging but useful steps was the creation of a **strategic change canvas**—essentially a map of what the agency felt were the most important outcome areas or interim destinations that drive or affect the ultimate goal. Inevitably, there were a good number of these, and use was made of the categorization set out in the Annie E. Casey foundation paper, separating out **impact, influencing,** and **leverage** areas. This illustration was set out earlier in Figure 4.3.

The program team in the field came together to define a set of practical change statements for each outcome area. This was used to develop the change canvas and was particularly helpful in the design of a balanced set of practical metrics of progress for each program.

We can see that the range of factors or outcomes on this map is much broader than the scope of the agency's likely interventions. Clearly, it does not have the expertise, capacity, or resources to intervene on several of these areas. The diagram in Figure 4.3 provides an indicative sense of how these outcome areas flow through to the ultimate goal "Supporting trade and enterprise in Africa to accelerate pro-poor growth." As indicated in this diagram, we did not seek to map all the various relationships and interconnections between the factors. This would be far too complex. This level of interconnection would be explored more productively at a specific project level.

Although we do not attempt to describe the full range of proposed future programs here, the intention was to map each program on to the same strategic canvas described above. Thus, the canvas provided a shared tool to communicate internally and externally the key focus of a particular program, as well as indicating what indirect areas of benefit might be and how they might be tracked over time. This is illustrated in Figures 4.7 and 4.8.

One good example is the market-linked program (Figure 4.7). This is an expanded and improved continuation of an initiative that had already proved very successful in Uganda. This program is in partnership with the Ugandan government, and supported by Irish Aid and Trade Mark East Africa. It seeks to help micro, small, and medium enterprises in Uganda by building their confidence and skills to enable them to export regionally, while at the same time helping build the capacity of the Uganda Export Promotion Board to support and develop these activities in the future.

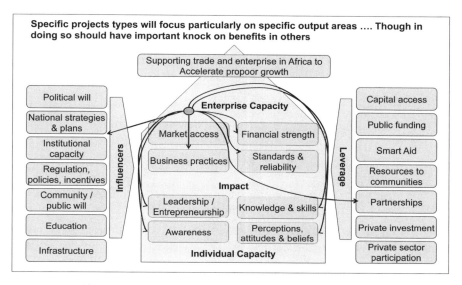

Figure 4.7 Example Program A: Market-Linked Program

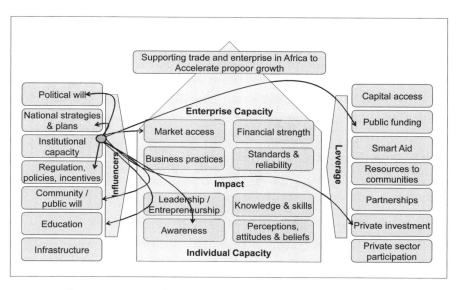

Figure 4.8 Example Program B: Institutional Capacity Building

A Set of Proposed Interventions

As Traidlinks began to define the range of programs it felt it could contribute to its ultimate goal, it first sought to be clear and candid about what it could bring to the table. In summary, it felt it could contribute through:

- Access to deep private sector expertise
- A commercial ethos in everything they did
- East Africa understanding
- Practical expertise in helping local firms progress
- Ability to open doors, convene and join the dots between different stakeholders
- A genuine partnering approach—both with firms and also with key government bodies—in everything they did

Based on these contributions, it defined three broad program areas, each with a number of potential projects. These mapped closely on to the three segments of the summary flywheel model described earlier.

Notes

1. Craig Valters, "Theories of Change in International Development: Communication, Learning, or Accountability?" Justice and Security Research Programme Paper 17 (London, LSE, 2014).

2. Duncan Green, http://www.oxfamblogs.com and draft book *How Change Happens*, forthcoming October 2016.

3. Anjana Ahuja, "The Fight Against Ebola Now Needs a Social Front," *Financial Times*, October 5, 2014; https://next.ft.com/content/15bf9afc-4b0d-11e4-b1be-00144feab7de.

4. Organizational Research Services, "Theory of Change: A Practical Tool for Action, Results and Learning," Annie E. Casey Foundation (2004); http://www.aecf.org/m/resourcedoc/aecf-theoryofchange-2004.pdf.

5. AMREF Business Plan: Transforming communities from within by imporving the health of women and children, (October 2011) http://amref.org/silo/files/amref-business-plan.pdf, p. 23. (The actual text is as follows: "AMREF strives to close the gap between the communities and formal health systems. It does so by partnering with the very poor, the most vulnerable and the most remote communities; and by helping to strengthen the formal health system throught building its capacity.")

6. James Crowley and Morgana Ryan, *Building a Better International NGO: Greater than the Sum of the Parts* (Boulder, CO: Kumarian Press, 2013), 23–24.

7. Ibid., 9–42.

8. Nicholas Rees, Jingqing Chai, and David Anthony, "Right in Principle and Practice: A Brief Review of the Social and Economic Return of Investing in Children," UNICEF working paper (New York, UNICEF, 2012).

9. Agnès Poirier, "Philippe-Joseph Salazar: The Philosopher Whose Essay on Isis Has Shocked and Enlightened," *Observer*, November 29, 2015; http://www.theguardian.com/world/2015/nov/29/philippe-joseph-salazar-essay-paris-attacks-isis.

10. Dominique Moisi, *The Geopolitics of Emotion: How Cultures of Fear, Humiliation, and Hope Are Reshaping the World* (New York: First Anchor Books, 2010).

11. William Easterly, *The White Man's Burden: Why the West's Efforts to Aid the Rest Have Done So Much Ill and So Little Good* (New York: Penguin Press, 2006).

5

Working with and Alongside the Private Sector

Many countries in the developing world remain very poor. As William Easterly articulated so simply, "Poor countries are poor because their incomes are too low and are insufficient to meet basic needs and pay taxes to allow governments to invest in the kinds of education, health and opportunities that citizens might aspire."[1] If they are to progress, incomes have to grow substantially.

There are some positive signs. Some developing countries have seen encouraging growth rates over the past decade or so, well above the levels in the developed world, especially since the financial crisis that began in 2008. Many large global firms see the developing world not just as sources of cheap raw materials and labor, but as a source of business growth, with an expanding consumer base in terms of numbers and spending capacity. Firms like Unilever, Procter & Gamble, and Diagio have long seen Africa and other parts of the developing world as central to their future business plans in terms of revenue, profit, and a place to site future operations.

Foreign direct investment (FDI) in developing countries has grown dramatically through new greenfield investments (though admittedly from a very low base), expanding existing business operations and equity stakes in high-potential local companies. In 2012 for the first time, the developing country share of total global FDI exceeded that of developed countries. According to a 2014 OECD report,[2] FDI represented by far the biggest international capital inflow into developing countries (US$600 billion in 2012 or 60 percent of all international capital flows to developing countries). All this brings new and ultra-scarce capital as well as new technologies and know-how, which are all essential for long-term progress.

Consistent with this trend, donors such as DFID, the EU, DFAT, and

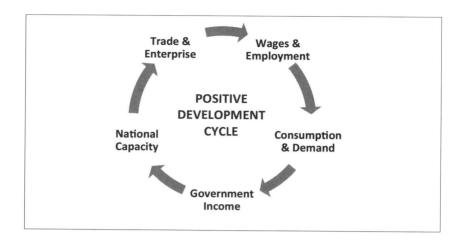

USAID are increasingly seeing trade and enterprise as integrated parts of the fight against poverty. A number of donor governments have been reviewing their overseas aid goals and priorities and are seeking to integrate their aid budgets more closely with their foreign trade objectives.

In addition to its key role in trade and enterprise, the private sector (be it local, national, or multinational) is making increasingly significant contributions to many parts of the traditional development process. It is bringing new technologies and know-how; investing in much-needed research in areas such as health, nutrition, and sustainable agriculture; and accelerating the financing and construction of infrastructure such as roads, ports, power systems, and communications. The following box sets out an illustrative range of recent case examples.

As a result, we are seeing a significant enhancement in the profile of enterprise and trade and in the role and potential contribution that the private sector can play. There are many new initiatives and forums for exchanging ideas and learning. Good examples include the Business Fights Poverty initiative (http://www.businessfightspoverty.org) and the Shared Value Initiative (http://www.sharedvalue.org). Though still in relatively early days, there is a growing list of good case examples and success stories.

Thankfully, a number of NGOs have become increasingly active in seeking ways of collaborating more closely with the private sector in all its guises, beyond traditional fundraising. The much-publicized example of Oxfam and Unilever working together[3] on supply chain initiatives was an early and much publicized example, though there have been many others. We published a significant piece of research in 2009[4] based on 350 face-to-

Examples of Accelerating Private Sector Engagement in the Developing World

Example of Private Equity Interest

"TGP, one of the world's biggest private equity houses, is making its first foray into Africa as it prepares to invest up to $1bn in Africa through a tie up with Sudanese billionaire Mo Ibrahim. The money will come from TGP Growth, the US firm's middle market platform, rather than from raising a specific fund for Africa, and will work with Mr. Ibrahim's $500m private equity fund, Satya Capital…. TGP joins other large US private equity houses, including Carlyle and KKR that have turned to Africa for the first time in recent years…. Many new investors are attracted by African growth rates above global averages, forecast at 4.5%" in 2015. A representative of TGP commented, "We look at Africa as one of the most growthful markets in the world: but also a market where you have to be very savvy and sophisticated about who you're dealing with."[5]

Collaboration to Tackle Development Challenges: Malaria

In June of 2015, two US Oil companies, Marathon Oil and Noble Energy, announced that they have teamed up with the government of Equatorial Guinea and invested millions of dollars into trials of a promising malaria vaccine (PfSPZ) "trying to help tackle one of Africa's biggest health scourges." "Other agencies involved in setting up the trials include the Swiss Tropical and Public Health Institute and Medical Care Development International, a US non-governmental organisation—as well as researchers from Tanzania, where another small trial has taken place." Despite some useful progress, this is a disease that kills nearly 600,000 every year. This is a mix of pure philanthropic activity combined with a long term commercial incentive to "eradicate a disease that affects about 10 per cent of the locals amongst its 900-strong workforce in Equatorial Guinea each year."[6]

Radical Partnerships to Give Newborns a Healthier Start

GSK and Save the Children's partnership aims to help save the lives of one million children.[7]

Corporate-NGO Partnership Helping India's Smallholder Farmers

In India, The Mosaic Company Foundation has partnered with the Sehgal Foundation, to support the "Krishi Jyoti," or "enlightened agriculture," program which lifts smallholder farmers out of poverty through investment in agricultural development, water management, and community initiatives.[8]

Partnerships to Increase Water-Use Efficiency: SAB Miller
"In many countries both the availability and quality of water are in decline as populations—and associated demand from agriculture, energy generation, industry and households—grow. The Water Resources Group (WRG), of which SABMiller is a member, estimates that the shortfall between freshwater supply and global demand could reach 40% by 2030, an average that conceals even more acute shortfalls in certain water-stressed countries. We have been partnering to improve water resource management and governance in many ways, for many years. We have joined forces with other companies, governments, donors, and civil society organisations, often in multi-stakeholder alliances. We have aimed to increase water use efficiency, improve water management and governance, and address the root causes of water risk. We have worked at the supply chain, watershed, and sometimes even national levels. Today, we have 14 water partnerships in 8 countries."[9]

Partnerships to Deliver SDGs
"SDG agenda includes explicitly stated efforts to involve stakeholders beyond member states—including charities, foundations and the private sector. Goal 17 directly addresses the importance of partnerships, calling for members to enhance global partnerships that mobilize and share knowledge, expertise, technology and financial resources."[10]

Paul Polman, Turbo Charging Development:
Making the SDGs a Reality
"In order to make the SDGs a reality transformative partnerships between business, civil society and government are essential. As UK Secretary of State for International Development, Justine Greening recently put it; 'We need to unleash new finance, expertise and innovation to turbo charge development . . . using the best in our resources, networks and know-how.' . . . Last week one such partnership—Transform—was announced by Unilever, the UK Department for International Development (DFID) and Clinton Giustra Enterprise Partnership (CGEP). Transform will see us join forces to create jobs, increase incomes, and improve the health and well-being of 100 million people in Africa and South Asia by 2025."[11]

face interviews with senior executives from over 120 large companies as well as more than 50 NGOs. The contributors were interviewed in their local countries, divided equally between North and South. We found that many international NGOs are putting considerable efforts into building up new capacity to collaborate more closely with the private sector, creating functions and devoting more management attention to this strand of their efforts.[12]

Some Uncertainty and Frustration

Despite considerable and encouraging progress, not all is rosy in terms of collaboration between NGOs and the private sector. One of the unfortunate consequences of the increased profile and debate has been the considerable and frankly unfortunate amount of new language and jargon—with an endless flow of terms like "convergence," "co-creation," "shared value," "fourth sector," "inclusive development," "private sector development" and several others bandied about with a fairly loose understanding of what these terms actually mean. It is fair to say that the emergence of such unnecessary and overly complex vocabulary has resulted in some confusion as well as a bit of resistance.

Within the NGO community, we frequently hear remarks like "I understand that this is an area which is important, and have given it some thought—however, it is not completely clear how and where to start. What precisely should we do differently in terms of focus, approach, or mix of activities?"

Some NGOs who were initially very positive about collaborating with the private sector and made a serious attempt to do so, give the sense of being somewhat underwhelmed or disappointed. Maybe expectations were overhyped? Perhaps there is still a lack of clarity and agreement on where the value is and what the collaboration opportunities really are. Perhaps there is not sufficient appreciation of the length of time needed to achieve results. Of course, in a number of NGOs, one does not have to scratch the surface very much to find a considerable amount of resistance and skepticism. The private sector is still regarded by some as the "evil or dark side," intent on making large profits at the expense of the poor and marginalized.

On the other hand, there's little doubt that within the private sector community some executives begin with a fairly mixed view of NGOs, their people, their approaches, and their capacities. Some are understandably confused by the complexity of the NGO landscape in terms of who's who and who does what. Others can easily be put off by the complexity of the language that NGOs use.

In this chapter we seek to address some fairly basic questions.

- Why does all of this collaboration really matter? In very simple terms, what is the relevance of trade and enterprise (and by consequence, the private sector) in the pursuit of economic and social development?
- What in practice has been happening with private sector involvement in development and humanitarian domains? What have we learned from efforts to stimulate enterprise and trade over the past three to five years?
- Where are the real opportunities or areas of connection? How can we segment and understand these opportunities better?
- What have we learned from collaboration efforts so far?
- What is really behind NGO reluctance to collaborate more closely with the private sector?
- What needs to happen to accelerate progress? What do NGOs need to do differently? What do private sector firms need to do differently?

Why Does Collaboration Matter?

To address this question, we divide our discussion into two separate underpinning topics. First, why should trade and enterprise, including the private sector, be at the heart of our development efforts? Second, do we have an obligation to stimulate progress beyond traditional aid?

Why Does Trade, Enterprise, and the Private Sector Matter?

How does trade and enterprise fit into the long-term development process? We illustrate this using the simple model in Figure 5.1.

More **enterprise and trade** (be it local, national, or international) should provide more **employment and wages**, increasing household income. As well as improving living standards and providing an increasing sense of self-worth, this increased household income will stimulate local **demand and consumption**, which will inevitably stimulate further enterprise and trade, as well as creating an atmosphere of confidence and ambition.

More jobs and more trade will increase **government income** by growing income tax or other taxes or duties. This should enable the government to invest in the provision of better public services (e.g., education and health) as well as investing in improvements to national infrastructure (roads, rail, ports). It should also encourage government to

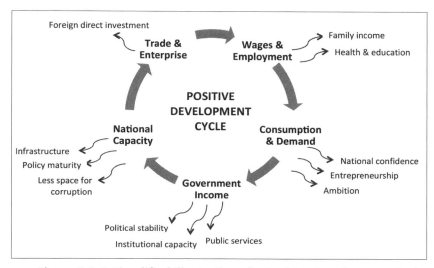

Figure 5.1 A Simplified Illustration of a Positive Development Cycle

strengthen policies and incentives to encourage further enterprise and trade.

This new investment with the cumulative learning from increased economic activity should enhance **national capacity** in a variety of ways, which will create a better foundation for future trade and enterprise. So the positive economic cycle continues. Of course, with an improving economic activity, increasing national capacity, and growing demand, we are likely to see an increase in FDI (greenfield or equity investments), which will further accelerate growth.

A positive economic cycle builds country and political confidence and should increase the expectation of decent governance and, all else being equal, reduce the plague of corruption, an issue that is widely accepted to be the biggest blockage to progress. There is strong evidence to suggest that a stagnant or declining economy provides a greater inclination to grab a bigger share of a "declining pie" while you can. An expanding pie should be good for all.

The private sector is at the core of enterprise and trade—micro, small, medium, and large local firms, as well as international firms—unless you are one of the remaining few who believe that a socialist/communist and centrally planned economy is the key to long-term prosperity. We need to help to get this development cycle moving, as well as remove important barriers or obstacles, including and especially with respect to our own actions and national policies.

Why Is This "Development Cycle" Broken?

The next logical question to ask would be why it is that in poorer countries in the developing world this development cycle seems to be broken, or at least not working as well as it seems to have been in strong performing countries. To tackle this question, we take a brief sojourn to explore the geographical, political, economic, and social history. This can be used to isolate some of the key factors that explain why these countries find themselves in their current plight. (We have tried to squeeze a lot of history into one or two paragraphs here.)

When we investigate context and history, we find that populations in developing countries are poor (relative to the developed world) because of a number of very practical and understandable reasons. Some of the factors are to do with climatic conditions. Some are to do with the effects of an unfair share of natural disasters (earthquakes, floods, etc.) that hit certain regions particularly hard. These natural factors are certainly very important. However, there are human-made factors as well. In Africa, the creation of what we now call countries or nation-states was a result of a drawing of boundaries by Europeans that happened a little over 100 years ago, agreed to at the infamous Berlin conference of 1884–1885. These boundaries grouped together African peoples with very different ethnic, religious, and political backgrounds. A good example is Nigeria, Africa's most populous country: an artificial construct of 250 ethnic groups and hundreds of languages, split between Christianity and Islam and created by British colonial decree. Quite a few of these countries were remotely managed colonies until the latter half of the last century and have little more than a half-century of experience as independent nation-states. Hence, they are still in their infancy, and it should be no great surprise that the maturity of their national infrastructure, governance, and the associated national institutions are nowhere near what is needed.

We also know that much of the developing world missed out on the extraordinary rapid economic gains that other parts enjoyed during the Industrial Revolution in the eighteenth and nineteenth centuries and was therefore not in a position to take full advantage of the subsequent waves of industrial and technological breakthroughs that followed. In fact, for a number of these developing countries (typically colonies), their mineral and human resources (for example, through slavery) were plundered to help feed the Industrial Revolution that took place elsewhere.

If all of that is not enough, we know that some of these countries were exploited as convenient places to carry out proxy wars. The battle for influence that went on in Angola during the Cold War exemplifies this. The clashes between the capitalist West and the socialist Soviet models played out in a number of African countries in the 1950s, 1960s, and 1970s. If we look further back, we note how that battle for supremacy between Christianity and Islam also played out in Africa. Over time Islam became dominant in the north, west, and along the Horn of Africa, whereas Christianity created a strong foothold in many countries in sub-Saharan Africa. The tension at the interface between the Christian and Islamic spheres of influence has been a source of social and political problems for many years, as illustrated by the split of north and south Sudan, the recent clashes in Mali, and the tragedies in northern Nigeria linked to Boko Haram.

In recent decades, the good intentions and progress enabled by international aid have been counterbalanced by barriers that have (somewhat cynically) been put in place by the same powerful, developed countries that have provided much of this aid. These barriers include tariffs, policies, quotas, regulations, and subsidies, particularly in sectors such as agriculture and fishing that are core to many pre-industrialized economies. In 2000, global agriculture subsidies in the West were six times the amount spent on international aid; when subsidies awarded to farmers in the United States, Europe, and Japan amounted to almost $1 billion a day.[13] These are the subsidies, together with tariffs and quotas, that make it virtually impossible for developing countries to compete in world markets. Even more damaging, these subsidies facilitate agricultural exports (often dumping) from rich countries and drive small farmers out of business even in their home countries. This threatens domestic food security, as well as undermining export potential.

To complete this difficult set of events, we are now beginning to understand that the brunt of the effects of climate change—rising temperatures, sea levels, and incidence of natural disasters—will be most extremely felt in the developing world, even though it is clear they have had almost no contribution to the CO_2 and other harmful emissions that have caused the change.

These are the inescapable facts that are too easy to let slip from our consciousness.

Our Duty to Stimulate Trade and Economic Development

What can we conclude from this brief recap of the history of these developing countries? First, we should not be at all surprised that the positive development cycle is often moving slowly, if at all, and can easily go into reverse for extended periods through a combination of luck and misfortune. This is illustrated in Figure 5.2.

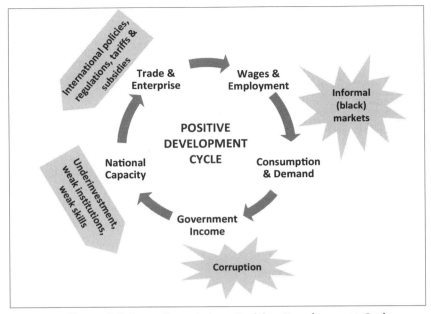

Figure 5.2 Impediments to a Positive Development Cycle

The second observation is that, to put it mildly, the very countries that provide aid are not devoid of responsibility for the current plight in many of these countries. This is not about attributing blame, but acknowledging that this is an issue of justice and fair play, not charity.

Yes, traditional aid is needed. It is vital to address the basic needs in humanitarian crises, which we know are increasing in frequency and severity. It is also essential to help in areas such as basic health and education for the poorest of the poor.

If we reflect on some of the root causes of poverty as summarized above, we can appreciate that **we have a responsibility to go beyond traditional aid to help accelerate trade and economic growth in these countries**. We need to see how else to put our shoulders to the wheel and stimulate enterprise, trade, and jobs, as opposed to inadvertently putting obstacles in the way of this process. As illustrated in Figure 5.3, this means new investment, fairer access to markets, and access to new technology and know-how. It means encouraging large private sector firms to invest to create jobs, build skills, and expand trade and enterprise in the developing world. It also implies dismantling the myriad of barriers and blockages that hinder these new economies participating in international trade. This will

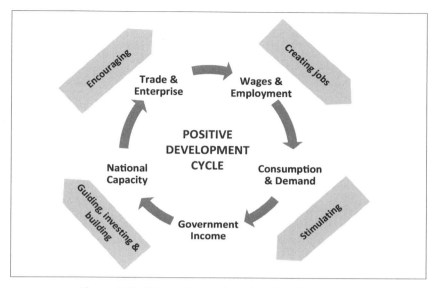

Figure 5.3 Stimulating a Positive Development Cycle

require changes in the policies, regulations, tariffs, and subsidies we impose in the developed world. That's the responsibility of our governments, our industries, our farmers, and us.

The difficult question is: what specifically needs to happen? What specifically does an NGO need to do differently?

What Has Been Happening in Terms of Private Sector Collaboration?

What are the main developments over the past five to ten years? As we summarize the key changes, it is useful to recognize that the spectrum of country contexts is extraordinarily wide. On one extreme, we have countries such as Kenya, Ghana, and Indonesia, which are making strong progress toward becoming middle-income countries despite retaining large pockets of extreme poverty. On the other hand, we have countries that are often classed as fragile or failed states (such Somalia, South Sudan, Mali, or Democratic Republic of Congo) where the level of progress is minimal and is often a case of one step forward, two steps back. Of course there are many countries that fall somewhere in between.

To generalize, however, we have identified ten key trends, which can be grouped into three broad themes (see Table 5.1).

- More global firms are seriously engaging in the developing world.
- Governments in developing countries are placing a greater emphasis and priority on enterprise, trade, and investment.
- NGOs and major donors are beginning to see enterprise, trade, and the private sector as something connected to what they do.

Theme: More Global Firms Are Seriously Engaging in the Developing World

Trend 1: Global firms increasingly engaging in the developing world as part of core business growth. In a global economic context of declining and nearly zero growth in mature, developed markets, many global firms are directing an increasing proportion of their growth investments to the developing world. This is true across all of the major sectors: consumer products (companies such as Unilever and Procter & Gamble), retail (e.g., Walmart and Carrefour), telecommunications (e.g., Vodafone and Motorola), financial services (e.g., Allianz), as well as extractive industries (e.g., Shell, BP, and Rio Tinto). This trend has now been fairly consistent over the past decade or more and is reflected in the higher rate of GDP growth in the developing world, compared to the developed world. According to the International Monetary Fund, sub-Saharan Africa expanded at an average GDP growth of 5.6 percent between 2000 and 2012—more than double the 2.2 percent of the 1990s.[14]

The involvement of the private sector is driven by a varying range of opportunities that can be grouped into four broad categories:

1. To access new customers and markets,
2. To source raw materials and natural resources,
3. To invest capital in greenfield or equity/merger and acquisition (M&A) investments, and
4. To site operations in locations with competitive labor markets.

Working and investing in these countries is not without risks. However, many large global firms are gradually developing a better understanding of the social, political, and regulatory issues that need to be addressed to succeed in these markets. In fact, many firms are still positively choosing these developing countries as growth routes as opposed to other, more developed markets. However, the investments are often initially

Table 5.1 Ten Key Trends in Private Sector Engagement in Development

Themes	Key Trends
More global firms are seriously engaging in the developing world	1. Global firms are increasingly engaging in the developing world as part of core business growth. 2. Major global (private sector) firms are increasingly linking philanthropy/CSR with core business activities/investments. 3. There are growing pots of external investment capital looking to invest in developing markets.
Governments in developing countries are more focused on enterprise, trade, and investment.	4. Local developing country governments are welcoming more enterprise, trade, and external investment. 5. There is a stronger emphasis on pro-poor, transformative growth. 6. Growing awareness of the importance of smaller local firms. 7. There is a better appreciation that progress is being hindered by a range of missing factors.
NGOs and major donors are beginning to see enterprise, trade, and the private sector as connected to what they do.	8. NGOs are slowly beginning to accept that economic growth and wealth creation should be center stage in the development process. 9. Major institutional donors are increasingly including enterprise, trade, and private sector dimensions in their plans. 10. NGOs are finding it challenging to choose between a daunting and potentially confusing set of collaboration opportunities with the private sector.

concentrated in certain countries and markets (e.g., Kenya, Ghana, South Africa, India, Indonesia, the Philippines) because of their size and attractiveness and perceived ease and risks of doing business.

However, it is fair to say that there is still a significant proportion of major global firms who remain reluctant to dip toes in the water, particularly in more challenging countries. This is partly due to a lack of familiarity, along with risks that result from political uncertainty in some of these new markets. However, as experience grows—and there is a growing population of business executives who have this kind of experience—we expect that the appetite to do business in developing markets will expand. This is especially true in countries that show themselves to be dependable and reliable places to invest.

Trend 2: Major global firms are increasingly linking philanthropy and corporate social responsibility (CSR) with core business activities/ investments. Companies are increasingly linking their more philanthropic investments with their core business goals and finding a synergistic relationship between them. In our research report in 2009 we developed a framework to illustrate this trend, identifying four levels of engagement (illustrated in Table 5.2). Over the past seven years we can see that this trend has continued to gather pace.

Trend 3: There are growing pots of external investment capital looking to invest in developing markets. These fall into four broad categories:

1. **Traditional providers**, the likes of the World Bank and African Development Bank or the Asian Development Bank (ADB). These mainly focus on infrastructure investments.
2. **Ethical funds**: There is a growing number of funds broadly labelled as "ethical investments" or "socially responsible" investments, which roughly means they are investments chosen to fit specified social or environmental good criteria.
3. **Social impact bonds** are another growing category. These bring private sector investment discipline with an explicit emphasis on social returns as well as acceptable financial returns.[15] A good example of this is the Dolma Impact Fund (http://www. dolmafoundation.org), a $20 million fund that aims to provide growth capital for small and medium enterprises in Nepal.
4. Finally, straightforward **equity funds** that focus specifically on developing markets (could be for large or small firms and may be focused on one or multiple sectors). These funds respond to the belief that much of the longer-term growth opportunities will come from the current developing world.

What all of this signifies is the increasing integration of the economies of the developing world into the global economy. Although this is generally very positive, we can expect to see some volatility in growth based on what is happening in the rest of the world. For example, there has been a recent slowing down in the growth of FDI in emerging markets, though this is expected to be a short term blip in a generally upward trend. The Institute of International Finance has projected that it expected all flows from foreign investors to developing countries, including investments in bonds and equities, direct investments, and official flows, to slow to $981 billion in 2015, though expected a rise to $1,158 billion in 2016.[16]

Table 5.2 Four Levels of Private Sector Investment in Developing Countries

Type of Investment	Typical Goals	Value Horizon
Philanthropy	• Do good — anywhere • Do good close to business operations • Employee engagement, development, commitment	Undefined/moral responsibility
Social investment/ CSR	• Contribute skills, technology, assets for social return (no direct payoff for firm) • Stimulus of social transformation	Prospective value (distant future)
Corporate	• Grow long-term market • Build sustainability image into brand • Link business and local markets • Develop/strengthen supply chain	Emerging value (tomorrow)
Business basics	• Competitive and sustainable operations and supply chain • Community support for operations • Healthy productive workforce • Influence regulatory environment	Embedded value (today)

What this and other reports allude to is the risk in grouping all developing markets in the same category. As investors gather more insight, they will unsurprisingly favor emerging markets with stable governments and progressive policies and incentives.

Theme: Governments in Developing Countries Are More Focused on Enterprise, Trade, and Investment

Trend 4: Local governments are welcoming more enterprise, trade, and external investment. Quite a few local governments in developing countries are increasingly welcoming international firms who wish to invest, create jobs, and make a profit. In fact, there are a number of examples of countries where foreign commercial investment is increasingly more welcome and appreciated than charitable help from NGOs. This is a sign of the change in attitude toward foreign commercial firms as well as increasing frustration toward the NGO community. We have heard this sentiment directly from several senior government representatives in a number of countries in east Africa.

Trend 5: Stronger emphasis on pro-poor or transformative growth. Economic growth is clearly a fundamental cornerstone of poverty alleviation. However, for this to happen, it is necessary to combine a range of growth-promoting policies with policies and practices that enable the poor to participate in that growth. If a country gets this combination right, growth and poverty reduction can be significant; if it gets it wrong, both may be stalled. We have seen firms like Industrial Promotion Services (the industrial development arm of the Aga Khan Fund for Economic Development) pursue large-scale enterprises in agriculture and other sectors, providing opportunities for small out-grower farmers to participate in global agricultural markets, at a scale and level of quality and reliability demanded by global markets.

This seems an obvious area where NGOs and private sector firms could team up to support. This point was emphasized by the outgoing head of the African Investment Bank, Donald Kaberuka,[17] who noted the importance of more inclusive growth and delivered a clear warning of the dangers of rising income inequality.

Trend 6: Growing awareness of the importance of smaller local firms (micro, small, and medium-sized enterprises). In much of the dialogue and case examples so far, there has been considerable emphasis on larger global firms. However, there is a growing appreciation that the biggest opportunity for enterprise and trade will be in micro, small, and medium enterprises (SMEs), helping them grow in their local markets, trade with neighboring markets, and prepare to compete in international markets. It is well known that this category of firms is the heartland of economic progress and often provides 70–90 percent of jobs in successful economies. This is sometimes referred to as the "missing middle" in developing markets. As illustrated in Figure 5.4, these firms sit in the middle tier of enterprise, below the very large global firms and above the micro, subsistence-level activities that are often the focus of many NGO livelihood programs. Figure 5.5 illustrates the intended direction of the pyramid of firms, based on the direction we aspire to relative to where we are today.

Trend 7: A better appreciation that progress is being hindered by a range of missing factors. There is a growing appreciation that what is missing is

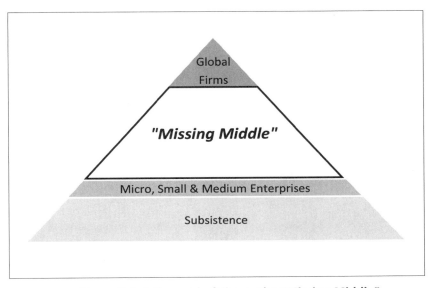

Figure 5.4 A Pyramid of Firms: The "Missing Middle"

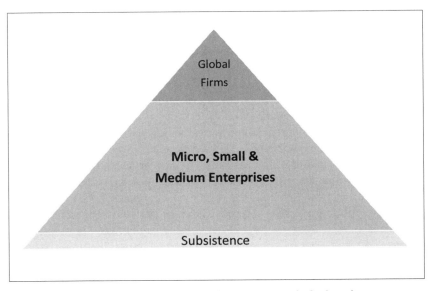

Figure 5.5 A Pyramid of Firms: Intended Directions

not just enterprise and trade but a range of facilitating factors that would enable trade and enterprise to grow. This includes the obvious infrastructural factors (roads, ports, telecommunications, power) as well as policy, appropriate regulation, and incentives. These deficits are often caused by a lack of institutional capacity within central and local governments—skills, resources, and know-how that we often take for granted in the developed world. Developing countries could benefit from some practical assistance in these areas.

Theme: NGOs and Major Donors Are Beginning to See Enterprise, Trade, and the Private Sector as Something Connected to What They Do

Trend 8: NGOs are beginning (reluctantly in some cases) to accept that economic growth and wealth creation should be center stage in the development process. The perception that wealth creation is somewhat uncomfortable or something separate from development is very slowly disappearing from NGO discourse, as organizations appreciate that economic development is a core part of the solution to long-term poverty and can offer much larger development progress than traditional aid alone.

Some NGOs still have considerable barriers to overcome. The challenge is not so much convincing organizations of the relevance of these two spheres of activity, but working out precisely what they should do differently. This question is discussed further in the next section of this chapter.

Trend 9: Major institutional donors are increasingly including enterprise, trade, and private sector dimensions in their plans. Many international donors have taken the opportunity to review their scope and priorities. This has been driven by a combination of factors, particularly by growing public scrutiny of international aid expenditure in the wake of the recent financial crisis. This scrutiny has resulted in donors seeking greater evidence of impact in what is often referred to as "the results-based agenda." As a result, in a good number of cases, trade, enterprise, and the private sector have become more central to tackling poverty. There is still a gap between principles and practice on the ground, as many of these donors are struggling to convert the new emphasis on trade and enterprise to practical investments. This is due to the significant momentum and comfort around the more traditional kinds of development projects that have been supported in the past.

Trend 10: NGOs are finding it challenging to choose between a daunting and potentially confusing set of collaboration opportunities. There is a massive—indeed, potentially daunting—scope and volume of opportunities in terms of geography, industry, and type and myriad companies to choose from. NGOs are realizing that collaborating with the private sector does not always fit into the kinds of programs they have been familiar with. The effort can be significant, the time scales long, and the tangible benefits not always simple to tie down.

Where Are the Real Collaboration Opportunities?

To begin this assessment, it is useful to remind ourselves of the priorities of some important stakeholders in the development process. We have identified four groups (see Figure 5.6):

- Developing country governments
- NGOs (international and local)
- National micro and SMEs in developing countries
- International/global firms

Figure 5.6 Four Groups of Stakeholders with Overlapping Interests and Priorities

The star in the center of Figure 5.6 is intended to signify areas of common interest, which should help point us to the most productive areas of collaboration. To begin, let's explore the priorities of these four groups.

Developing country governments have a fairly practical set of aims and priorities. They are often seeking out means to create stability, progress, and hope for the future. A typical agenda might include:

- Maintaining political and economic stability, which will assist with other priorities and help them stay in control
- Improving public services, such as education and basic health
- Stimulating economic activity, more jobs, higher household income (including to reduce or eliminate the reliance on aid hand-outs)
- Attracting external investment (infrastructure, enterprise, jobs)
- Maintaining their political support and popularity

Local micro and SMEs are often locked at a certain level of scale and ambition and seek an opportunity to break out of their current logjam in the quest for new growth opportunities and increased income and employment. The priorities are mainly around:

- Access to capital
- Access to new markets
- Access to technology and know-how
- Ability to meet standards and regulations in new markets
- Improving management systems and capacity

International private sector firms typically have a clearer set of business-driven priorities, which are essentially about accessing:

- Customer markets to expand their revenues, short- and/or long-term
- Raw materials for their global businesses
- Investment opportunities (new or existing)
- Competitive locations to locate operations in terms of skills, labor costs, and taxes

NGOs (international and local) come in many shapes and sizes and cover a range of aims and mandates. Typically, their priorities are centered on:

- Securing funds to pursue long-term humanitarian and development goals
- Sourcing technical solutions to development and humanitarian problems (often with insufficient budgets)

- Building the cooperation of a range of local and international stakeholders to allow them to implement programs
- Identifying innovative approaches to take successful programs to scale

What might be the areas of common interest? Looking across the four groups, we see that many of these priorities seem fairly complementary— at least there are not too many obvious conflicts. We expect that there is collaboration going on already, especially between certain combinations of stakeholders. For example, NGOs already collaborate very closely with a range of local stakeholders—beneficiaries, local community-based organizations, or local government bodies.

However, if there is to be progress in stimulating economic growth through enterprise and trade, as well as meeting the other basic development needs in poor countries, we believe much more focused and powerful collaboration is needed. This is a two-way process, including private sector support for development goals as well as NGO support for enterprise and trade.

Seven Key Areas for Greater Collaboration

We identify seven key areas that have enormous potential and where more collaboration between NGOs and private sector firms could be very helpful (see Table 5.3).

1. Reducing International Barriers to Enterprise and Trade. Earlier in the chapter, we touched on the barriers that get in the way of local enterprise and trade in developing countries. Some of these have to do with a political and economic history at the global level that may be difficult to address, at least directly. However, many of the barriers relate to policies, tariffs, regulation, subsidies, and incentives that need to be dealt with to provide a level playing field. In fact, one could argue that we need to create more favorable conditions, at least on a temporary basis, to give these poorer economies a leg up—akin to the support many new countries receive when joining the European Union.

2. Encouraging Appropriate Industries. In poorer developing countries with weak institutions, it can be difficult to join up the thinking, planning, policies, and incentives to encourage the right long-term industries. There could be an opportunity to help local governments and institutions select and encourage competitive, sustainable industries, and guide external investment toward the most productive areas.

3. Building National Workforce Capacity. Local governments often lack the capacity to provide training and build skills to meet the needs of local firms, especially for key growth industries. A good example of this is the dearth of practical vocational training. Another example relates to the broader education system. In some countries, local business leaders and entrepreneurs often criticize the balance of the basic education curriculum and approach, complaining that there is an abundance of rote learning and a desperate lack of problem-solving and critical thinking. They claim that for the small volume of students who progress to university, the education system produces a cadre of young graduates with a strong culture of entitlement and little sense of responsibility. This is an important constraint to economic growth and an area where help could be beneficial.

4. Strengthening Government and Institutional Capacity and Policy. NGOs and others are sometimes quick to throw stones at local government institutions without fully realizing the constraints on their funding, capacity, and cumulative experience. It can be useful to put yourself in the shoes of these institutions to understand how to help. They may require help to establish local policy and plans around enterprise and trade, to strengthen government capacity, to develop appropriate regulation, or perhaps to help simplify or reduce unnecessary rules and barriers to trade and enterprise.

5. Supporting and Encouraging Local Firms. Local micro and SMEs are often stuck at a certain scale of operations through a combination of practical barriers and a lack of basic resources. Collaboration could focus on:

- Helping micro enterprises make small steps to go beyond basic survival to becoming SMEs
- Helping SMEs grow and expand in their current markets and access new external markets (national or international)
- Helping local firms maximize the opportunities around local content, especially in the servicing of extractive industries, which is a growing segment in some developing countries

6. Encouraging/Facilitating Major Infrastructure Projects. This is an essential aspect of development, particularly to facilitate growing trade and enterprise. Infrastructure projects, such as roads, rail, power, or telecommunications, are large-scale, capital-intensive, long-term investments and demand government support and funding—funding that poorer countries typically cannot provide.

When you reflect on the four groups of stakeholders, it is easy to appreciate that these kinds of projects often fall between the cracks and, if they come to fruition, do so extremely slowly. Collaboration in the identification, planning, funding, and construction of these projects should be an area of focus for all stakeholders.

7. Creating Technical Solutions and Support to Key Development and Humanitarian Challenges. Last but not least, the private sector has the opportunity to do far more in a wider variety of ways to help local and international NGOs tackle the development problems that are core to their traditional mandate. This is the area where we have seen the most progress over the past decade, though far more collaboration could be beneficial. This could include doing more to provide technical solutions for a range of key health issues, such as malaria and tuberculosis, or the supply of medicines at a price that is realistic for poorer countries. It could include the exploitation of information and communication technology in all its applications to help with a range of challenges and opportunities.

Areas the Private Sector Should Avoid

private sector firms should stay clear of certain areas or simply provide philanthropic support to local NGOs that are better equipped to help. In particular, private sector firms should avoid:

- Carrying out development or humanitarian initiatives that have little connection with their core business, where they do not have the skills and expertise, and where they risk wasting their valuable business skills and resources to become amateur development or humanitarian workers.
- Participating in local enterprise and trade in a manner that is unsustainable, uncommercial, or just too short-term, which distorts local market dynamics for local firms.
- Seeking contracts or market share if it distorts local markets in a way that inhibits local firms from participating in business opportunities

What Should NGOs and Private Sector Firms Do Differently?

As discussed earlier, we acknowledge that there is some grounds for optimism. There has been undeniable progress in the emergence of enterprise, trade, and the private sector as a central (rather than peripheral)

Table 5.3 Seven Opportunity Areas for Deeper Collaboration Between NGOs and Private Sector Firms

Opportunity Area	NGOs Could Contribute	Private Firms Could Contribute	2016 Score (1–10)[a]
1. Reducing international barriers to enterprise and trade • International policies and regulation • Tariffs • Subsidies • Incentives	Independent voice on trade justice	Respected voice from industry on benefits of stimulating global trade	3/10
2. Encouraging appropriate industries • Imagining and encouraging sustainable and competitive industries • Guiding/steering external investment	Local context understanding and insight, long-term relationships, independence	Practical insight about which industries have best long-term potential	1/10
3. Building national workforce capacity • Depth and relevant skills • Practical vocational training • Problem solving	Local context understanding and insight, long-term relationships, independence	Investment capital, international understanding, and credibility	2/10
4. Strengthening local government capacity and policy • Government capacity • Government policy • Corruption	Local context understanding and insight, long-term relationships, independence	Access to new know-how, new technology, partnerships, longer term contracts	3/10

5. Building local firms • Micro to sustainability to SME • SME to growth and new markets • Local content	Local context understanding and insight, long-term relationships, independence	Collaboration to expand business ventures nationally and internationally	2/10
6. Creating essential infrastructure • Roads, rail, ports • Energy and telecommmunications	Local context understanding and insight, long-term	Financing and project planning	2/10
7. Creating technical solutions and support to key development and humanitarian challenges • Medicines and nutrition • Telecommunications • Power and solar	Deep understanding of the practical problems and needs of poor communities	Finance and technological know-how to bolster NGO efforts	4/10

Note: a. Authors' estimated scoring of degree of collaboration so far (as a challenge!).

part of the development process. There are some valuable examples of practical collaboration between NGOs and private sector firms. There is a higher profile on this whole area, particularly in public forums such as Business Fights Poverty and the Shared Value Initiative, which draw attention to key opportunities and provide a space for shared learning. Finally, a number of the large institutional donors, such as USAID, DFID, and others, have embraced enterprise and trade as an important part of their development agenda. All of this is encouraging.

However, progress on large-scale collaboration is disappointing. Our subjective scoring in Table 5.3 is perhaps a bit "tongue-in-cheek" but is probably not far off the mark. What do various stakeholders need to do differently to speed up progress and results? First, let us examine the issues from the perspective of NGOs.

Challenges and Resistance from the NGO Community

Despite the encouraging efforts and progress, there is a seam of uncertainty and resistance to the idea of collaborating more with the private sector. Why is that? In our day-to-day work with the NGO community, we have found that resistance falls broadly into three camps:

- Camp 1: Trade, enterprise, and the private sector collaboration is great—the answer to everything.
- Camp 2: private sector collaboration is important, but practically we are not clear what should be done differently and are underwhelmed about what it has achieved so far.
- Camp 3: The private sector is made up of evil exploiters, and while we will play along, we really should have nothing to do with them.

The resistance is rooted in a number of understandable conflicts, some of which are real, some perceived. These could be: a conflict of mission and values, a conflict of goals and time horizons, a conflict of time, a conflict of language, a conflict of expertise and approach, a conflict of results and potentially the most serious—a conflict of trust. These are expanded and reviewed in Table 5.4.

The point is not that collaboration is too difficult, but that NGOs and private sector firms have important differences. Some of these differences can be bridged through cumulative experience and working more closely together; others can lead to complementary approaches that can be productive for both parties.

Table 5.4 Potential Collaboration Conflicts Between NGOs and Private Sector Firms

Conflict	Comment	Our Response
Conflict of mission	• Our missions are fundamentally different— private sector is just about profit and shareholders	May be framed differently— but not necessarily contradictory
Conflict of values	• Our values are fundamentally different—ours are about caring, solidarity, justice, participation, etc. • Profit is not an easy concept for us	Maybe not as different as one might think
Conflict of goals	• Our goals and objectives are just too different	Challenge worth exploring if there are complementary longer-term goals
Conflict of time horizon	• We care about longer-term sustainable impact— private sector is about profit today	Not true—long-term growth and results is key to shareholder value
Conflict of time	• If had more time I would engage more, but I just do not have the time given the demand of today's programs/donors and number of urgent humanitarian crises	This is a challenge—an issue of focus and prioritization
Conflict of language	• Private sector does not understand our language	This is often valid, maybe need to simplify
Conflict of experience/habits	• Familiar with private sector as donors to our programs • Not familiar with private sector firms as contributors/participants to typical programs	Will take time and some learning
Conflict of expertise and approach	• I don't understand what goes on in private sector firms • Designing development and humanitarian programs requires comprehensive knowledge and expertise. Private sector staff will not get it	Good—think of complementary expertise, two-way learning, and building on each other's methods

Continues

Table 5.4 Continued

Conflict	Comment	Our Response
Conflict of results	• Where we have tried to engage with the private sector in the field, the results have been either underwhelming or hard to define. We cannot justify to most of our donors.	It can take time, and an approach to measuring impact might need to evolve
Conflict of trust	• Not sure I really trust private sector firms' motives—feeling they will exploit the poor and vulnerable at the first opportunity.	Valid concern, but most good firms and their shareholders appreciate long-term success in terms of the triple bottom line (society, environment, financial)

Challenges from the Perspective of Private Sector Firms

From the perspective of the private sector, particularly from the larger international firms, we can also see some significant barriers. Some have to do with the nature of the development landscape and resource constraints and some to the levels and experience of NGO staff. These can be illustrated by some typical quotes we have often heard from private sector executives.

> The NGO development and humanitarian landscape is too complex—there are far too many organizations; most are far too small and too unprofessional to collaborate with. It is almost impossible for us to work out who is the best agency to work with.

> NGOs are not willing to take time to understand what we do, our strategies and plans, and where the opportunities might be—we need to spend twelve to eighteen months to discuss, learn, and find out where collaboration might be most productive. Sometimes, they seem much more comfortable taking a $50,000 grant for a project that they can go away and implement in isolation.

> They are hampered by the constraints and expectations of their current donor set. They simply do not have the time and resources to explore new avenues around trade and enterprise.

> The individuals we interact with are too junior and inexperienced. The people who are tasked with private sector engagement are too far down their hierarchy, probably because enterprise, trade, and the private sector are too far down their list of priorities.

So what exactly needs to happen to light a fire under the pot of collaboration, dramatically accelerate progress for the benefit of development and humanitarian programs, and kick-start enterprise and trade for the benefit of the poor? We start with advice that applies to both NGOs and private firms and then make some specific comments for each sector.

Messages for NGOs and Private Sector Firms

Be as clear as possible about the **target collaboration area** and end goal, for example, by picking from the kinds of opportunity areas listed in Table 5.3. There are so many firms and NGOs out there, the options for potential partnership are numerous. Being as clear as possible about the target area will help bring focus and increase the chances of success.

Be prepared to invest in relationships and take the **time to build trust**. This can take a while—be patient! Trust and personal chemistry are important ingredients for success in all collaborations. It is much easier to build a trusting relationship if the managers and staff who will also be working together get along.

Think big, even if the start is small. If ambitious goals are the starting point and are eye-catching at national or international levels (e.g., to transform specific industry sectors), there might be half a chance of staying committed. It may also be helpful to encourage other key contributors to join in.

Specific Messages for NGOs

The kinds of projects where collaboration might be effective **could look very different** to traditional NGO programs; they might be on a different scale and have very different metrics of success. It may take time and effort to shape these projects. Be aware of the core competencies of your organization and consider the different ways these may be utilized.

It may be necessary to participate in **new collaborative organizational models**, outside of your normal organizational structure. Shoehorning these new opportunities into your current organizational ways of working might not be the best way.

Specific Messages for Private Sector Firms

Be realistic. Recognize that NGOs are hampered by lack of funding for program activities that fall outside the traditional model as understood by their donors. Hence, the private sector may need to provide some funding support to help ambitious NGOs engage in the area of trade and enterprise. This might mean combining a spoonful of philanthropy to allow the collaboration to progress.

Drop any hint of arrogance. Our honest experience is that the caliber of staff in NGOs is absolutely no different to what one might see in any other sector. In fact, we believe there is typically a higher proportion of qualified, experienced, and motivated professionals in this sector than we might find in a typical private sector firm.

Stick with an opportunity area once identified. private sector firms are accustomed to turning investment up and down on specific initiatives as conditions and other priorities dictate. This can sometimes be harder for NGOs; for example, temporary gaps in funding can result in the loss of learning and capacity.

Conclusions

We hope we have managed to highlight some of the key areas for collaboration and reflect on what is at stake and how these sectors might move forward together. Here are the key conclusions we can draw from this analysis.

We strongly believe that more **trade and enterprise is central to the long-term development**. The private sector is a central part of that process. This includes international firms as well as smaller local enterprises—be they farmers, small out-growers, or micro and SMEs.

The West has a **duty as well as an opportunity to encourage enterprise, trade, and private sector activity** in the developing world. There is some culpability for the weakness of trade and enterprise in these countries—hence the call to help goes beyond charity to social and economic justice.

NGOs have an opportunity and obligation to contribute. NGOs may not always be central to the process of economic growth, enterprise, and trade, but they can help, or at least not get in the way. NGOs will do an enormous disservice to those they seek to serve if they do not do their utmost to encourage trade and enterprise and general economic growth. This also means being helpful to the growth of private sector firms, small and large.

Thankfully, the perception that wealth creation is somehow uncomfortable or separate from international development is slowly disappearing from the NGO mind-set. They are beginning to see the private sector as relevant actors in the development equation, though real action on the ground is still lagging behind. However, the majority of large NGOs are investing to build capacity to collaborate more closely with the private sector, beyond traditional fundraising.[18]

The private sector can also be an invaluable **provider of innovative solutions** and new technologies to help increase the impact and effectiveness of a range of development and humanitarian programs.

If we look at the bigger picture, there are **at least seven focused areas** where we believe collaboration between private sector firms and NGOs could be productive. These are:

1. Reducing international barriers to enterprise and trade.
2. Encouraging appropriate industries.
3. Building national workforce capacity.
4. Strengthening government and institutional capacity and policy.
5. Building local firms.
6. Encouraging/facilitating major infrastructure projects.
7. Creating innovative technical solutions to key development and humanitarian challenges.

Collaboration between NGOs and private sector firms, at local and international levels, **is still in its infancy**. Both sides need to respect this and allow space and time to interact and learn. Where collaboration is happening, we can see that companies are much more likely to engage with NGOs via philanthropic investments, and much less likely via core business activities.

Initiatives and efforts in the **South are beginning to lead this overall agenda**. Despite increasing discussion around international partnerships, the majority of interesting collaboration opportunities seem to be emerging from bottom-up ideas, primarily in developing countries. So far, at least, local needs and ideas trump global initiatives. However, local efforts can benefit from international support and nourishment to achieve material scale and impact.[19]

Despite the range of areas of collaboration described here, NGOs also have a duty to be knowledgeable and independent to ensure they have the ability and the **legitimacy to raise issues of exploitation or unfairness**, as larger firms explore opportunities in terrains and social and political contexts that are new to them.

Notes

1. William Easterly, *The White Man's Burden: Why the West's Efforts to Aid the Rest Have Done So Much Ill and So Little Good* (New York: Penguin, 2006).

2. Development Co-operation Report 2014, *Mobilising Resources for Sustainable Development* (Paris: OECD, 2014). "Note that foreign direct investment is investment by individuals or firms from one country into another, either by buying an existing firm (through mergers and acquisitions), setting up a new operation (greenfield investment), or by expanding the operations of an existing business. The three main components of FDI are equity investment, intercompany loans, and reinvested earnings."

3. Robert J. Crawford and N. Craig Smith, "Unilever and Oxfam: Understanding the Impacts of Business on Poverty, "European Academy of Business in Society," INSEAD Case Study (2008).

4. James Crowley and Cristina Alzaga, *Connecting Business and Development: The "Rubik's Cube" of Cross Sector Collaboration* (London: Crowley Institute, 2009).

5. Katrina Manson, "TPG to Invest up to $1bn in Africa with Satya Capital," http://www.ft.com/cms/s/0/0026695c-1437-11e5-9bc5-00144feabdc0.html #axzz49rOcjkhs.

6. Andrew Ward, "Hopes Rise for Malaria Vaccine as Oil Companies Fund Trials," http://www.ft.com/intl/cms/s/0/7b95d69e-1c03-11e5-8201cbdb03d71480.htm l#axzz49rOcjkhs.

7. Pauline Williams and Simon Wright, "Radical Partnerships to Give Newborns a Healthier Start," Business Fights Poverty, October 26, 2015, http://community .businessfightspoverty.org/profiles/blogs/pauline-williams-and-simon-wright-radical-partnerships-to-give-ne.

8. Pooja O. Murada, "Corporate-NGO Partnership Helping India's Smallholder Farmers," August 6, 2015, http://community.businessfightspoverty.org/profiles /blogs/corporate-ngo-partnership-helping-india-s-smallholder-farmers.

9. David Grant, "Partnering to Sustain Access to Safe, Clean Water for All", Business Fights Poverty, June 22, 2015, http://community.businessfightspoverty.org /profiles/blogs/david-grant-partnering-to-sustain-access-to-safe-clean-water-for-all.

10. Fiona Koch, "How Successful Partnerships Will Fuel Agenda 2030", 1st October, 2015, Business Fights Poverty, http://community.businessfightspoverty .org/profiles/blogs/how-successful-partnerships-will-fuel-agenda-2030.

11. Paul Polman and Mark Gunton, "Turbo Charging Development—Making the SDGs a Reality," Business Fights Poverty, October 2, 2015, http://community .businessfightspoverty.org/profiles/blogs/paul-polman-turbo-charging-development-making-the-sdgs-a-reality.

12. Morgana Ryan, Shaun Richardson, and Paul Voutier, "Business in Development Study, Funded by AusAID," Accenture and Business for Millennium Development (2012).

13. Wole Akande, "Agricultural Subsidies in Rich Countries," Globalpolicy.org, *Yellow Times*, April 6, 2002; https://www.globalpolicy.org/component/content /article/162/27731.html.

14. Javier Blas, "Commoditites: Destination Africa," *Financial Times*, November 10, 2013.

15. The Center for Global Development and Social Finance, "Investing in Social

Outcomes: Development Impact Bonds—The Report of the Development Impact Bond Working Group" (2013).

16. Jonathan Wheatley, "Capital Flows to Emerging Markets Seen at Post-2009 Low," *Financial Times*, May 28, 2015.

17. William Wallis and Maggie Fick, "Nigerian Akinwumi Adesina Wins African Development Bank Top Job," *Financial Times*, June 2, 2015.

18. Crowley and Alzaga, *Connecting Business and Development*.

19. Ibid.

6

Why NGOs Have So Much Trouble with IT

Historically, NGOs have tended to adopt a minimalist, "get-by" approach to IT (information technology). With a few notable exceptions, the culture and incentives in the sector have not been conducive to significant new investments, either to support core operations or to help strengthen programs. However, as we noted in our previous publication, *Building a Better International NGO*, the "changes and new possibilities that information and communications technologies can bring offers the opportunity to transform most areas of international development"—front and back office.[1] NGOs are now operating in a digital world with a very different technology context.

It is impossible to ignore the extent to which lives are being touched by technology. People have a growing expectation of access to information and services at the touch of a button. Across all sectors, organizations are continuously seeking to adapt to these evolving expectations. The international development and humanitarian sector is no different. NGOs, often with a legacy of disparate and disconnected IT solutions, are beginning to appreciate and respond to the changing expectations of donors and supporters, staff, partner organizations, and the beneficiaries they are trying to help. At the same time, we've seen the sector struggle to effectively embrace and implement technology. This raises the question: why do NGOs have such trouble with IT?

We believe there are two important reasons for this. First, many NGOs began life as grassroots, issue-based organizations, nimble and responsive to achieve their vision and with little interest and patience in processes or formalized ways of working. Staff were passionate about their work in the field and tended to regard processes and technology as

159

necessary evils or peripheral. Senior leaders in most NGOs often came from program and campaigning backgrounds and had deep development expertise but limited or no experience working with technology. In this environment, there was no serious priority placed on using technology. The result was often basic, piecemeal, and outdated use of IT.

The second reason is related to the way the sector measures performance, particularly in relation to the metric of percentage of expenditure on direct programs versus overhead costs. This measure acts as a disincentive to investing in IT, particularly when it relates to strengthening enabling processes. In recent years, NGOs have experienced very rapid growth, in many cases through an increase in major institutional grants. They are now considerably larger, with more complex and diverse operating footprints, but haven't made the internal investments required to effectively manage at their size and scale. This growth has resulted in a more unfavorable balance of restricted to unrestricted income, which makes it even more difficult to embark on these kinds of investments. Too often NGOs choose to forgo investment in IT systems and processes because it is accounted as a nice-to-have "overhead" by donors and by NGOs themselves. This is aptly summarized by the Bridgespan Group article "Stop Starving Scale."

> NGOs have grown into global conglomerates managing, in some cases, hundreds of programs in dozens of countries. While outwardly successful, it's a pattern of fragmented growth that feeds the programmatic branches and starves the operational core. Individual program "branches" grow without commensurate growth in the "core" management capabilities and systems required to maximize their impact in the most efficient manner.[2]

With the current speed of technological change, the world in which NGOs operate has fundamentally changed and is likely to keep changing at a rapid pace. NGOs should be encouraged to invest in their organizational capacity, build the systems and processes that enable leadership and staff at all levels to capture and use data to monitor and steer the organization, use technology in their development programs, and communicate effectively with donors, with supporters, and within the organization. This requires donors, the public, NGO boards, leadership, and staff to think differently about the value and power of technology.

- **Technology needs to be seen as strategic** rather than purely operational.
- **Technology needs to be seen as an enabler of development impact rather than an overhead**.
- NGOs need to have **senior, experienced IT knowledge within their organization and at the leadership table**.

In the past few years, we have noticed that international NGOs have begun to implement new strategic IT systems. A good example is in the area of customer relationship management (CRM) systems, particularly to help in fundraising and public engagement in an increasingly digital world. There have also been moves to implement better program and project management systems (PPMS) to support international work. A PPMS is usually set up to manage an NGO's entire program department (i.e., the life cycles of all the development programs, including budget and actual expenditure) and not just donor reporting requirements.

However, only a limited number of large NGOs have used common technology and ways of working across their entire international family. This should be seriously considered for the advantages this brings in terms of global access to data and knowledge sharing, making it easier for staff from different entities to work together, as well as cost savings in implementation and support. We hope more NGOs will look at IT strategy at an international family level. This would represent a considerable shift from the current norm with a proliferation of standalone, incompatible solutions.

As NGOs embark on these projects, we seek to learn from the lessons, successes, and failures that have occurred to date in the hope of supporting successful change in the future. The material in this chapter is relevant for local and international NGOs. For international NGOs it is relevant at all levels of the international NGO family, including the international secretariat, affiliates and members, and regional and country offices. Obviously, for a global implementation it is important to be aware of the politics and cultural challenges that exist and factor these in when planning the project.

We review some common issues that NGOs encounter when changing their IT systems and some practical mitigations to consider. A later section explores what a "typical" technology change project looks like, providing a simplified illustrative example of the key elements in a project life cycle. We provide key tips for NGO leaders to work with and use technology successfully. The final section contains pragmatic answers to some frequently asked questions.

Why Do NGOs Have so Much Trouble with IT?

In Chapters 1 and 2 we introduced some ideas and suggestions on the art and science of navigating change, structured around four levels of thinking. We've found that many of the challenges NGOs encounter with IT projects occur at Level 1, the basics. The good news is that these problems are fairly tangible and can be addressed in particular by ensuring important steps are not missed. Often when things go wrong, it is because key actions, checks, and governance structures have not been put in place. Once you know what these things are, it's not difficult to plan for and include them. Sometimes mistakes are made due to inexperience. This is understandable, as it's difficult to predict and plan for something when you haven't done it before and don't know what to expect.

The points highlighted here are primarily focused on IT projects but can also be applied to programs. We ask readers to think carefully about whether the scale of their IT change can be managed as a project or needs to be a program. When it is a program, consider the additional complexity and how the challenges and mitigations may need to be adjusted. For example, if you have a solution that is rolling out to multiple entities in a global international family, it may be necessary to create a multilayer steering committee structure.

The following are some specific issues, root causes, and suggested responses, organized around some of the key areas we introduced in Level 1 thinking in Chapter 1.

Vision, Drivers, and Benefits

Too often IT change projects have poorly framed vision and drivers. With a weak or absent business case, it becomes difficult to build momentum and support for the project, as there is no compelling evidence to justify the effort and investment.

Often the vision and drivers are poorly framed because the project is:

- Rushed from start to fit within a financial cycle and limited amount of earmarked budget with a general perception that it is best to just "get on with doing the project"
- Originating from the IT department and is only defined with a "technical vision"
- Conceived for negative reasons when the old IT system is collapsing, and misses the positive opportunity that new technology provides
- Not based on a business case or clear articulation of why the change is happening, or only evaluates the new solution and not the status quo solution

It is important to invest time at the beginning to frame the project from a holistic perspective, showing clearly how technology enables and enhances the NGO's ability to achieve its core objectives. Then build a business case that shows the benefits in tangible terms. The business case may need some robust consideration. For example, if the current IT system is outdated and no longer able to support the business but is significantly cheaper than the new solution being contemplated, it's important to evaluate the new solution and the risks associated with the status quo. As the project progresses, track the key measures of success to ensure the project delivers on the stated project vision and objectives.

Authentic Leadership

Leadership in a technology context presents two distinct challenges for NGOs. At a senior NGO leadership level, technology is often ignored and does not have a voice at the board or in the senior executive team. The IT lead is often a relatively junior position and housed under finance or programs with limited profile and influence. A shift needs to occur so that IT is no longer just a "keep the lights on" operational activity but is viewed as an important topic at leadership level. In the future, successful and innovative NGOs will have a knowledgeable and respected IT person as a full-fledged member of the senior team. They will be someone who can help look at IT strategically, working with each of the business functional leads to keep pace and embrace new possibilities and continually reviewing the ways technology can enable the organization to function better and have greater impact. This also applies at the international level—it is not enough to elevate IT just within the national entities.

Second, it can be difficult to get business and IT leaders within the organization to work together. The result is that IT projects are either led by IT alone, or alternatively the business takes the lead without involving the IT department. In either case the result is suboptimal. As discussed in the matrix approach in Chapter 3, we ask leaders to wear two hats when considering IT projects: that of your department and that of the organization as a whole. Considering both views will help ensure your decisionmaking is rounded, and you are able to show leadership that extends beyond the boundaries of your immediate team.

Clear and Consistent Communication

Clear and consistent communication is vital across the project life cycle. Some common challenges we've seen include:

- Communication is piecemeal, lacking a clear or compelling vision.
- Communication is not consistent among leadership (at worst there is obvious hostility from some in the leadership team towards the change).
- Communication is not coming from the most senior leadership level, so staff perceive an absence of senior commitment.

To mitigate these potential issues, messages need to be easy to understand and communicated often and consistently. They need to be tied to the vision and drivers for the change, be simple to understand, and resonate with staff. Leaders must be comfortable with what they are being asked to communicate, otherwise it will appear disingenuous and staff members will quickly lose faith in the change.

Ideally communications about the project should come from the business and IT leadership and at very senior levels. IT change works best when it is seen as enabling the whole business, rather than being as technology for its own sake. When implementing a system for one functional area that has connections with other areas, ensure that leadership from all affected functions consistently talk positively about the change using common language and messages.

Selection and Continuity of the Right People

Although there is a temptation to focus solely on the technology in IT change projects, in reality it is the *people* aspects that drive success or failure. Staffing the project team can be a big challenge for an organization that is resource constrained and busy. Overlay that with the fact the technology is new and the current staff don't have relevant experience. Daunting! It can be risky to rely on vendor staff (i.e., from the IT software vendor(s) or from implementation consulting vendor(s)) with insufficient understanding of the agency's ways of working; this can result in a solution that is not compatible with the business need. Furthermore, once the system is live there will be insufficient internal staff with the requisite skills and knowledge to support the new solution. The other risk is to allocate staff to work part-time on the project while expecting them to continue their day job. In a worst case, this can result in staff burnout and resignations.

To mitigate these risks, choose staff that you think have the best chance of learning and adapting their skills to work with the new technology. Once you've identified them, commit to them and to the organization by allocating them 100 percent to the project and backfilling their current role. This can be a great opportunity for staff development—for the individuals assigned to the project and the person who has the opportunity to step up in the backfill role. You may also need to invest in IT training. Software vendors usually offer courses that teach people how to configure and maintain the system. This should be in addition to end-user training, which is also very important.

Set up a combined project team with the vendor(s)/implementation partner (could be the same) and your internal staff. Have a well-defined team structure where each person's role is clearly articulated. This is a great way for NGO staff to develop the skills they will need to support the solution once it is live and once the external resources have departed. It's also a good way to ensure the implementation partner understands the business and ways of working. Inform the vendor/implementation partner that they are expected to transfer knowledge to train the staff who will be the future support team. Include this requirement in the contract with the vendor if possible.

Embracing technology also means embracing the fact the organization may need to value staff with different skills from those they have today. Consider opportunities to borrow employees from other organizations, including from other members of your international NGO family. There are a number of useful benefits. You gain an employee with the skills and experience needed, as well as insight into how others operate in the sector, even if their practices are somewhat different. There are also benefits for the employee who might gain a useful career development opportunity. For the other organization, it offers the chance to obtain insights into how others work, allowing for sharing of good practices.

In addition to the options discussed above, recruiting one or more new staff is advisable if there are insufficient skilled resources in the organization.

Resistance and Barriers to Change

NGO culture is often characterized by a high level of open dialogue, where staff are very comfortable voicing their opinions and concerns. Hence, when implementing a new change project, it is no surprise that the volume of resistance and objections can be plentiful. In addition, we know that NGO staff are passionate about their organization's vision, mission, and their ability to be agile and responsive as needs dictate. When embracing a major IT-driven change project, staff may be suspicious that it could enforce rigid processes and ways of working that restrict responsiveness.

A potential consequence of this is that leadership and the IT project team overcompensate by trying to keep everyone happy. This can result in the new IT system becoming a hostage—in trying to please everyone, you end up making the system overly complex and heavily customized. This is one of the most common pitfalls we see NGOs make during IT implementations. NGOs go with an existing "out of the box" software product (versus a custom build), but will then try to build their old ways of working into the new system. This sounds fairly logical, but the reality is that for many NGOs, their current ways of working are not based on a sophisticated and enabling IT system and have many legacy quirks. It is better to minimize customization and adopt as many of the standard design features of the new system as possible. It is a fallacy to believe that by trying to replicate the current ways of working you will minimize the impact on your staff. In reality the result is a heavily customized system that is complicated to navigate and is likely to be very difficult and costly to maintain, support, and upgrade.

This risk is often exacerbated (1) when the project lacks good governance structures, (2) when there is not a clear vision, and (3) where senior leadership are not fully versed in the key drivers and benefits sought. Addressing these important areas will help mitigate these risks.

Basic Project Management Disciplines

In Chapter 1 we considered twelve basic project management disciplines. Although all are important for NGO IT change projects, there are several in particular that we repeatedly see missed or inadequately addressed.

Governance and Steering Arrangements. This is a particularly critical area. Too often we see projects fail because of a lack of project governance. By "lack of governance" we mean one or more of the following:

- No project steering committee for IT change
- Insufficient business representation or IT representation
- Insufficient geographic representation (if the solution is going to multiple countries and regions)
- Steering committee members and/or process and data owners not committed and don't take the role seriously
- High turnover of steering committee membership over the project life cycle
- No supporting ownership structures outside the steering committee (e.g., process owners and data owners)

Do not start an IT project (even the early stages like selecting the software vendor or implementation vendor) without having established a project steering committee. Ideally, this would have senior leadership representation from IT, from the business function where the IT change is occurring and potentially other business functions that will use the new system. If the new system is to be implemented across multiple regions, it should also have representation from more than one location.

However, keep the number of members on the steering committee to a manageable level.

The steering committee should meet regularly with clear roles and responsibilities. Members must also understand that they are expected to attend and participate in decisionmaking. Let them know that they are making decisions for the good of the organization as a whole, not just their own department or function.

Equally critical is the concept of process owners. A common theme across the sector is the lack of standard processes and ways of working. This appears to be because organizations originate as grassroots movements, seeking to be responsive to the needs of beneficiaries, donors, and supporters. Yet for an IT implementation to be successful, a degree of discipline and process standardization is required. There needs to be a single point of decisionmaking. To this end, have a very clear view of the high-level process map that will define the scope boundaries for the IT system implementation. Identify senior or relatively senior staff to be process owners for each key process area and ensure that they are empowered to be the final point of decisionmaking. This does not mean others are not consulted; in fact, it's important that they *are*.

Data owners, who may or may not be different people from the process owners, play a key role with regard to data integrity. As the process owners are responsible for the process design, the data owners are accountable for the design of data usage in the new system. They have a say in the way information is taken from existing (legacy) systems and created in the new system. This is an important role because a new system populated with poor data won't work.

Developing a Robust Business Case and Securing Necessary Approvals. Too often projects start with completely the wrong foundation because there is a pot of money available that needs to be spent within a particular timeframe. Projects that start like this struggle to succeed. We strongly recommend the development of a business case for all IT projects. This should be updated as the project progresses. Avoid defining a budget at the outset that doesn't reflect the scope of the solution. Can you actually get the system for the money available? If not, can more funds be found, or can the scope be reduced? Only once there is a balance between available budget and project scope should the project begin.

Signing a time and materials contract with the vendor or implementation partner can lead to significant cost challenges. This is especially the case where the requirements in the request for proposal have been poorly defined. Avoid signing a time and materials contract if key steps have not been executed prior to contracting (for example, setting up a project steering committee, developing a well-defined project vision, and gathering preliminary scope and requirements that clearly define the project scope). Otherwise you significantly increase the risk that the costs will exceed the initial estimate. If the vendor is only willing to contract on a time and materials basis, consider contracting for a smaller piece of up front work to define the scope and provide a basis for a fixed price contract for the main implementation.

Project and Program Team Selection, Orientation, Training, and Support. Appointing the right people to key roles can be a big factor in the success or failure of an IT change project. Select a project manager who has some prior IT system implementation experience, even if it is with a different technology. NGO IT implementations are often much smaller in scale in terms of total number of users than for large commercial implementations, so it is not always necessary to hire someone who has had large-scale experience (they are often very expensive). It might be worth considering someone with five to eight years of experience in more junior roles on complex implementations. Importantly, they must be experienced in IT project life cycles and understand all areas (change management, business process design, testing, data conversion, security, infrastructure, etc.).

Resource Planning. In addition to what was discussed already, there are a couple of resource planning pitfalls to consider. Data conversion and in particular data clean-up activities are almost always underresourced— don't underestimate the amount of effort involved. These are time-consuming and frankly tedious but essential activities. At the end of the day, the best designed system can still have a substandard implementation if the data quality and data converted into the system is poor. Invest the time!

Finally, plan well in advance how the system will be supported once it is implemented. This includes business support, technical infrastructure as well as security/access support. Plan ahead to make sure staff learn as much as they can. If part of the support is going to be outsourced, make sure this is well planned and that service level agreements are defined. Allocate the necessary budget to provide a sufficient level of support, including a budget for ongoing enhancements.

Basic Elements of an IT Project

So far we have discussed technology change but haven't yet considered the question: what does an IT change project look like? There are many different methodologies for technology implementations and we seek not to investigate each or recommend a specific approach. Regardless of whether your organization is using an agile or waterfall approach (see the box on Development Methodology), a combination of both, or some other approach, the important thing is that you select a development methodology with clear phases and activities and a thorough project plan by which the project will be managed.

What we want to do here is demystify IT projects for those who are not familiar or have very limited experience with them. Figure 6.1 is a simplified illustrative example of the phasing and key activities for implementing technology change. This diagram is not intended to imply that every implementation is the same, nor that every phase and activity must be done.

Please note that for large complex technology changes (for example, multi-entity, multi-geography, multi-function) it may be necessary to add a program management layer over the top of one or more projects implementing the change. (See Chapter 1 for more details about program management.)

Although Figure 6.1 is structured for a system implementation like

---

Development Methodology: What's in a Name?

Two common types of IT project development methodology are *waterfall* and *agile*.

Waterfall: The "traditional" approach based on linear development with distinct project stages (analysis, design, etc.), often with clear checkpoints between each stage.

Agile: An iterative approach to development with an emphasis on working in teams during multiple construction iteration cycles (sprints). Each cycle has a workshop component to design the solution plus development and testing activities.

Factors that may influence the development methodology used include IT product being implemented, complexity, extent of integration with other existing systems, time and scope to go live, and availability of business users to participate in the project.

Phase	0) Concept / Feasibility	1) Inception / Analyse	2) Design & Build	3) Test & Deploy / Transition	4) Production Support
			Construction Iterations		
Important activities	Before starting, ensure there is guidance via an: • IT strategy; and • Executive sponsorship and project governance. Feasibility: • Vision and objectives • Scope and high level requirements • Business case • Vendor selection • Vendor contracting • Initial plan and budget • Initial stakeholder mapping • Project team selection & training	• Detailed project plan and project budget • Risk / issue management process defined • Stakeholder mapping, communications plan, Training strategy • Success measures defined • Process model (As-Is/To-Be) confirmed • Process and data owners appointed • Detailed requirements gathering • Conversion, interfaces strategy with inventory • Test strategy	• Detailed functional and technical design • Role mapping and job definition • Solution Design (including Architecture, Integration and Security / Authorization Model) • Solution Development (including Architecture, Integration and Security / Authorization Model) • System configuration development • Data conversion extract / upload development • Data clean-up • Unit testing	• System testing and system fixing • Trial/Mock conversion and extra data clean-up • User Acceptance Testing (UAT) with security testing • Train the trainer, then end user training • Post go-live support strategy and planning • Go live checklist (steering committee reviewed) • Cutover, including data conversion • Go Live	• Transition from initial post go live support to business as usual support including system, user, process support and upgrades • Process and system improvements • Ongoing training as required • Measure success
Ongoing	*Governance / Steering*				
	Project Management				
	Communications				
Top tips	Governance Team selection	Future business needs vision	Avoid customisation	Business ownership Rigor Cutover checklist	Planning for support Perseverance

Figure 6.1 Example Phases and Activities for IT Implementation for NGOs

CRM or an enterprise resource planning solution, it can also be adapted for an information communication technology for development or application development. The actual duration of each phase will vary depending on factors such as the type of IT change, the implementation methodology, and the scale of reach.

Project Phases

The **concept/feasibility phase** is used to determine if the technology change being considered is the right approach for the organization and, if so, to ensure the project begins on a solid footing. Before starting, consult the organization's IT strategy to help narrow the range of options for consideration (for example, don't consider technology that is incompatible with the current IT landscape). If, as is the case in many organizations, there is no IT strategy, invest time to do a high-level audit of existing technology and consider how any new IT might fit within the existing architecture and also meet the strategic needs of the organization. It is a good idea to do a scan of the technology being used by other members of the international NGO global family (if applicable) to see if there might be opportunities to use existing solutions and/or do a combined project.

Tip: Ensure there is executive-level sponsorship and establish a governance body (for example, a steering committee) for the feasibility phase, even if its composition is modified for the subsequent implementation. The governance body is necessary because it functions as the main point of accountability to decide whether the project will progress. If the IT project implementation is going to take place across multiple regions and multiple departments, then take time to pick the right stakeholders for the steering committee to ensure broad representation.

Once the IT strategy has been consulted and the governance established, resources can be devoted to determining the vision of the project and the scope and high-level requirements. These need to be fairly clear to allow the development of a vendor selection criteria and also a Request for Proposal (RFP) process if the organization decides to run one. They are key inputs for the business case, which will guide the steering committee in its decision about whether to progress to the next stage. Note that depending on the type of technology change project, there may be multiple vendors involved as technology provider(s) and implementation partner(s). Invest the time to do due diligence on the vendors.

Develop a high-level plan and budget that will present an initial view of the project and can be further refined in the next phase.

Tip: Build a project team that includes some vendor resources and a mix of IT and business staff from your organization. This helps establish joint responsibility for the project and provides ample learning opportunity for staff through close engagement with the vendor(s). It ensures that vendor staff have good exposure to those who really know the way the organization operates. Consider the skills your staff members currently have, the skills you need for the project, and the extent to which those skills can be developed in existing staff versus the need to recruit or contract external resources.

The **inception/analyze phase** focuses on developing the details behind the high-level feasibility assessment. This means setting the project boundaries and also selecting the process and data owners who will become part of the project governance and decisionmaking. It also involves developing the project plan and budget. The project budget should contain reasonable contingency plans. These elements together are important because they will provide a basis for determining a mandatory versus a "nice-to-have" requirement. This will be important in this phase and during the design and build phase, when the number of requirements may increase and the pressure to customize and build complexity into the new system grows.

It is essential to know which stakeholders will be affected by the project. This is an important input to the development of the communication strategy and helps shape a strong, clear message about how the change will enable the achievement of the organization's vision.

Tip: Ensure the message is not too technical and really reflects the vision and focus of the organization. Assuming most people in the organization are not particularly excited by IT, the message needs to focus on how the technology will enable the organization to do better and achieve more. If it is multi-geography the messaging needs to factor in sensitivities about headquarters and field relationships. It should be framed so that it is not interpreted as a headquarters solution being forced on field staff.

The **design and build phase** is when the detailed design of the new processes and system takes place. As part of this, the team will articulate how the organization will run using the new IT solution. They will determine how and what data will be moved from the current (legacy) system to the new system, what roles and access people will have, and how the new architecture fits with the existing IT landscape. It is essential to develop an adequate level of documentation about the new solution design, as a solid foundation to subsequent phases.

Tip: Resist the temptation to build old ways of working into the system. Use the established governance structures to challenge the prioritization of requirements so as to limit the need for customization. Resist the temptation to focus on how unique your organization is. Look for ways to make the most of the standard, well-developed ways of working. Keep the solution as simple as possible.

The **test and deploy/transition phase** provides multiple opportunities to test the robustness of the new system configuration, the data conversion approaches, and interfaces with other systems.

Tip: Ensure the business is actively involved in conversion testing and User Acceptance Testing (UAT). This can be a useful way of helping the business become very familiar with the new system and start to take ownership. Ideally the UAT would use trial converted data, as this is a particularly important step for implementations that are using the waterfall methodology. At this point the new system with actual business data will be available for review by the business. For agile implementation approaches, the business will already have had the chance to see the system. Regardless of the methodology, the UAT is the point where staff are responsible for reviewing the solution and indicating whether they accept it and can work with the new system, processes, and converted data. We recommend using a formal sign-off process for testing to help drive business engagement and ownership. For each UAT scenario, the relevant process owner(s) would participate in the test and then be asked to sign off at the completion of the UAT. The sign-off is important because it is an acceptance by the process owners that they believe the new system design will be able to support the business operations in their process area.

Tip: This part of the project often feels time pressured as delays from early in the project start to pile up. Maintain rigor in testing approaches, especially with data conversion.

Tip: As part of the preparation for transitioning into the new system (a process known as *cut-over*) it is important to develop a cut-over checklist. The checklist identifies the minimum items that must be in place in each area (functional design, conversion, interfaces, change management, security, etc.) for the new system to go live. This is a key document for the steering committee to review in the lead-up to making the final decision about switching the new system on and the old system(s) off.

If your organization has elected to use an agile approach, it is likely that the design and build phase and the test and deploy activities will be consolidated into a series—often referred to as *construction iterations*. Put simply, an iteration is a mini–design, build, and test loop that allows for quick development and display of the solution in a way the waterfall approach does not. Many of the activities outlined for the design and build phase and the test and deploy transition phase are relevant with an agile approach but structured in a different way to the waterfall approach.

Tip: If you are using an agile approach, create a base level of documentation to support further development and support of the solution. Without good documentation, it is difficult to answer questions later in the project about how and why the system was designed in a particular way.

Once the excitement of going live has passed, the **production support** phase focuses on keeping the production system running; making improvements, modifications, and upgrades to the system as required; and ensuring the system and processes meet the needs of the organization. Key considerations in establishing production support include determining whether the infrastructure or application support will be done in house or outsourced and deciding where the support team will sit in the organizational structure.

Tip: Begin planning for production support well before the project goes live. Too often this is overlooked in the rush to get the project over the line, and as a consequence the valley of despair (refer to Chapter 1) is deeper and longer than it needs to be. Allocate sufficient budget for support, including ongoing enhancements.

Tip: Persevere! It can be a bumpy ride immediately after the system goes live, but be determined and resilient. Make sure there are knowledgeable people available to support the organization and measure success to show benefits as quickly as possible to help people see the value in adopting the new ways of working.

Key Considerations for IT Success

We recommend reviewing the practical hints and tips for navigating change in Chapter 1. Although they relate to change projects in general, they are very relevant for IT change initiatives. In addition, based on our experience supporting a range of IT projects, we highlight five particular considerations that we feel are important to help NGOs use technology more effectively.

1. Reposition IT as a Strategic Opportunity
2. Reimagine a Technology-Enabled NGO
3. Develop a Good IT Strategy and Roadmap

4. Reposition Technology in the Organization
5. Discipline to Ensure Simplicity and Consistency

Reposition IT as a Strategic Opportunity

It is unfortunate that IT is typically considered an overhead rather than program cost, as this can drive the wrong investment decisions. This is a difficult area for individual NGOs to tackle. Much more needs to be done. Don't shy away from hard discussions. As much as possible, try to explain to donors why significant investment in IT is important and ultimately enables your organization to achieve its mission and strategy more effectively. This is a difficult issue for organizations to argue because leaders are caught in a bind. Underinvesting in technology threatens the long-term success and impact of the organization, but to be perceived as overinvesting in overhead can reduce donor support. Fortunately there appears to be a growing global voice[3] to highlight this issue. Much more needs to be done, and we welcome continued involvement by the international NGO peak bodies (such as BOND, ACFID, Interaction, InsideNGO, Dochas, NetHope) to educate people about why a change is necessary. Technology can be strategic!

Reimagine a Technology-Enabled NGO

Reimagine your organization through the lens of IT, allowing technology to play a key role in achieving your organization's vision and mission. Ensure that leaders from across the organization regularly talk to and collaborate with the IT department to find ways technology can increase reach and impact. Technology-enabled business should become a senior management and board-level agenda topic.

Develop A Good IT Strategy and Roadmap

A technology strategy, even if only a high-level strategy is possible, is an important roadmap for NGOs to obtain the most out of technology across the organization. Significant savings and efficiencies can be achieved through an integrated approach to technology at both the global international NGO family level and within an individual entity. Although we do not always advocate a centralized, standardized approach, there is value in being aware of what is already in place across the organization, what the longer-term strategic vision is, and how reusable and compatible technology can help.

Reposition Technology in the Organization

This should be done both structurally and culturally, as an enabler to achieve the first two points.

IT leadership: IT must be elevated within the organization. We strongly recommend NGO leadership teams include at least one person with deep technology skills. (Note: this is not the same as having someone responsible for technology but not skilled in the area.) We also suggest the NGO board includes one person with technology strategy skills. Contemplate a technology subcommittee of the board to seek out ideas and opportunities to use technology to enhance the impact of the agency.

Organizational structure and connection: Too often IT functions are duplicated in different parts of the organization and completely disconnected. For example, we have seen organizations that have headquarters-level IT departments in both finance and international programs and then additional IT departments in the regional and country offices. This can work if the departments have a good relationship with each other and collaborate, but it is a waste of resources and money when they are standalone and disconnected. Consider unifying IT as a horizontal line of expertise/responsibility in a matrix approach (as suggested in Chapter 3). This would mean that IT staff members wear two hats, one reporting to their immediate geographic/functional lead and one to the overall IT department lead.

IT culture: Culturally IT is often seen as an operational function that maintains the Internet, telephones, and other basic hardware. This needs to change to a world where IT is a strategic enabler of the organization's mission. If senior leadership can change their attitudes and behavior toward IT, it will go a long way to changing the tone and the culture across the organization. Talking about how IT improves programs and increases impact helps shift staff mind-set. Having non-IT leaders talk about how their area is enhanced by technology is also useful.

Discipline to Ensure Simplicity and Consistency

Without fail, every NGO we've worked with likes to give the impression that they are somehow unique. As controversial as this statement may be, we believe most NGOs are not! In reality, an overemphasis on being unique can compromise an agency's reach and impact. We see it in the lack of knowledge exchange and sharing, which results in constant reinvention of the wheel. Internally, NGOs should be closely aligned with each other, but too often they operate as standalone departments with poor interconnectivity. The consequences are double handling, missed information, and lost opportunities to learn and improve reach and impact.

The focus on being unique affects the way NGOs approach technology. Although we've mentioned this already with regard to individual IT projects, it is also worth mentioning in the context of organization-wide IT and IT strategy. Too often we see isolated IT solutions being selected for individual departments rather than using technology solutions that already exist. Avoid focusing on being unique, don't look for heavily customized solutions, and don't look for new standalone solutions when there already are existing ones. Keep it simple!

Frequently Asked Questions

How do NGOs differ in their approach and use of IT compared with other organizations?

On the whole, we believe there are more similarities than differences between NGOs and other organizations. However, the following are a few specific areas where NGOs exhibit some particular sector traits.

- For NGO boards and leadership, IT is often an afterthought rather than front of mind. The result is that technology is under-used—seen as operational only and not strategic. Technology has long been regarded as very strategic for many firms in the private sector.
- Few NGOs have a technology strategy,[4] so there is no overarching roadmap to guide them away from making costly investments in incompatible technology solutions.
- NGOs have an unhealthy tendency to think of themselves as being very unique. This seems to result, time and time again, in overly complex and costly IT system solutions with significant amounts of customization.
- There is sometimes a bias away from the leading, generic technology solutions as some staff perceive these to be too business/commercially oriented and counter to the ethics of the organization.
- NGOs often try to do a lot more with a lot less, implementing IT across many geographic locations but with a skeleton project

team. As a consequence, governance, change management, and data conversion activities tend to be under-resourced. This can have a big impact on the longer-term success of the new system and associated ways of working.

How do I ensure a technology project that is started will actually be completed?

Put very simply, focusing on good governance plus strong project management will result in good scope management. Effective governance is the means by which it is possible to steer and make timely decisions about the project. Project management is the means by which the project timeline/roadmap, key milestones, and budget are properly mapped out. A well-selected and resourced project team is also important. Make sure that the solution being designed and developed remains within the budget and timeline while still meeting the business needs. When this starts to get out of sync, the issues should be raised to the correct level of project governance to discuss and make choices where necessary.

A clear and compelling vision for the project that really speaks to the staff and shows them why this IT change project is vital for the organization is also very important. This is the motivating glue (see Chapter 3) that keeps staff interested and willing to invest time, often over and above their day job, to see the project go live and adapt to the new ways of working.

Always include a project budget contingency, even for the best, most detailed project plans! There are numerous ways to calculate contingency that we do not cover here. For a simple approach, we suggest considering a range, especially for projects where there is considerable scope uncertainty in the early phases—for example, a contingency could be in the range of 10 to 20 percent of the overall project budget.

Once the technology project is completed, how do you ensure the technology is used?

A number of key steps need to occur prior to the project going live to increase the likelihood that the new tools and ways of working will be used. Build business ownership throughout the project life cycle, making it clear that the solution belongs not to the project team but to the organization. This can be done via constant, clear communications and by active stakeholder management. Know who the key influences are in the organization, get them (and as many other staff as possible) involved at various stages in the project, especially around solution design, testing, data conversion, and training.

Keep the new solution simple. Rather than investing in customization, invest in change management and training to help staff quickly learn and appreciate the new system and ways of working. We have seen some good examples of this with CRM systems, where the improved analytical capacity has enabled staff to better analyze and manage their interactions with supporters and donors. Measuring success and sharing success stories with staff will highlight the benefits of the new system and encourage others to try new ways of working.

Identify key performance indicators that show how the system is being used. Ensure the support team is tracking these and actively discussing the results with the steering committee, especially in the first six months after going live. This proactive tracking will help identify any areas where system uptake is not meeting expectation and mitigating actions can be identified.

Is there a way to bring the cost and risk of big IT projects down?

IT implementations can be perceived as very costly, especially if the previous system is basic and therefore cheap in comparison. The hiring cost for contractors or vendor staff with skills in a particular IT product can seem exorbitant when compared with internal salaries in the NGO. At the same time the project may feel like a collection of big risks. There are a number of factors that can influence the risk profile and total cost of the IT project. They fall into four main areas.

Strategic level
- Have an IT strategy and keep it current. Such a document provides an overview of all the technology in the organization and how technology enables the agency. Any new technology investments should be checked against the strategy to avoid costly mistakes of investing in solutions that are incompatible or don't meet long-term strategic objectives.
- Make the most of being part of a global family and seek opportunities to learn from others. Tap into forums that allow you to share insights from other NGOs. This can have a big influence in how you design and implement your project and may help avoid costly pitfalls.

Scope management
- Have an 80/20 mind-set. Be willing to accept a solution that is an 80 percent fit, as most often the final 20 percent contains the high risks, complexity, and ultimately the cost overruns.
- Pay attention to data privacy and security in the solution design. Ensure new IT systems and processes have robust security that protect against breaches as these can be costly and very damaging to an organization.
- If there is an apparent budget and scope gap, it may be necessary to make the hard decision to delay the IT change project rather than risk starting and not being able to finish.
- Make sure there is a defined risk and issue management process and that reviewing risks is a standing agenda item for the project steering committee.

Resourcing
- Invest in a good project manager you can trust to manage the project scope and budget. Make sure they are supported by an engaged steering committee.
- Depending on the location of the project, there might be options to resource project support from other locations where the skills are available at a lower cost.
- Consider the skills needed to support the project and the scale of the project. If you have a relatively small implementation, it is possible to recruit new staff who have prior experience on very large, complex implementations but in a more junior role than the one you are recruiting them for. This can work because they are likely to be cheaper than a more senior resource, and they should be able to adapt to the role you have for them based on their prior experience.
- Consider recruiting one or more resources with business analysis skills if you don't already have employees with this skill set. Business analysts are important in technology projects as their key skill is the ability to interpret business requirements into technical specifications, thus providing a bridge between the business and IT departments.
- Outsourcing. Consider options to have an outsourced/shared services solution.

Vendor relationships
- Build relationships with IT vendors. Depending on the type of IT

you are implementing, you may have licensing costs, support costs, and so on. Are there ways you can build a relationship with a vendor that might result in lower costs (for example, can you negotiate as a global international NGO family rather than a single entity?)? Can you use a peak organization like NetHope, Techsoup, or others that may be able to help your organization access discounted rates?

- Avoid time and materials contracts with vendors unless you have watertight scope, and even then consider it very carefully.
- If you select the software provider to also be your implementing vendor, be very tight on scope management as there is a risk of high levels of customization.

Why don't affiliates/members of the same international NGO family develop and share common technology?

International NGOs should be considering, and where applicable adopting, family-wide common technology approaches. There are a few successful examples where international NGOs have done this, but overall it's disappointing that more haven't. An obsession with uniqueness even within the same international NGO family as well as complex board/senior management governance structures combine to be the biggest impediments to shared technology. While each international NGO family member/affiliate has their own local board, often with greater power and influence than the global family board, it is very difficult to achieve common technology and ways of working. This can diminish what the global family NGO can achieve. Furthermore, as the world becomes increasingly interconnected, the stakeholders who interact with international NGOs are going to expect them to be interconnected too, and currently far too many are not. Those international NGOs who have been able to roll out technology across their global family may soon find they have a significant advantage.

Why can't someone else develop and run systems for multiple NGOs?

Just as international NGOs should be considering IT strategy and common technology approaches across the entire family, organizations should be considering options for shared services. There are many potential benefits to this approach, not least cost and efficiency savings. Up to now there has been limited uptake, something we hope will change in the future. Toby Porter sees the potential for "the emergence of locally owned and run social businesses, in countries with large NGO presence and activities" that provide services to NGOs.[5] It would be very interesting to see this developed.

Unfortunately, until NGOs are willing to put less focus on their uniqueness and boards and leadership start to embrace different ways of working, it may be some time before we see significant examples of IT shared services for NGOs.

How do we ensure that the development drives our IT systems rather than the other way around?

Consider establishing a governance body that reviews all change projects for the organization (some call it a project review board). This is essentially a group of cross-functional leaders (business and technology) who act as a review and steering group to oversee all proposed change project ideas (not just technology ones). They ensure all projects at the concept stage have a clear vision and benefit to the organization and fit within the strategic direction. They also pick up any duplications where a newly proposed project overlaps with another. Any project that is reviewed and approved by a project review board can be assumed to fit well within the organization's development drivers. This would be a valuable first checkpoint for IT projects to ensure they serve the organization's mission *before* any intensive work starts in the feasibility phase.

Having the right project vision is critical. Articulate a vision and objectives about how the project supports the organization's development goals. State this at the outset and repeat it often. Define project measures of success to illustrate how the project will support the development goals. When setting up the project team, process owners, data owners, and other staff involved in the project, create a balance of business and technology staff plus some with business analysis skills. Getting this mix right will be a foundation for a balanced technology solution to support development outcomes. Balance is the key. Too much control by business resources, especially those with limited or no IT experience, can result in a suboptimal system design. Too much control by IT resources can result in a technology-heavy solution that doesn't meet the business needs.

Active business involvement in the project from the beginning is important. The more you involve the business, the greater the level of ownership felt and also the more likely the solution will meet business needs. Business involvement can take many forms. Here are a few suggestions:

- Business representatives on the project team (discussed in detail already)
- Business representatives appointed as process owners and data owners (select people who are respected in the organization and will invest the time to do the role with rigor)
- Business representatives involved in workshops and testing to both design and check the system
- Potential to use "super users" (business staff, over and above process and data owners) who are involved with the project and can act as additional support once the system is live and be involved in end-user training
- Regular project communications that articulate a compelling vision for staff that resonates with the organization's overall vision and mission
- Measure success as quickly as possible and share success stories

It is difficult to convince our donors and supporters that investment in IT is a good use of resources, and we have limited unrestricted income to self-fund IT investment. What can we do?

We have already said a lot in this chapter about the issues with overhead investment, and we acknowledge the sheer scale of the challenge in influencing public perception on this matter, in particular about IT being strategic. It may be a very slow journey to change public opinion, yet NGOs need to invest in IT now. What can organizations do? Consider some of the cost-saving measures mentioned earlier as a way to reduce the overall cost of an IT change project. NGOs could also try one or more of the following.

- Include an IT component in grant proposals with a strong story about how IT will bring value to the grant implementation. This is most relevant for information communication technology for development but more difficult for operational support solutions.
- Approach new and different donors who have a background in technology or an understanding of the value of technology.
- Depending on the composition of your board and their reach with your donors and supporters, consider asking board members to represent and lobby on behalf of the organization.
- Approach donors with a compelling story about the value of IT and offer to match funding to the amount they are willing to give.

- Engage with the peak body in your location to seek their support on raising the profile and educating on this issue (a peak body is the organization that represents and advocates for NGOs, for example in the United States there is Interaction and InsideNGO, and in Australia there is ACFID, the Australian Council for International Development).

I'm personally uncomfortable with IT as I have no prior experience and I have limited time or interest to learn more. What can I do to quickly gain a base level of knowledge?

Consider finding a technology "reverse mentor."[6] There is much emphasis on looking at more experienced, more senior people to act as mentors, but when it comes to technology, there is merit in considering youth mentoring.

Recruiting the right IT skills into the organization can also give reassurance that you will be provided with information for decision-making in a manner that is easy to understand for your level of knowledge.

Use your network and talk to others in your international NGO family, outside the family, and outside the sector if relevant. If you are going to be engaged with a particular software product or vendor, ask the vendor to arrange a site visit to one of their previous clients. These site visits can be a way to invest minimal time for maximum learning.

How do you get the organization excited about technology?

Communication is key. Have leadership team members and other senior staff talk about how technology enables the organization to achieve its vision and mission, particularly with regard to campaigning or programming impact. Share success stories from other organizations, not necessarily about how the IT implementation was done but about the results it achieved and how it enabled the organization to achieve better impact. Consider sending non-IT staff to events focused on the benefits of technology so they can learn from others and share their insights on their return. A good example is CRS, who have been hosting an information communication technology for development conference once or twice a year since 2010 and share many resources online.[7] Organizations like NetHope also provide great forums and online resources for members to learn about the benefits of technology.[8] InsideNGO holds regular forums and also a large annual conference with a focus on strengthening the operational and management capacity of international NGOs.[9]

Notes

1. James Crowley and Morgana Ryan, *Building a Better International NGO: Greater than the Sum of the Parts?* (Boulder, CO: Kumarian Press, 2013).

2. Jeri Eckhart Queenan, Jacob Allen, and Jari Tuomala, "Stop Starving Scale: Unlocking the Potential of Global NGOs," Bridgespan Group, April 15, 2013, p. 4.

3. Queenan, Allen, and Tuomala, "Stop Starving Scale"; Dan Pallotta, "The Way We Think about Charity Is Dead Wrong," TED Talk, March 2013, https://www.ted.com/talks/dan_pallotta_the_way_we_think_about_charity_is_dead _wrong?language=en; Crowley and Ryan, *Building a Better International NGO*; Bryan Breckenridge and Anne Maloney, "Why Fund Tech for Nonprofits?" Box.org, n.d., http://www.techsoup.org/SiteCollectionDocuments/blog-why-fund -tech-for-nonprofits-white-paper-pdf.

4. Breckenridge and Maloney, "Why Fund Tech for Nonprofits?"

5. Toby Porter, "Can We Future-Proof Our NGOs?" Devex, January 15, 2016, https://www.devex.com/news/can-we-future-proof-our-ngos-87596.

6. Don Tapscott, "Why My Kids Are My 'Reverse Mentors,'" August 11, 2015, http://dontapscott.com/2015/09/why-my-kids-are-my-reverse-mentors/.

7. See http://www.ict4dconference.org/; http://www.ict4dconference.org/archive.

8. See http://solutionscenter.nethope.org.

9. InsideNGO, https://www.insidengo.org/mission.htm.

7

Making Sense of Mergers in the Development and Humanitarian Sectors

In recent years, there has been a growing clamor for consolidation in the international development and humanitarian sectors. This is an extraordinarily crowded landscape, with many large, medium, small, and tiny organizations with overlapping objectives, capacities, and programs. Not only does this create a very complex landscape for donors, it can also make for a highly confusing and chaotic environment for stakeholders and beneficiaries. Why can't these organizations combine their efforts and expertise to simplify the sector, save costs, and deliver assistance more effectively?

We have seen some good examples of this in the past, such as the high-profile merger of Merlin and Save the Children announced in 2013. There have been several cases where smaller national NGOs have joined up to become a member of a larger international organization, confederation or federation. An example is Novib (Netherlands Organization for International Development), which became an affiliate of Oxfam International in 1996 and renamed as Oxfam Novib in 2006. There were similar journeys for two local Australian NGOs, Community Aid Abroad and Australia Freedom from Hunger Campaign, which merged in 1992. The newly merged entity then became a member of Oxfam International, changing their name to Oxfam Australia. Often when this happens, the new members retain their own local governance as well as participating (sometimes reluctantly) in the governance of the new international federation or network. The various kinds of organizations, federations, and networks that have developed from this process have been reviewed and critiqued in *Building a Better International NGO*.[1]

187

At a tactical level, we are seeing some isolated case-by-case movement in this direction with the growing popularity of consortia and coalitions, where donors combine their resources related to a specific set of goals and often demand that contributing NGOs come together to support larger-scale and more integrated programs. Some of these are structured around particular places, for example, in dealing with the complex needs of a particular country—such as Somalia. Others are organized around a particular issue, such as the battle against malaria in Africa. However, these are still the exceptions rather than the rule, and more often than not these consortia will disband once the program has come to an end.

However, at an overall strategic level, the number of mergers is fairly minimal. Where they have occurred, they have often arguably been a marriage of convenience, with one agency in some difficulty and a merger being a pragmatic solution for both parties.

In our view, there is strong logic in favor of much more transformative consolidation. There are many substantive reasons to support this argument, such as economies of scale, economies of scope or skill, or just the need to dramatically simplify an overcrowded and complex NGO landscape. Whatever the specific arguments, the benefits can be boiled down to more impactful programs, reduced costs, meeting unmet need, and increasing the possibility of innovative breakthroughs in the fight against poverty and injustice. In the next section we discuss some of these rationale in more detail and map each of the typical arguments on to these potential benefit areas.

We also pause to reflect on what we judge to be some more questionable arguments and reflect on the likelihood of these coming to the fore in this sector. We review some of the very significant and troublesome intrinsic barriers to consolidation, and then explore what might be done to overcome these challenges.

We need to progress with caution. Combining two or more organizations is a tremendously demanding and high-risk task, with many opportunities to trip up. Success requires planning, effort, discipline, and strong leadership. Despite the compelling case for more consolidation, experience from the private sector shows that mergers and acquisitions can prove challenging, often produce underwhelming results, or simply fail.

Later in this chapter, we examine the key phases of any merger process, as well as the important strands of work that permeate each of these phases. Then we discuss some of the typical risks that can come into play in these situations and suggest some very practical responses.

Consolidation Rationale and Barriers

Key Arguments in Support of Consolidation

When evaluating the specific rationale for any possible combination, it is useful to establish a clear set of goalposts. These goalposts can be anchored around four very straightforward benefit areas. First we are seeking **better-quality programs** with stronger and more sustainable impact, perhaps benefiting from complementary sets of interventions, complementary expertise, or complementary stakeholder relationships. Next we would like to achieve improved **cost efficiency** at all stages of the program cycle, for example, by spreading fixed costs over a larger scale and volume of programs. We would like to be able to better address **unmet need** that cannot be reached by either organization today and is not likely to be met by others. Finally, we want to increase the opportunity for **innovative breakthroughs** and the ability to help bring them to material scale.

We can see that these benefit areas are derived, individually or collectively, from a number of factors or arguments. There are at least six that deserve particular consideration:

1. Economies of scale, scope, and skill for fixed/overhead costs.
2. Economies of scale, scope, and skill within program countries.
3. Synergies across funding streams.
4. Complementary expertise and organization capacity.
5. Ability to attract, use, and develop the best people.
6. Achieving minimum efficient scale to be a credible contributor.

Table 7.1 sets out a summary mapping of each argument to the four benefit areas introduced above. As we review the mapping, we can see that all of these arguments contribute in some way toward all of the four criteria.

1. Economies of scale for fixed/overhead costs. Large NGOs are increasingly facing a difficult dilemma. On one hand, there is a growing clamor for more impactful programs, adapted more precisely to local context, with greater controls, stronger monitoring and evaluation, and more comprehensive engagement with stakeholders, beneficiaries, and other local bodies. Meeting these expectations is costly and involves developing and maintaining key technical expertise, strong management, and investment in professional robust systems and processes. All of this implies higher (predominantly fixed) costs at international and local levels. On the other hand we are seeing an ever-growing scrutiny of costs, particularly costs

Table 7.1 Typical Arguments Mapped to Four Key Benefit Areas

Factors that Could Contribute to Four Benefit Areas	Cost Efficiency	Impactful Programs	Unmet Need	Innovation/ Breakthroughs
Economies of scale, scope, and skill for fixed/overhead costs	●	●	O	O
Economies of scale, scope, and skill within program countries	O	●	●	O
Synergies across funding streams	O	●	O	O
Complementary expertise or organizational capacity	O	●	O	O
Ability to attract, use, and develop the best people	O	●	O	O
Achieving minimum efficient scale to be a credible contributor in broader partnerships and coalitions	O	●	O	O

relating to management and administration, fundraising, and back-office functions. NGOs somehow have to learn to manage within this tricky conundrum.

Consolidation seems a logical way of responding to this challenge. It could help by providing a means of spreading what are largely fixed overhead and back-office costs over a broader portfolio of programs and countries. It could also help justify essential new investments in systems and capacity that is vital for the future success of any modern agency.

2. Economies of scale within program countries. The fixed or overhead costs of operating in any developing country can be considerable, potentially in excess of $1 million per annum—just to secure the local expertise and capacity to be a credible and reliable long-term contributor. NGOs need a deep understanding of the local social, political, and economic context. They need to invest in local relationships to develop trust and build capacity for program design, monitoring and evaluation, technical support, finance, HR, and IT. In practice, you can't hop in and out of a program country overnight: this is neither efficient nor effective. Building local trust and capacity takes coordination and investment, and is unlikely to be justifiable unless there is a sufficient volume of program activity. Otherwise the ratio of direct to indirect costs for any individual program risks being both indefensible and unsustainable.

To address this challenge, some NGOs, even very large ones, are starting to refocus their attention on a smaller subset of program countries, in some cases reducing from more than fifty to a handful of key priority countries.

A merger or combination at a local level could help resolve these issues by providing a number of potential benefits. For example, it could:

- Reduce in-country costs through rationalizing offices, management positions, support infrastructure and functions, and technical support.
- Simplify the relationship management workload with a range of local stakeholders—for the benefit of the local partners as well as the NGO.
- Simplify the crowded situation in some program countries where there are many NGOs competing for local stakeholder attention, which risks creating an inefficient, confusing, and chaotic environment for local beneficiaries and stakeholders alike.

3. Synergies across Funding Streams. Merging to create a larger agency with a combined funding stream can create additional flexibility and resilience, especially where there is the opportunity to optimize the combination of institutional funding (typically restricted) and private funding (typically unrestricted) to best effect. There are a number of potential advantages.

First, institutional donors often prefer their contribution to be complemented by funding from the NGO concerned, as it signals a deeper commitment from the organization. Hence, a larger source of private funding could help attract more institutional grants.

Second, access to private funding is very useful for NGOs because it allows them to respond quickly to new crisis situations, well before it may be feasible to organize a direct fundraising call for that particular need—recognizing that it can often take some time to bring a new crisis to the attention of public and donor governments. Médecins San Frontières' impressive ability to respond so quickly to the Ebola outbreak in 2013 in West Africa was a good illustration of this.

A combined income stream can also help smooth out the peaks and troughs in donor funding. Securing a balanced and reliable flow of funding is essential for all NGOs, and a constant challenge as donors evolve their priorities and criteria in response to changing public and government attitudes. Depending on one or a few major donors can be a considerable risk. Indeed, many institutional donors are more comfortable funding larger programs, where they are one of several supporters, often in some form of consortium. This approach provides a degree of reassurance that a program is more likely stronger if others are also willing to fund it. It allows each donor to support a broader set of programs, diversifying their portfolio of projects, and thus hedging their own reputation risk.

Finally, private funding can be valuable for meeting the costs of core operations, such as basic infrastructure, management, and other supporting functions. Few institutional donors are keen to finance these requirements.

4. Complementary expertise or organizational capacity. Merging to create a larger agency can be a way to provide a more tailored and flexible selection of interventions for a particular local context, beyond what a small NGO can manage on its own. Frequently, NGOs will have built up a depth of expertise and a reputation in a certain area, such as health, education, or emergency. As the needs of particular countries evolve, NGOs may feel it necessary to develop new areas of expertise and capacity. This can be done organically over a period of time, though this can be slow and require considerable investment. A merger can be a practical and faster way to do this.

5. Better able to attract, use, and develop the best people. The primary assets of any NGO are its people; its cumulative knowledge, learning, and know-how; its relationships; and its reputation. Hence, the ability to attract, develop, and retain the best people is the most important single success factor for any NGO. In this regard, NGOs are comparable to any professional services firm.

This is a particularly sensitive topic in respect to mergers. On one hand, a merger can bring considerable benefits since larger agencies can offer more secure careers, tailored to each individual's area of interest and ambition, with the flexibility to grow each person's expertise and contributions as their careers develop. This explains why larger, established agencies can find it easier to attract specialist talent than smaller, less well-known agencies. (This point is explored in greater detail in the discussion on the benefits of a matrix organization model in Chapter 3.)

On the other hand (as we discuss in more detail later in this chapter), merger integration can be a very challenging and high-risk time in the life of any organization. Unless the transition is well managed, there's a good possibility that some of the best people might be distracted or demotivated or even leave during the integration process.

6. Minimum efficient scale to be a credible and effective contributor.
We have already noted that the development and humanitarian arena is a
complex and populated space, with an enormous number of organizations
of all sizes, and with very good intentions, competing for the attention of
both donors and local stakeholders. Add to this the view that the days of the
independent NGO operators, ploughing their own furrow in rural areas in
the poorest developing countries, is the exception rather than the norm. Not
only are there grave doubts about the efficacy of this approach, there is a
declining list of countries where local governments will continue to allow
NGOs to work in such a way.

Modern, large-scale development programs need combined efforts,
ideally led by local government bodies, involving credible local
stakeholders as well as relevant private-sector firms (local and
international). NGOs can contribute, but they may require a minimum scale
of operation to be regarded as useful and credible, to be taken seriously by
donors, and to be a worthwhile partner for local stakeholders. A dramatic
wave of consolidation may be necessary to get to that place.

Increasingly, larger NGOs realize they can have more impact when
working together to implement joint programs. As a result the number of
partnerships, coalitions, and consortia is growing. One good example is
the Global Fund (http://www.theglobalfund.com) to tackle AIDS,
tuberculosis, and malaria, which mobilizes and invests nearly US$4
billion a year to support programs run by local experts in countries and
communities most in need. Another example is a consortium in south
central Somalia implementing a four-year grant secured by Save the
Children (lead agency) and implemented with ACF, Concern Worldwide,
and Oxfam.

As we outline these arguments, we add a note of caution. Size is *not* the
only criteria that local stakeholders and donors need to consider. Indeed,
there are plenty of contrarian examples of very small niche and innovative
organizations that have an impact far in excess of their size in terms of funds
or numbers of staff.

Examples of Some Questionable Criteria

What are some of the more questionable criteria that one might come across
when considering mergers? One would expect (or hope) that these are more
prevalent in the private (business) sector than in the development and
humanitarian sectors. Nonetheless, it is helpful to be on guard for any of
these kinds of drivers. These are summarised in Table 7.2, which includes
some of our reflections on each.

Table 7.2 Questionable Arguments in Favor of Mergers

Arguments	Our Response
Use the merger to fix fundamental problems in an agency's approach or management capacity	Best to address fundamental issues head on; a merger is a very disruptive process and unless there is sound rationale, there is a risk that a merger may just distract from the problems that need to be tackled.
Use the merger to further the career ambitions of a CEO or chairperson	Ambitions of individuals or their careers should never be the driving force of a merger— individuals come and go.
To get the upper hand over a competitor you have found problematic in the marketplace	If another agency is proving more successful at addressing key funding streams, they are likely to be doing something right; better to improve own capability and results to be more competitive. Also, competition between NGOs for funding is a good thing: it helps raise the performance bar for all.

Key Barriers to Mergers in the Development and Humanitarian Sector

The barriers to mergers are many. A number are specific to this sector, and several mirror what one comes across in any sector (see Table 7.3).

1. Lack of typical drivers for consolidation around revenue, profit, and shareholder value. First it is useful to note the fundamental differences with the dynamic in the private sector, where we see frequent mergers and acquisitions. Many of the drivers that are important in that sector—such as revenue and profit growth, shareholder value, growth for its own sake, or the need to gain a competitive edge—are not as relevant in the development and humanitarian sector and do not make a defensible rationale for consolidation. Hence, we can see that one of the first barriers is the absence of the kinds of drivers that might be the case in the private sector.

2. Conflicting philosophies about development. Each NGO will have its own set of values, approaches, and methods that have been developed and refined over decades of experience. A valid worry is that an NGO's particular approach and the nuances around how it works could be diluted or lost during a merger. This could result in loss of valuable learning. It could also result in a subsequent loss of talent, particularly those key people who may resent the changes implied.

Table 7.3 Selected Barriers to Consolidation and Possible Responses

Barriers	Response
Lack of typical drivers for consolidation around revenue, profit, and shareholder value	• Focus on impact and cost efficiency • Quantify both as rigorously as possible
Conflicting philosophies about development	• Accept that developing a unified theory of change is likely to be an important foundation step to unlock the integration benefits. However, it is essential to have a thoughtful, professional process to combine insights and learning, being diligent to build on the combined best rather than deferring to the customs of the biggest. • Develop a combined knowledge database on unified process/system
Wasted investment in key enabling systems and processes	• Accept that unifying key processes and systems is likely to be a core part of integration, unlocking the practical benefits of a larger integrated agency (e.g., in finance, performance management, HR, knowledge management) • Define clearly, as part of detailed integration planning, the cost and other benefits of integration as well as the inevitable investment that will be required to unify systems and processes
Fewer positions for key executives and other senior directors	• Professional process to establish new integrated leadership team (transparent and fair) • Carefully managed transition • Maintain input of previous executives in other ways where possible (but beware of risks)
Board reluctant to lose their influence and/or independence	• Professional process to establish new, skills based, integrated board • Carefully managed transition • Maintain input of previous board members in other ways where possible (but beware of risks of a shadow board!)

3. Wasted investment in key systems and processes. Investing in strengthening enabling systems such as finance, HR, and knowledge management is a considerable challenge for all NGOs. If an agency has made good progress, or perhaps are midway through an important investment, its employees may fear that all their efforts will be wasted in the course of an integration process.

4. Fewer positions for key executives and other senior officers. As is the case in any merger, a combined entity will (most likely) have one chair, one chief executive, one program director, one finance director, and so on. Hence it is likely that the merger may not be welcomed by all of the current leaders from the organizations, given that some will lose their jobs. It takes a brave individual or team to recommend a merger that could result in their own redundancy.

5. Board reluctance to lose their influence or independence. Board members understandably tend to get emotionally committed to their particular NGO. They value the feeling of making a useful contribution to the mission and goals of their agency. Consolidation is bound to challenge the status quo, which can be uncomfortable in itself, and will inevitably result in a reduced number of available board positions. Where a board has the occasional member (if we are being candid) with a reasonable amount of ego and self-importance, do not be surprised if they show a limited appetite for consolidation. This concern is on top of the current trend toward smaller, skills-based boards, which will already result in a considerable reduction in the number of available board positions.

Stages of an Integration Process

Often a small number of crucial choices are likely to have a major impact on how the integration process proceeds. These choices affect how the organization feels about the integration process and will have a major bearing on the ultimate success or failure of the combined entity. These are very practical choices; although fairly easy to articulate, they require considerable thought. The more agencies consider and address them in advance of concluding the merger transaction, the better.

Examples of Crucial Choices in Merger Planning

Pace of integration: How much integration will we seek to implement during the first twelve to eighteen months immediately after the transaction? What will be tackled in subsequent stages? Which parts of the agency will be unaffected?

Appointments: How do you manage the tricky and sensitive appointments process to the new unified structure, particularly for key leadership roles? Will this be done quickly based on the best information available? Will there be a formal application process with interviews? What are the merits of a more considered or staggered set of appointments over the first three or four months? (Those who have lived through a serious merger will appreciate that the HR function is often stretched and truly tested during a merger integration process.)

Communication: How much do we communicate before the deal, when the rumor mills may be working overdrive—particularly when we know that keeping plans confidential can be even more difficult than in the private sector? How bluntly and honestly should we communicate once the deal is announced, about what we know, what we half know, and particularly what we don't yet know? How do we ensure consistent communications to staff across the two merging entities? Will there be job losses? If so, will they be voluntary or compulsory redundancies? Will some jobs be relocated to different locations? In the uncertainty and anxiety of a merger situation, unsurprisingly staff members tend to worry about very basic questions: Do I still have a job? If so, where will it be? Will my pay change? Who will my boss be? Who will my new colleagues be? Is my pension still safe?

Setting the tone: What are the key principles or ways of working that the new leadership wants to emphasize, bearing in mind that there is a short and fertile time window for leadership to establish clear ground rules for the new entity? If this is not utilized, it may take a long time to achieve the same end once the integration process has begun.

Leadership style and standards of behaviors: The weeks and months leading up to and directly after a merger transaction is a unique period in the life of any organization. The entire workforce will go through a whirlwind of emotions with a mix of excitement, anticipation, and fear. Senior leadership is significantly more in the limelight during this sensitive period, compared to normal times when most employees are at best only vaguely aware of who the leadership teams are and what they actually do. This is a one-time opportunity to establish your reputation, the expected standards and behaviors, and the leadership style you and your team would like to be known for. Of course, as the old saying goes, actions speak more loudly than words!

Stages of a Merger Integration Process

Here we discuss the typical key phases of any merger process and explore the main activities and priorities that are likely to come to the fore at each stage. Every transaction will have its own particular nuances.

Predeal planning: This is the phase before the negotiation starts in earnest. It is likely to involve some closely guarded analysis, using the best available (sometimes limited) data, typically comparing a particular combination with potential alternatives. This phase can last several months or longer, and confidentiality is essential. The work is normally carried out by a handful of carefully selected individuals, typically senior executives and board members, though it could involve some off-the-record discussions with key personnel from the other party, recognizing that mergers in this sector are likely to be friendly. For a range of obvious reasons, hostile takeovers are extremely unlikely in this sector.

Deal closure: This is the phase during the weeks or months leading up to the transaction. By now, leadership is broadly convinced of the merits of the transaction. This is an extremely sensitive stage, again involving a handful of key individuals selected from senior executives and board members—although some key functional experts may get involved to deal with critical legal, HR, IT, or important programmatic issues. Confidentiality continues to be essential to ensure inaccurate information does not leak out and particularly to ensure that both organizations are able to continue their day-to-day program delivery and other ongoing work.

First three to four weeks, immediately post deal: The three or four weeks immediately after the announcement of the deal is an absolutely critical stage. During this time, the leadership team must come to a clear position on the kinds of crucial choices outlined above, if they haven't already done so. There are a number of important tasks to progress at pace. These are usually coordinated by a carefully selected group of approximately five to eight people, with a mix of the key functional skills— HR, program, finance, IT, communications, legal, and so on. This group can draw from other key specialists as needed, but generally it is better if both workforces are encouraged to get on with their day jobs (sometimes, this is easier said than done).

By the end of this period, the leadership team should have a high-level blueprint showing what the combined organization will look like after integration, indicating broadly what is expected to be integrated, what will be left as is (at least during the first wave of the integration process), and what might be spun off into a separate entity. In addition, they will need to establish the new transition leadership structure(s), showing clearly how day-to-day management of both organizations will proceed in tandem with the detailed integration design and planning work. Another key output is a practical transition plan, with a clear roadmap for the first three to four months. Finally, they must select the leaders who will be responsible for the detailed integration design and planning work in the next phase.

First three months, integration design and planning: This is the intensive and detailed design/planning phase for the new combined entity.

Those entrusted to lead this phase are typically released from their normal responsibilities to concentrate on this important task, and should have full access to all available operational and financial information. The positioning of these roles is very important to create the right incentives and atmosphere. In particular, those who lead the design planning stage should feel they have the opportunity to be appointed to key positions—after the cutover, once the detailed integration planning work is complete. Encouraging a degree of cooperation and competition between the leaders of the integration design teams and those entrusted to continue to run day-to-day operations can sometimes be a healthy part of the selection process.

From three to eighteen months, making the integration happen: This is the period when most of the hard and detailed integration work takes place. This often involves a sensitive redundancy program (voluntary or involuntary). There may be significant efforts to unify the structures and processes across a range of functions. This will probably demand careful consultation, communication, and project management. It might also involve some training and/or investment to migrate both organizations to the same processes and systems. Some of this work might need to be phased to align with the feasibility of relocating staff into the desired physical premises or timed to take account of the expiration of existing contractual constraints.

Strands of Work Through Each Phase of Integration Process

A number of important strands of activity flow through each phase. Each of these will come into the spotlight during particular intensive periods. They include:

- **Executive governance** (thinking through the new integrated board structure and executive leadership arrangements, during and after transition)
- **HR** (dealing with crunch issues such as appointments, trade unions, pay, pensions, and redundancies)
- **Finance** (keeping on top of cost and income implications, as well as integration investment requirements)
- **Internal communications** (need to provide regular updates, develop trust)
- **External communications** (with regulators, customers, suppliers, and the general public, potentially in all locations where the two agencies operate)
- **Legal and contracts** (dealing with critical license and other key

Table 7.4 Mapping of Key Strands of Work Against Stages of an Integration Process

	Predeal Planning	[Closure] First Three Weeks	First Three Months	[Cut Over] Three to Eighteen Months
Leadership and Governance	• Small tight core team of key executives and board members • Focus on combination logic and benefits and possible blockages and risks	• Transition oversight board • Articulating and communicating logic • Dealing with surprises	• Transition oversight to emerging new unified leadership team • Helicopter view of logic in practice and benefits tracking • Dealing with surprises	• Single unified structure after full cutover • Benefits tracking
HR/People	• Plan for key executives and roles • Hypothesis of HR integration strategy • Contingency planning	• People model/mapping • Appointments/streaming approach • Unions • Pay and pensions	• People model/mapping • Appointments/streaming approach • Unions • Pay and pensions	• Implementing new integrated HR management processes (performance management, training, career development, etc.)
Finance	• Robust model of projected costs and benefits • Assumptions	• Refined model of projected costs and benefits • Better access to key people/numbers	• New integrated budget and plans	• Normal financial controls
Internal Communications	• Careful management of confidentiality—very tight control	• Honest and direct communication	• Honest and direct communication	
External Communication	• Tight control	• Key customers, suppliers, and partners • Careful management of external media	• Maintain dialogue	• Maintain rhythm

Legal and Regulation	• Key issues/constraints	• Key issues/constraints	• Key issues/constraints	
Infrastructure and Services	• Key issues/constraints	• High-level blueprint	• Detailed blueprint and integration plan • Support to other integration design teams	
IT and Enabling Systems	• Hypothesis	• High-level blueprint	• Detailed blueprint and integration plan • Support to other integration design teams	• Follow-through
Key Milestones	• Assemble core transition team and transition	• Select and mobilize integration design teams	• Approve new integration plans and new detailed structures	• Cut over to new plans and fully unified responsibility structure

Note: Gray highlighted entries are areas of emphasis/focus at each stage in the process.

legal or contractual aspects that can get in the way of the integration process)

- **IT and enabling systems** (unifying IT systems for critical areas such as finance, HR, or monitoring and evaluation can be important for the integration process. This could be dealt with as part of the previous strand(s), but sometimes merits attention as a key strand in its own right.) Finally, some form of program management unit can be very useful in coordinating all of the different contributions.

The nature of the work will evolve throughout the phases and will inevitably get into much more detail after the closure of the deal, particularly in the detailed design of the combined structure and operations. Table 7.4 provides an overview of how each strand might map on to the successive phases of an integration process.

Risks, Success Factors, and Some Hints and Tips

Possible Risks

There are a large number of potential risks in any merger integration process. Unsurprisingly, many of them are around people. This can be an extraordinarily uneasy time in the life of any organization, with many competing and conflicting emotions that have the potential to disturb the normal atmosphere or sense of confidence. Important risks include the following:

1. Wild rumors can lead to **misleading or incorrect information**. In a world of uncertainty, if leadership do not provide the expected flow of information, someone else is likely to make up the answers to the questions that are worrying the staff. These answers may be inaccurate or incorrect, causing confusion and building potential barriers to a successful integration process.

2. Some of the **best staff might leave** because they feel excluded or not included in a way that they expect.

3. Some of the **best people freeze and their performance declines** because they do not know where they stand or do not feel part of the process—allowing their engagement and commitment to the combined organization to dissipate.

4. **Staff lose respect and trust for senior leadership**, which in turn can have negative impact on the success of the integration process and in the performance of the new combined entity in the years to come.

5. **Staff lose confidence in the logic of the merger** and as a result do not feel a sense of ownership and commitment toward the combined agency.

6. The **biggest partner in the merger rules the roost,** and despite attempts to the contrary, its philosophies, approaches, and systems are allowed to dominate. The new entity does not build on the combined knowledge and know-how of both agencies. This can be a considerable risk in mergers in all sectors.

7. Key **customers, suppliers, partners, and external stakeholders are left in a vacuum**, with zero or insufficient information. Mergers have an unfortunate tendency to make organizations very inward-focused, which is understandable in light of the sensitive internal integration choices and issues that come up. As a result, there is a risk that customers and stakeholders do not get their normal levels of attention and can be left uncertain as to what to expect in the future.

8. In the quest to keep everybody happy and supportive, senior leadership **fails to grasp the short window of opportunity** (twelve to eighteen months) to move the organization to a new level of performance. This can happen, for example, if leadership makes rash or popular promises (e.g., ruling out redundancies) that tie the hands of the teams who will carry out the detailed integration design process. The full benefits of the integration are probably not achieved; in the extreme case, no meaningful integration takes place.

Hints and Tips

The following is a selection of hints and tips that may help mitigate the risks described here.

- Remember: **people are the main assets of a development agency**. They can walk out the door very easily, and the best ones will walk quickly because they probably have plenty of options. This is one of the key reasons that mergers and acquisitions in the professional services sector have proved to be particularly problematic.

- A **down-to-Earth and honest approach to internal communications** is always best. Say what you know, acknowledge what you do not yet know, and communicate the logic and vision for the combined organization clearly and simply. Communicate regularly and through a variety of channels to ensure messages get through. Use whatever combinations of direct email, brown-bag lunches, cascade briefings (face-to-face or virtual), memos, or whatever works best. Honesty, consistency, and authenticity are the order of the day—no need for overly polished addresses, which carry the risk of being immediately contradicted by subsequent actions or messages.

• **Don't rush the appointment process** for key roles. An effective approach is to assign equivalent leaders from both organizations' complementary tasks, allowing them time to feel their way into the new situation and demonstrate their potential through observation and contributions, rather than relying on some rushed and questionable interview process. For example, Exec A from NGO X could take line responsibility for day-to-day activities of NGOs X and Y, while Exec B from NGO Y could be tasked with leading the integration design team. This approach can create a very constructive tension, allowing executives from both sides the opportunity to step up and show their worth in the first few months of the integration process.

• **Don't overpromise**, or promise what you can't deliver, or make promises that will constrain the performance of the organization down the road. How staff feel at the end of the integration process matters more than how they feel in the early days. If you paint an overly rosy picture (e.g., saying there will be no redundancies), you may well undermine trust and close down options in the months to come.

• Detail matters. For example, be diligent in **mapping every single staff member** from both organizations onto a common template and making sure they are treated fairly and professionally. This seems to be a very detailed point, but ensuring that no one is forgotten is essential.

• The merger process is a challenge but also an exciting **window of opportunity** to move both organizations to a new level of performance and achievement. If done well, the integration process can enable management and staff to visualize and make a leap to new levels that normally might either be difficult or take a very long time. If you don't grasp this opportunity, it will probably not arise again! The worst of all results is for both agencies to get dragged down to the lowest common denominator of the performance of either.

• Do not forget about the leaders and **staff of entities that are not planned to be affected** by the merger, at least in the first wave of integration. Ensure you communicate regularly with them and keep them informed or involved in the process. Everyone likes to be included—it is human nature. In some real situations in mergers, we have watched some great people stagnate in anticipation of the unknown.

• **Half-life rule:** unless you have achieved 50 percent of the benefits in the first twelve to eighteen months after the deal, there is a high chance that you will never see anything like the full benefits.

Conclusions

What are the main conclusions of this short overview of some of the key drivers and challenges related to consolidation and mergers in the development and humanitarian sectors?

The Logic for Consolidation Is Compelling

- Mergers can provide the opportunity to reduce cost, improve program quality, increase reach, and make breakthrough initiatives more likely to succeed.
- Mergers can provide a window of opportunity for both organizations to reach a level of performance not easily achievable on their own.
- They can give NGOs the scale and scope to be effective contributors in the larger development process (though we appreciate this argument is tricky to quantify).

Barriers Are Considerable

There are some very significant barriers. It will take tremendous courage and resolve from visionary leaders in the sector to make transformative consolidation happen.

Proceed with Care and Diligence

- The track record of mergers across all sectors is not always positive—there are a number of considerable risks if not properly executed. Progress with due care and diligence. Be very clear about what you are seeking to gain from the merger, and don't lose sight of this throughout.
- There is no single magic formula. Success simply demands careful planning, management discipline, and honesty throughout the process. There is no reason mergers based on sound, strategic logic cannot be successful.

People Are the Critical Aspect of Any Merger

People are the core asset of any organization, especially for an NGO. This is the key aspect to get right in any integration. If you can take the entire management and staff with you, then success is entirely possible.

To end, we think it is helpful to keep one particular point in mind. The capacity of good people to deliver results, even in the most difficult of situations, is often staggering. As you endeavor to strengthen your organizations in so many different ways, which we encourage and salute, bear in mind that it is the quality and energy of your staff that matters most of all. Good staff members can make good things happen when given half a chance. Hence, whatever the change you are pursuing, success will come from creating an environment that attracts, encourages, enables, and supports these great people.

Note

1. James Crowley and Morgana Ryan, *Building a Better International NGO: Better than the Sum of the Parts?* (Boulder, CO: Kumarian Press, 2013).

Bibliography

Abell, Derek. "Strategic Windows," *Journal of Marketing*, 42 (July 1978): 21–28.

Abetti, Pier A. "Jack Welch's Creative Revolutionary Transformation of General Electric and the Thermidorean Reaction (1981–2004)," *Creativity and Innovation Management*, 15, no. 1 (2006): 71–84.

Ahuja, Anjana. "The Fight Against Ebola Now Needs a Social Front," *Financial Times*, October 5, 2014; https://next.ft.com/content/15bf9afc-4b0d-11e4-b1be-00144feab7de.

Cain, Susan. *Quiet—The Power of Introverts in a World That Can't Stop Talking* (London, Penguin, 2012).

Collins, Jim. *Good to Great: Why Some Companies Make The Leap . . . and Others Don't* (New York: Collins Business, 2001).

Collins, Jim. *Good to Great and the Social Sectors: A Monograph to Accompany Good to Great* (London: Random House Business Books, 2006).

Crawford, Robert J., and N. Craig Smith. "Unilever and Oxfam: Understanding the Impacts of Business on Poverty," European Academy of Business in Society, INSEAD Case Study (2008).

Crowley, James, and Morgana Ryan, *Building a Better International NGO: Greater than the Sum of the Parts* (Boulder, CO: Kumarian Press, 2013).

Crowley, James, and Cristina Alzaga. *Connecting Business and Development, The "Rubik's Cube" of Cross Sector Collaboration* (London: Crowley Institute, 2009).

Drucker, Peter F. *Age of Discontinuity: Guidelines to Our Changing Society* (London: Heinemann, 1969).

Easterly, William. *The White Man's Burden: Why the West's Efforts to Aid the Rest Have Done So Much Ill and So Little Good* (New York: Penguin, 2006).

Gladwell, Malcolm. *The Tipping Point* (New York: Little, Brown, 2000).

Goffee, Rob, and Gareth Jones. *Why Should Anyone Be Led by You?: What It Takes to Be an Authentic Leader* (Cambridge, MA: Harvard Business School Press, 2006).

Haire, Mason. *Modern Organizational Theory* (New York: John Wiley & Sons, 1959).

Hamel, Gary, *Leading the Revolution* (New York: Plume, 2002).

207

Kegan, Robert, and Lisa Laskow Lahey. "The Real Reason People Won't Change," *Harvard Business Review* (November 2001).

Kotter, John P. "Leading Change: Why Transformation Efforts Fail," *Harvard Business Review* (March–April 1995).

Kübler-Ross, Elizabeth. *On Death and Dying* (New York: Routledge, 1969).

Organization for Economic Co-operation and Development (OECD). Development Co-operation Report 2014, *Mobilising Resources for Sustainable Development* (Paris: OECD, 2014).

O'Reilly, Charles A., and Jeffrey Pfeffer. "Southwest Airlines—Case Study," *Harvard Business Review* (January 1995).

Merrill, David W., and Roger H. Reid, *Personal Styles and Effective Performance* (New York: CRC Press, 1981).

Moïsi, Dominique. *The Geopolitics of Emotion: How Cultures of Fear, Humiliation, and Hope Are Reshaping the World* (New York: First Anchor Books, 2010).

Nokes, Sebastian, Ian Major, Alan Greenwood, and Mark Goodyear. *The Definitive Guide to Project Management: The Fast Track to Getting the Job Done on Time and on Budget* (London: FT Prentice Hall, 2003).

Porter, Michael E. *Competitive Advantage: Creating and Sustaining Superior Performance* (New York: Free Press, 1985).

Queenan, Jeri Eckhart, Jacob Allen, and Jari Tuomala. "Stop Starving Scale: Unlocking the Potential of Global NGOs," Bridgespan Group, April 15, 2013.

Ryan, Morgana, Shaun Richardson, and Paul Voutier: "Business in Development Study, Funded by AusAID," Accenture and Business for Millennium Development (2012).

Valters, Craig. "Theories of Change in International Development: Communication, Learning, or Accountability?" Justice and Security Research Program Paper 17 (London, LSE, 2014).

Index

Abell, Derek, 54
ability: motivation and ability segmentation, 48–50
accelerators (investment and aid), 119
Accenture, 37
accountability: developing a high-performance organization, 65, 68(table); selecting the right mix of approaches, 39(table); self-evaluation template for high-performance organizations, 80(table); types of change, 42
Acholi people, 96–97
adaptability style dimension, 50–53
administrative capacity: Organizational Life Cycle model, 46–47; Save the Planet careers, 76–79
Adolescence phase of organizations, 47
advocacy programs: remit and levels of decisionmaking for lines of expertise, 73(fig.)
Africa: growing involvement of global firms in development, 136–139; private equity interest, 127; proxy wars, 132–133
Aga Khan Fund for Economic Development, 140
agency-level theory of change: ambitious goals, 95; analyzing local contexts, 95–97; architecture of, 91–101; articulating the ultimate goal of your agency, 107; assessment frame-work, 107; becoming a trusted friend and advisor, 112–114; beliefs and assumptions, 94; building local trust, 111–112; change canvas, 97–99, 107; command-and-control management, 105; contextual issues, 88; fitting into the broad components of an NGO, 100–101; hierarchies of theories of change, 90–91; hope and momentum, 116; infrastructure development, 115–116; internal consultations, 108; intervention types, 108; leadership's gap in understanding, 104; overcoming organization resistance, 101–106; recognizing the agencies' legacy and baggage, 114; reflecting on past learning, successes, and failures, 106; return on social investment, 111; shifting the program focus, 115–116; strategies, interventions and principles, 99–100; stretch ideas and disruptive thinking, 109–116; stretching ambition, 110–111; summary, 100; supporting trade and enterprise in Africa, 118–119; synthesis of learning, 94, 119–120; understanding innovation, 105–106; weak practices and habits in research and learning, 105
agendas: aligning disconnected agendas and priorities, 40–42

209

agile methodology, 170(box), 174–175
aging process of organizations, 45–47
agricultural sector: ambitious goals, 95; the developing world's exclusion from subsidies, 133; India's enlightened agriculture, 128; remit and levels of decisionmaking for lines of expertise, 73(fig.)
ambition: agency-level change goals, 97; private sector-NGO partnerships, 153; questionable drivers for development-humanitarian sector mergers, 194(table)
amiable people, 51–53
AMREF Africa, 100
analytical people, 51–53, 55–56
Angola, proxy war in, 132–133
approach to change: aligning with context and content, 42–44; appraising the best approach, 30; choosing the best approach, 37–39; content, context, and, 1–2; selecting a mix of approaches, 39(table)
appropriate industries, 145, 148(table)
approval for change project, 22
assertiveness style dimension, 50–53
assessment of change, 107
Australia: development-humanitarian sector mergers, 187
Australia Freedom from Hunger Campaign, 187
authentic leadership, 15–16, 164

ballast in the workforce, 49
barriers to change: agency-level theory of change, 101–106; changes in information technology, 166–167; command-and-control management philosophy, 105; donors' understanding of change, 103; identification and analysis of, 31; organizational inertia, 104; resistance and, 20–21
basics of navigating change: authentic leadership, 15–16; clear and consistent communication, 16–17; information technology, 162–175; overcoming resistance and barriers to change, 20–21; project management disciplines, 21–25; selection and continuity of the right people, 17–

20; trust building, 25–26; understanding drivers and benefits, 12–15
battle of cultures, 3
BCG's Growth Share Matrix, 59
beliefs and assumptions about change: agency-level theory of change, 92, 93(table), 94; developing a theory of change, 106–107; supporting trade and enterprise in Africa, 120–121
benefits of organizational change: careful articulation of drivers and, 30; clarifying drivers and, 12–15; developing a high-performance organization, 67; tracking, 24–25
blockers in the workforce, 49
boards: elements of organizations, 2
budgeting: basic project management disciplines, 24; bringing IT project costs down, 180–181; causing local friction, 113; cost efficiency in development-humanitarian sector consolidation, 189–192; ensuring IT program completion, 179; global lines of expertise, 77; strands of activity during development-humanitarian sector integration, 199–202
Building a Better International NGO (Crowley and Ryan), 35, 44, 63, 66–67, 69–70, 159, 187
business basics: development driving IT systems, 183–184; levels of investment in developing countries, 139(table); vendor relationships with IT vendors, 181–182
business case: building a robust business case, 22; project management in IT projects, 168–169, 172–173; push and pull, macro and micro dimensions, 38(fig.)
business goals, linking corporate social responsibility with, 138

Cain, Susan, 16
capacity: challenges to agency-level change, 87; developing a high-performance organization, 66; example program for institutional capacity building, 123(fig.); increasing institutional capacity for development, 142; ordering and prioritizing the

components of change, 35–36; Organizational Life Cycle model, 46–47; private sector collaboration to build workforce capacity, 146, 148(table); as questionable driver for development-humanitarian sector mergers, 194(table); trade and enterprise in long-term development, 131; types of change, 42

career development: remit for lines of expertise, 74

Carlyle Fund, 127

casualties of initiating change, 26

challenges to NGOs, 4, 7–9; agency-level theory of change, 101–106; management and staff as obstacles to change, 17–20. *See also* barriers to change; resistance to change

change canvas: agency-level theory of change, 92, 93(table), 107; factors affecting the longer-term goal, 97–99; supporting trade and enterprise in Africa, 122

change process: balancing enabling and motivating glues, 44–45; ordering and prioritizing the components of change, 35–36; practical steps for the leadership structure, 29–31; practical suggestions for, 25–29; structuring and phasing, 22–23; utilizing the social styles model of people, 51–52; Valley of Despair, 26–27. *See also* basics of navigating change

children and infants: private sector development partnerships, 127

Christianity: African conflicts over religion, 133

climate, 3; climate conditions breaking a positive development cycle, 132–133; impact of climate change on economic growth in the developing world, 133; remit and levels of decisionmaking for lines of expertise, 73(fig.)

Clinton Giustra Enterprise Partnership (CGEP), 128

Cold War: proxy wars, 132–133

collaboration: purpose of a theory of change, 89. *See also* development-humanitarian sector merger; private sector-NGO partnerships

Collins, Jim, 10

command-and-control management philosophy: barriers and challenges to agency-level theory of change, 87, 102; inadequacy of, 66–67, 105

communication: articulating drivers and benefits, 30; articulating strategic shifts, 18(table); authentic leadership utilizing, 15–16; clarity and consistency, 16–17; crucial choices in development-humanitarian sector merger planning, 197; developing an approach and plan, 31; having the hard conversations, 26; planning and management, 24; purpose of a change canvas, 99; purpose of a theory of change, 89; risk factors in development-humanitarian sector mergers, 203–204; strands of activity during development-humanitarian sector integration, 199–202

communications technology: encouraging excitement about information technology, 185; ensuring technology utilization, 179–180; lines of expertise mapped to geography, 70(table); push and pull, macro and micro dimensions, 38(fig.); remit and levels of decisionmaking for lines of expertise, 73(fig.). *See also* information technology

communist system, disintegration of: motivation and ability, 48–50

Community Aid Abroad, 187

community of practice, 72

community-based organizations (CBOs), agency-level change and, 86, 88

complexity, managing, 10–11; aligning agendas and priorities, 40–42; aligning context, content, and approach to change, 42–44; choosing the best change approach, 37–39; high-impact leadership, 41–42; ordering and prioritizing the components of change, 35–36; from static to dynamic thinking, 55

concept/feasibility phase of IT change, 172–173

construction iterations, 174–175

content of change: approach, context, and, 1–2, 42–44

context of change: aligning with content and approach, 1–2, 42–44; analyzing local context, 121; applying dynamic thinking to navigating change, 58–60; architecture of agency-level theory of change, 92, 93(table); assessing and understanding local contexts, 107; becoming a trusted friend and advisor, 112–114; careful appraisal and articulation, 30; contextual factors in agency-level change, 85–88; deeper appreciation of, 10–11; encouraging the local private sector, 115; framework for analyzing local contexts, 95–97; hierarchies of theories of change, 90; high-impact leadership, 41(table); motivation and ability segmentation, 48–50; ordering and prioritizing the components of change, 36; Organizational Life Cycle model, 45–48; selecting the best intervention for the context, 110–111; social style model, 50–53; understanding and strengthening organizational glue, 44–45. *See also* agency-level theory of change
context-analysis framework, 121
contingency planning, 24
continuity of key individuals in the change team, 19
coordination: working with the scope and scale of change, 8–9
core team, selection and continuity of, 17–20
corporate investment in developing countries, 139(table)
corporate social responsibility (CSR), 138, 139(table)
cost management, 24
country programs: developing a high-performance organization, 68(table); hierarchies of theories of change, 90, 91(table); Save the Planet careers, 78–79; self-evaluation template for high-performance organizations, 80(table)
country teams: developing a high-performance organization, 68(table); self-evaluation template for high-performance organizations, 80(table)

critical path analysis, 23–24
culture of fear, 114
culture of hope, 114
culture of humiliation, 114
culture of information technology, 177
customer relationship management systems, 161–162
cut-over process, 174

decisionmaking: contextual issues with agency-level change, 88; developing a high-performance organization, 65, 68(table); having the hard conversations, 26; purpose of a theory of change, 89; push and pull, macro and micro dimensions, 38(fig.); remit for lines of expertise, 73(fig.), 74; self-evaluation template for high-performance organizations, 80(table); social styles model of people, 52; timing of actions, 54
The Definitive Guide to Project Management (Nokes et al.), 21
demand and consumption, stimulating, 130–131
Department for International Development (DFID), 128
dependencies, 23–24
design and build phase in IT projects, 173–174
development sector: becoming a trusted friend and advisor, 112–114; breaking the positive development cycle, 132–133; contextual factors in agency-level change, 85–88; growing involvement of global firms, 136–139; infrastructure development, 115–116; IT project development methodology, 170(box); key trends in private sector engagement, 137(table); positive development cycle, 131–133, 131(fig.); private sector contributions to, 126, 129, 137(table); the shifting profile of poverty, 2; stretching ambitions for progress, 110; utilizing the social styles model of people, 52
development-humanitarian sector merger: barriers to, 194–196; crucial choices in merger planning, 196–197; growing popularity of, 187–

188; implementation, 199; process phases, 197–199; questionable drivers for, 193–194; rationale for consolidation, 189–193; risk factors and risk mitigation, 202–204; strands of activity during the integration, 199–202

disruptive thinking, 109–116

donor community: accepting IT investment, 184–185; articulating strategic shifts, 18(table); barriers and challenges to agency-level theory of change, 87, 102–103; developing barriers counterbalancing, 133; driving change, 13(table); including private sector and enterprise dimensions, 142; NGO awareness of the value of enterprise, 142; NGO investment in strategic IT systems, 161–162; power relationships in agency-level change, 86; responsibility for economic inequality in developing countries, 134–135; selecting the right mix of approaches, 39(table); self-evaluation template for high-performance organizations, 81(table); signs of global economic growth, 125–126; synergies across funding streams in development-humanitarian sector mergers, 191–192

drivers of organizational change: articulating and clarifying benefits and, 12–15, 30; barriers to development-humanitarian sector merger, 194–196; clear communication of, 16–17; obstacles and barriers to development-humanitarian sector mergers, 193–196; poor framing of vision and drivers for IT change, 163; social style model, 50–53

Drucker, Peter, 54

dynamic thinking, 54–60

Easterly, William, 125

Ebola virus, 96–97

economic growth: areas of progress, 3; emphasizing infrastructure growth, 142; emphasizing pro-poor growth, 140; global firms' engagement with the developing world, 136–139;

increasing private sector engagement in Africa, 127; positive development cycle, 131–132, 131(fig.), 132–135, 134(fig.); signs of global growth, 125–126; supporting trade and enterprise in Africa, 118–124. *See also* private sector-NGO partnerships

economies of scale, 189–191

education programs: remit and levels of decisionmaking for lines of expertise, 73(fig.)

elements of successful change, 1, 10–11. *See also* approach to change; basics of navigating change; content of change; context of change

emergency programs: remit and levels of decisionmaking for lines of expertise, 73(fig.)

employment and wages: importance of trade and enterprise in long-term development, 130–131; private sector collaboration to build workforce capacity, 146

enablement management: remit and levels of decisionmaking for lines of expertise, 73(fig.)

enabling glue, 44–45

enabling processes: selecting the right mix of approaches, 39(table)

enterprise and trade: accelerating economic growth in the developing world, 133–135; as anti-poverty element, 125–126; challenges and resistance to private sector-NGO partnerships, 150–152; donors including private sector and enterprise dimensions, 142; eliminating international barriers, 148(table); encouraging appropriate industries, 145, 148(table); importance in long-term development, 130–131; local governments' concentration on enterprise and trade, 139–140; NGOs' increasing awareness of the value of, 142; reducing international barriers to, 145; remit and levels of decisionmaking for lines of expertise, 73(fig.)

entrepreneurial bias, 46–47

entrepreneurial capacity, 46–47

equity funds, 138
ethical funds, 138
executives: aligning disconnected agendas and priorities, 40–42; barriers to development-humanitarian sector merger, 195(table), 196; private sector-NGO partnerships, 129; strands of activity during development-humanitarian sector integration, 199–202
expertise, lines of, 69–72, 73(fig.), 76–78
expressive people, 51
extroverts: leadership style, 16

failures, program, 103, 106
fear, the culture of, 114
field staff: developing a high-performance organization, 68(table); involvement in governance, 29; social styles model addressing tensions among leaders, 52
financial management: Save the Planet career, 76–78
flywheel approach to economic development and pro-poor growth, 119(fig.)
focus of the program, 110
foreign direct investment (FDI), 125–126, 138–139
funding access: as challenge to organizational change, 9; change canvas, 97–98; customer relationship management systems, 161–162; increasing difficulty of, 2–3; purpose of a theory of change, 89; remit and levels of decisionmaking for lines of expertise, 73(fig.)

gender programs: remit and levels of decisionmaking for lines of expertise, 73(fig.)
General Electric (GE), 7
geography, mapping lines of expertise to, 70(table), 71
Geopolitics of Emotion (Moïsi), 114
Gerstner, Lou, 7
Gladwell, Malcolm, 54
global firms: identifying private sector-NGO collaboration opportunities, 143–144. *See also* private sector; private sector-NGO partnerships

Global Fund, 193
global leadership teams, 72–74
glue, organizational, 44–45, 67
goals: ambitious goals for agency-level change, 95; architecture of agency-level theory of change, 92, 93(table); articulating the ultimate goal of your agency, 107; clear communication of, 16–17; creating a high-performance international organization, 63–64; day-to-day goals and targets, 28; defining change drivers, 14–15; poor framing of vision and drivers for IT change, 163; stretching goals, 119
Goffee, Rob, 16
good soldiers in the workforce, 49
Good to Great (Collins), 10
governance: as challenge to organizational change, 9; ensuring IT program completion, 179; establishing clear steering arrangements, 23; identifying private sector-NGO collaboration opportunities, 143–144; local governments' concentration on enterprise and trade, 139–140; ordering and prioritizing components of change, 37; project management in IT projects, 167–168; push and pull, macro and micro dimensions, 38(fig.); review and management disciplines, 31; taking time to design the structure, 29; water-use partnerships, 128
government income: role of trade and enterprise in long-term development, 130–131
governments, local: power relationships in agency-level change, 86
Green, Duncan, 88
Greening, Justine, 128
Growth Share Matrix, 59
GSK, 127

Haire, Mason, 46
Hamel, Gary, 54
headquarters leadership: developing a high-performance organization, 75; social styles model addressing tensions among leaders, 52. *See also* executives; leadership

health programs: development-humanitarian sector mergers addressing, 193; malaria eradication, 127; remit and levels of decisionmaking for lines of expertise, 73(fig.)

Hewlett, Barry, 96–97

hierarchies of theories of change, 90–91

high-impact leadership, 41–42

high-performance organizations: architecture of, 67–72; career examples, 76–79; components of, 64–67; differences from line structures, 72–81; horizontal lines of expertise, 69–71; implementation choices and considerations, 75–76; key benefits, 67; remit for different lines of expertise, 71–72; strengthening through self-evaluation, 80–81(table)

hope, the culture of, 114

horizontal lines of expertise, 69–71

humanitarian sector: becoming a trusted friend and advisor, 112–114; private sector-NGO collaboration solutions, 147; utilizing the social styles model of people, 52. *See also* development-humanitarian sector merger

humiliation, the culture of, 114

IBM, 7

Ibrahim, Mo, 127

identity/branding: self-evaluation template for high-performance organizations, 81(table)

impact of an outcome, 97–98

implementation: choices and considerations for high-performance organizations, 75–76; context of agency-level change, 87; development-humanitarian sector merger, 199; donors' understanding of agency-level change, 103; lack of lasting progress, 54; remit for different lines of expertise, 71–72

inception/analyze phase of IT change, 173

India: growing involvement of global firms in development, 136–139; private sector agricultural partnerships, 128

Industrial Promotion Services, 140

Industrial Revolution, the developing world's exclusion from, 132

Infancy phase of organizations, 46–47

influencers in outcomes, 97–98

information technology (IT): basic project elements, 170–175; basic project management disciplines, 167–169; considerations for successful initiatives, 175–178; development driving IT systems, 183–184; different organizational approaches to, 178–179; encouraging excitement about, 185; ensuring program completion, 179; ensuring technology utilization, 179–180; history of NGO challenges with, 159–161; importance at the leadership level, 164; importance of clear and consistent communication, 164–165; increasing personal knowledge and expertise, 185; international sharing of common technology, 182–183; merging humanitarian and development sectors, 190–191; new strategic systems, 161–162; NGO reluctance to invest in, 160–162; phases and activities for IT implementation, 171(fig.); poor framing of vision and drivers for change, 163; project and program team selection, orientation, training, and support, 169; project phases, 171(fig.), 172–173; repositioning in an NGO, 177; resistance and barriers to change in an IT team, 166–167; robust business case for IT change projects, 168–169; staff knowledge about, 165–166; strands of activity during development-humanitarian sector integration, 202; vendor relationships, 181–182

infrastructure: increasing availability for external funding, 138; private sector-NGO collaboration opportunities, 146, 149(table); role of trade and enterprise in long-term development, 130–131; shifting the focus to, 115–116

innovation: cost efficiency in development-humanitarian sector consolidation, 189; misunderstandings about what comprises, 105–106

Institute of International Finance, 138–139

institutional capacity building, 123(fig.), 146
interconnection in an integrated system, 35–37, 36(fig.)
interim destinations, 107
internal learning: agency-level theory of change, 108; architecture of agency-level theory of change, 92; purpose of a theory of change, 89
Internet economy, organizational rhythm and, 59–60
interventions: advantages of merging humanitarian and development sectors, 192; agency-level theory of change, 99–100; architecture of agency-level theory of change, 92, 93(table); developing a theory of change, 108; selecting the best intervention for the context, 110–111; supporting trade and enterprise in Africa, 124
introverts: leadership style, 16
investment: accelerators for investment and aid, 119; in development markets, 138–139; examples of accelerating investment in the developing world, 127–128; foreign direct investment, 125–126, 138–139; local governments' concentration on enterprise and trade and, 139–140; Return on Social Investment, 111
Islam: African conflicts over religion, 133

jargon of private sector-NGO partnerships, 129–130
Jones, Gareth, 16
journey management: aligning disconnected agendas and priorities, 40–42; defining a journey, 34; managing complexity, 33–34
justice over charity, 115

Kaberuka, Donald, 140
Kegan, Robert, 7
Kenya: careers in high-performance organizations, 76–78
Kenya First Assurance Ltd., 127
KKR fund, 127
knowledge management: articulating strategic shifts, 18(table); line and matrix structures, 74

Krishi Jyoti (enlightened agriculture) program, 128

Lahey, Lisa Laskow, 7
leadership: articulating strategic shifts, 18(table); as barrier to agency-level change, 104; choosing the best change approach, 37–39; crucial choices in development-humanitarian sector merger planning, 197; developing a high-performance organization, 66; differences between line and matrix structures, 72–74; elevating information technology, 177; high-impact leadership, 41–42; implementation choices and considerations for high-performance organizations, 75–76; importance of authentic leadership, 15–16; incorporating new individuals into change teams, 19–20; IT at the leadership level, 164; leadership style, 16; ordering and prioritizing the components of change, 35–36; overcoming resistance and barriers to change, 20–21; practical steps for the change process, 29–31; push and pull, macro and micro dimensions, 38(fig.); risk factors in development-humanitarian sector mergers, 202–203; Save the Planet, 77; selecting the right mix of approaches, 39(table); self-evaluation template for high-performance organizations, 81(table); social styles model addressing tensions among leaders, 52. *See also* executives
learning: agency-level theory of change, 108; architecture of agency-level theory of change, 92, 93(table); purpose of a change canvas, 99; purpose of a theory of change, 89; reflecting on past learning, successes, and failures, 106; synthesis of, 94, 119–120; weak practices as barrier to agency-level change, 105
legacy and baggage, organizational, 114
legitimacy driving change, 13(table)
levels of thinking about change: basic elements, 10–11; managing complexity, 33–44; organizational con-

text, 44–53; organizational rhythm, 53–60
leverage in outcomes, 97–98, 122
line structure of an organization: challenges to agency-level change, 87; inadequacy of command-and-control management philosophy, 66–67; key differences of matrix structures from, 72–81
lines of expertise: candidates and categories for, 69–71; remit and levels of decisionmaking, 71–72, 73(fig.); Save the Planet career, 76–78
local business, 146, 149(table)
local customs and beliefs, 96–97

macro-level change implementation, 38
malaria programs, 127
management: aligning disconnected agendas and priorities, 40–42; articulating strategic shifts, 18(table); as challenge to organizational change, 9; challenges to NGOs, 8; elements of organizations, 2; overcoming resistance and barriers to change, 20–21; project management disciplines, 21–25; selection and continuity of the right people, 17–20. *See also* program management
market-linked programs, 123(fig.); global engagement of the private sector in development, 136–139
markets: increasing availability for external funding in developing countries, 138–139
matrix approach: command-and-control management philosophy as barrier to change, 105; developing a high-performance organization, 66–67; types of change, 42. *See also* high-performance organizations
McKinsey's 7-S Framework, 59
mentoring: increasing personal knowledge and expertise of IT, 185
Merlin, 187
micro, small, and medium enterprises (SMEs), 140–141, 149(table); identifying private sector-NGO collaboration opportunities, 143–144; private sector-NGO collaboration opportunities, 146

micro-finance programs, 149(table); remit and levels of decisionmaking for lines of expertise, 73(fig.)
micro-level change implementation, 38
milestones: basic project management disciplines, 23–24; developing a roadmap, 30; push and pull, macro and micro dimensions, 38(fig.)
Millennium Bridge, United Kingdom, 55–57
Moïsi, Dominique, 114
Mosaic Company Foundation, 128
motivating glue, 44–45
motivation and ability segmentation, 48–50

natural disasters, 2; breaking a positive development cycle, 132–133
natural frequency, 55, 56(box), 58
Novib (Netherlands Organization for International Development), 187
nutrition programs: ambitious goals, 95; framework for analyzing local contexts, 95–97; Save the Planet, 76–78

obstacles to change. *See* barriers to change; resistance to change
operational responsibility, 72
Organizational Life Cycle model, 45–48
organizational model: architecture of a high-performance matrix organization, 67–72; challenges to agency-level change, 87; developing a high-performance organization, 65–67; prioritizing changes, 36–37; selecting the right mix of approaches, 39(table); self-evaluation template for high-performance organizations, 81(table)
organizational rhythm: applying dynamic thinking to organizations, 58; basic elements of change, 10–11; for different organizational parts, 59; dynamic thinking and navigational change, 58–60; importance of recognizing, 53–54; from static to dynamic thinking, 55–58
organizations: articulating strategic shifts, 18(table); elements and definition of, 2; journey management, 33–34; understanding and strength-

ening organizational glue, 44–45.
See also high-performance organizations
orientation: IT change teams, 169; project and program team, 23
outcomes: architecture of agency-level
theory of change, 92, 93(table);
assessment framework, 107; change
canvas, 97–99; developing a theory
of change, 107
overhead costs: benefits of merging
humanitarian and development sectors, 189–190
Oxfam, 126, 187, 193

pacing change, 27–28
PAEI dimensions of organizational life
cycles, 46–47
performance, individual: barriers to
agency-level theory of change, 102;
remit for different lines of expertise,
72. *See also* high-performance
organizations
performance, organizational: driving
change, 13(table); IT investment,
160–161; Organizational Life Cycle
model, 46–47; push and pull, macro
and micro dimensions, 38(fig.);
selecting the right mix of approaches, 39(table); types of change, 42
philanthropy, 138, 139(table)
philosophy as barrier to development-
humanitarian sector merger, 194,
195(table)
PLAN-IMPLEMENT-FIX+REFINE
approach, 43
planning the change process: communications program, 17; developing a high-
performance organization, 65,
68(table); developing a roadmap, 30;
development-humanitarian sector
merger, 197, 198–199; horizontal and
vertical alignment in high-performance organizations, 75; milestones,
critical path analysis and dependencies, 23–24; self-evaluation template
for high-performance organizations,
80(table); working with the scope and
scale of change, 8–9
PLAN+PLAN+PLAN-IMPLEMENT
approach, 43

Polman, Paul, 128
Porter's Five Forces, 59
positive development cycle, 131–132,
131(fig.), 132–135, 134(fig.)
poverty: accelerating trade and economic growth in developing countries,
134–135; context of agency-level
change, 87; emphasis on pro-poor
economic growth, 140; framework
for analyzing local contexts, 95–97;
the shifting profile of, 2; signs of
global economic growth, 125–126;
supporting trade and enterprise in
Africa, 118–124
power relationships: agency-level
change, 86–87
priorities: aligning disconnected agendas and priorities, 40–42
private equity interest, 127
private sector: articulating strategic
shifts, 18(table); emphasis on pro-
poor economic growth, 140; encouraging the local private sector, 115;
levels of investment in developing
countries, 139(table); lines of
expertise mapped to geography,
70(table); linking corporate social
responsibility with business goals,
138; local governments' concentration on enterprise and trade, 139–
140; micro, small, and medium-
sized enterprises, 140–141; NGOs'
acceptance of the enterprise role in
growth, 142; potential lines of
expertise, 69(table); power relationships in agency-level change, 86
private sector-NGO partnerships: areas
for private sector firms to avoid, 147;
areas of common interest, 145; challenges and NGO resistance to, 150–
152; challenges and private sector
resistance to, 152–153; contribution
to global economic growth, 126, 129;
examples of accelerating investment
in the developing world, 127–128;
identifying collaboration opportunities, 143–147; increasing engagement
of global firms, 136–139; increasing
scope and volume of opportunities,
143; key areas for greater collaboration, 145–147; opportunities for

improving the results, 147–150; pro-poor economic growth, 140; realistic goals for, 153–154; trade and enter-prise in the development process, 130–131; uncertainties and frustra-tions, 129–130

production support phase of IT projects, 175

professionalization of processes and systems, 74–75

program and project management sys-tems (PPMS), 161–162

program design: hierarchies of theories of change, 91(table); purpose of a change canvas, 99

program management: defining a pro-gram, 34; of IT change projects, 170–171; program as journey rather than set of projects, 33–34; project versus program, 22–23. *See also* management

program quality, 13(table)

program type: potential lines of expert-ise, 69(table); remit and levels of decisionmaking for lines of expert-ise, 73(fig.)

progress reporting, 24

project management: basic project man-agement disciplines, 21–25; defining a project, 34; IT change projects, 167–169; project structure and key team members, 30; project versus program, 22–23; push and pull, macro and micro dimensions, 38(fig.)

pro-poor economic growth, 140

proxy wars: exploitation of the develop-ing world, 132–133

public services: role of trade and enter-prise in long-term development, 130–131

pull-style change implementation, 37, 39(table)

push-style change implementation, 37, 39(table)

Quiet–The Power of Introverts in a World That Can't Stop Talking (Cain), 16

regional leadership: Save the Planet careers, 78–79; social styles model addressing tensions among leaders, 52

regulation: global engagement of the private sector in development, 136–137

relationship building: becoming a trust-ed friend and advisor, 112–114

religion, conflicts over, 133

reputation: elements of organizations, 2

research and learning as barrier to agency-level change, 105

research question, 94

resistance to change: agency-level theo-ry of change, 101–106; changes in information technology, 166–167; identification and analysis of, 31; management and staff as obstacles to change, 17–20; multiple waves, 28; overcoming resistance and barri-ers to change, 20–21

resonance, 55

resource management: donors' accept-ance of IT investment, 184–185; global engagement of the private sector in development, 136–139; increasing institutional capacity for development, 142; information tech-nology approaches, 181; IT change teams, 169; lines of expertise mapped to geography, 70(table); potential lines of expertise, 69(table); push and pull, macro and micro dimensions, 38(fig.); remit and levels of decisionmaking for lines of expertise, 73(fig.); wasted investment as barrier to develop-ment-humanitarian sector merger, 195–196, 195(table)

resource planning, 24

responsiveness style dimension, 50–53

results-based agendas, 87, 142

Return on Social Investment (ROSI), 111

rhythm. *See* organizational rhythm

rights-based organizations: improving local connections and conversations, 112

risk management: basic project manage-ment disciplines, 24; contextual issues with agency-level change, 88;

development-humanitarian sector
merger, 202–203; high-impact leadership, 41(table)
roadmap, 30, 176–177
robust business case, 22

SAGMiller, 128
Salazar, Philippe-Joseph, 112
Satya Capital fund, 127
Save the Children, 127, 187, 193
Save the Planet, 76–79
science and engineering: natural frequency, 55, 56(box), 57–58
scope and scale of change, 8–9
sector-level theory of change, 90,
91(table). *See also* agency-level theory of change
security, national, 2–3
segmentation framework: motivation
and ability, 48–50
Sehgal Foundation, 128
self-evaluation template, 80–81(table)
7-S Framework, 59
Severn Bridge, United Kingdom, 55–57
small enterprises. *See* micro, small, and
medium enterprises
social impact bonds, 138
Social Style Model, 50–53
Somalia: development-humanitarian
sector merger, 193
South Africa: Save the Planet, 76–78
Southwest Airlines, 7
Stable phase of organizations, 47
staff: advantages of merging humanitarian and development sectors, 192;
aligning disconnected agendas and
priorities, 40–42; building a governance structure, 29; as challenge to
organizational change, 9; developing
a high-performance organization,
64–65; elements of organizations, 2;
IT knowledge, 165–166; lines of
expertise mapped to geography, 71;
overcoming resistance and barriers
to change, 20–21; planning a communications program, 17; project
and program team selection, 23; risk
factors in development-humanitarian
sector mergers, 202–204; scheduling
in line and matrix structures, 74;
selection and continuity of the right
people, 17–20; self-evaluation template for high-performance organizations, 80(table)
stakeholder analysis, 24
stakeholder communication, 89
standardization of processes and systems, 74–75
stars in the workforce, 48–49
static thinking, 54–59
steering and guiding change, 12; project
management in IT projects, 167–168
strategy: articulating strategic shifts,
18(table); IT change as a strategic
opportunity, 176; new strategies as
drivers for change, 13(table); organizational approach to information
technology, 178–179
stretch ideas, 109–116
stretching goal, 92, 93(table), 119
successful change, 7
summary: agency-level theory of
change, 100; architecture of agency-
level theory of change, 92,
93(table); supporting trade and
enterprise in Africa, 118–119
support: aligning disconnected agendas
and priorities, 40–42; IT change
teams, 169; project and program
team, 23
Sustainable Development Goals (SDG),
128
synergies across funding streams, 189,
190(table), 191–192
synthesis of learning, 94, 119–120
systems: articulating strategic shifts,
18(table); challenges to agency-level
change, 87; developing a high-performance organization, 65–66; interconnectedness in integrated systems,
35–37; push and pull, macro and
micro dimensions, 38(fig.); remit for
different lines of expertise, 72; standardization and professionalization
of processes and, 74–75

takeaways: authentic leadership,
16(box); change leadership,
20(box); choosing the best change
approach, 39; drivers for change,
15(box); high-impact leadership,
42(box); journey management,

34(box); ordering and prioritizing components of change, 37(box); organizational glue, 45(box); organizational life cycle model, 47(box); organizational rhythm, 60(box); project management, 25(box); recognizing staff resistance, 20(box); social styles analysis, 53(box)
target collaboration area for private sector-NGO partnerships, 153
targets: day-to-day goals and targets, 28; push and pull, macro and micro dimensions, 38(fig.)
teaching: Save the Planet careers, 78–79
team selection: aligning disconnected agendas and priorities, 40–42; basic project management disciplines, 23; IT knowledge and staffing, 165–166; selection and continuity of the core team, 17–20
team-based environment in high-performance organizations, 75
technology: potential lines of expertise, 69(table); private sector-NGO collaboration for humanitarian and development challenges, 147; private sector-NGO collaboration opportunities, 149(table); spurring economic growth, 3. *See also* information technology
test and deploy/transition phase of an IT project, 174–175
TGP Growth, 127
theory of change, 3–4; articulating change at the agency level, 83–85; articulating strategic shifts, 18(table); articulating the problem for agency-level change, 86(fig.); context factors, 85–88; hierarchies, 90–91; personal perspectives, 84(box); purpose of, 89; synthesis of learning, 94, 119–120; what it is not, 89–90. *See also* agency-level theory of change
timing of organizational change: context in agency-level change, 86–87; exploiting organizational rhythm, 53–55. *See also* organizational rhythm
tracking change, 98(table)
trade. *See* enterprise and trade

training: IT change teams, 169; project and program team, 23; purpose of a theory of change, 89
Transform partnership, 128
transformative economic growth, 140
trustbuilding: agency-level theory of change, 109–110; becoming a trusted friend and advisor, 112–114; building long-term trust, 25–26; improving local connections, 111–112; private sector-NGO partnerships, 153

Unilever Group, 126, 128
United Kingdom: private sector-NGO partnerships, 128
User Acceptance Testing (UAT), 174–175

Valley of Despair model, 26–27, 27(fig.)
Valters, Craig, 88
victory, declaring too soon, 26–27

WASH (water, sanitation, and hygiene), 95
water resources: private sector-NGO partnership programs, 128
Water Resources Group (WRG), 128
waterfall methodology, 170(box)
Welsh, Jack, 7
Why Should Anyone Be Led by You?: What It Takes to Be an Authentic Leader (Goffee and Jones), 16
workforce: attracting talent to develop a high-performance organization, 68(table); crucial choices in development-humanitarian sector merger planning, 196–197; motivation and ability segmentation, 48–50; private sector collaboration to build workforce capacity, 146, 148(table); social style model, 50–53. *See also* executives; leadership; management; staff

About the Authors

James Crowley is a business advisor with more than 25 years' experience with a variety of large private-sector companies and more recently, with a range of agencies in the international development sector. After an earlier career as an offshore engineer and an MBA at London Business School, James joined Accenture's strategic consulting practice in 1989 and became a partner in 1997. He worked across a range of strategy and organization change issues for energy, consumer products, high tech, and public-sector companies, including international clients such as SmithKline Beecham, Hewlett Packard, Shell, British Gas, as well as a range of energy companies. Up to 2005, James led Accenture's strategy practice in the United Kingdom and Ireland and was the European practice lead for Mergers, Acquisitions and Alliances for many years.

He formally left Accenture's commercial consulting practice in 2005 to focus on strategic and organizational performance issues in the international development sector. However, he has continued to work extensively with Accenture's not–for–profit practice, Accenture Development Partnerships. Over that time, he has led a range of assignments on strategic issues for clients such as Plan International, African Medical Research and Education Foundation (AMREF), World Vision, Amnesty International, Catholic Relief Services, Voluntary Service Overseas (VSO), Traidlinks, ACF, and Trocaire.

In parallel with his ongoing advisory work, James invests a portion of his time on new independent research to stimulate new ideas around the effectiveness of large international NGOs, as well as new collaborative approaches between development and private-sector organizations. The first of these was released in 2009 in collaboration with World Vision and Accenture Development Partnerships, "The Rubik's cube of cross-sector collaboration" (www.thecrowleyinstitute.org). In 2013, working with Morgana Ryan, James finalized a series of new research papers in a book titled *Building a Better International NGO: Greater than the Sum of the Parts?* This has been widely reviewed and appreciated by leaders in the sector across the world and is available on Amazon.com and other online channels.

James holds an honours degree in engineering from University College Cork, a master's in offshore engineering from University College London, and a MBA from London Business School.

Morgana Ryan is a management consultant with experience across a range of strategic, business process, and IT assignments spanning the private and development sectors. Her early career focused on business process transformation for large utility and international oil companies, including Energy Australia and Shell Exploration and Production. This gave her the opportunity to work in Australia, the Middle East, Europe, and Asia.

Morgana has spent nearly a decade working in the international development sector, applying her skills and experiences with Accenture Development Partnerships (ADP), a non-for-profit organization within Accenture. Having led the ADP Asia Pacific practice, Morgana then moved to be the global lead for Organizational Strengthening, overseeing ADP's work on strategy, structure, and operations.

Morgana has been privileged to work with some of the world's largest international NGOs at multiple levels; designing and implementing improvements at international headquarter/secretariat, regional, and country levels, as well as with local national organizations. This work has largely focused on how complex international NGOs with limited resources can operate to achieve more together, particularly when faced with significant geographic and programmatic footprints. Clients include Oxfam International, Amnesty International, Plan International, Childfund Australia, Fred Hollows Foundation, Catholic Relief Services, World Vision, and Save the Children.

In addition to her consulting work, Morgana is also on the board of an Australian NGO, Infoxchange.

Morgana holds an honours degree in economics from Monash University at Clayton, Australia, and is a graduate of the Australian Institute of Company Directors.

Morgana and James have been collaborating since 2008, sharing commercial and development sector experiences to produce practical research papers focused on NGO performance. The first of these was published as a book in 2013 titled *Building a Better International NGO*.